Men of the Bible

ELIJAH

HIS LIFE AND TIMES

BY

Rev. W. Milligan, D.D.
Professor of Divinity and Biblical Criticism, Aberdeen.

WIPF & STOCK · Eugene, Oregon

Wipf and Stock Publishers
199 W 8th Ave, Suite 3
Eugene, OR 97401

Elijah
His Life and Times
By Milligan, William
Softcover ISBN-13: 978-1-7252-9751-7
Hardcover ISBN-13: 978-1-7252-9752-4
eBook ISBN-13: 978-1-7252-9753-1
Publication date 1/19/2021
Previously published by Fleming H. Revell Company, 1887

This edition is a scanned facsimile of
the original edition published in 1887.

CONTENTS.

CHAPTER I.

ISRAEL IN THE TIME OF ELIJAH, AND THE FIRST APPEARANCE
OF THE PROPHET (1 KINGS XVII. 1) 1

State of Israel—First appearance of Elijah—Gilead—Elijah's
training—Civil condition of the Northern Kingdom—Its religious
condition—Ahab and Jezebel—Peculiar sinfulness of the idolatry
of the time—Importance of the era—Elijah comes forth—His
outward appearance—His message and its nature—Elijah withdraws from Ahab—Light from the Apocalypse—Witnessing to
facts, and theology.

CHAPTER II.

THE TRAINING AND DISCIPLINE OF ELIJAH (1 KINGS XVII. 2-24). 19

Second stage of Elijah's work and preparation for it—Lessons to
be learned by the prophet—Dependence upon God, and fellowship with man in suffering—The brook Cherith—Elijah there
miraculously sustained—Learns dependence upon God—The
brook dries up—The prophet is sent to Zarephath—Learns fellowship with man in suffering—Second great lesson as to the
wideness of God's plan and His large and universal love—Again
miraculously sustained—Widow's child raised to life—Lesson of
the incidents at Zarephath—The mission of God wider than we
think—Need of similar lessons now—Importance of the means
by which Elijah was taught—Value of action.

CHAPTER III.

ELIJAH'S WORK OF REFORMATION (1 KINGS XVIII. 1-40) . . 40

Elijah enters upon his work of reformation—Effect of drought on
Israel and Ahab—Difficulty of the part which Elijah had to act—
Soreness of the famine—Persecution of Jezebel—Fears of Obadiah
—Elijah meets Obadiah—Presents himself to Ahab—Arrangements for the contest with the prophets of Baal—Carmel—The
place and its associations—The contest—The prophets of Baal
and their failure—Elijah's address to the people—His arrangements for the sacrifice—His prayer—The answer—Effect upon
the people—The slaughter of Baal's prophets at the Kishon—
Restoration of Israel to the Covenant.

CONTENTS.

CHAPTER IV.

ELIJAH AND THE BREAKING UP OF THE DROUGHT (1 KINGS XVIII. 41-46) 61

Delay in the fulfilment of the promise—Necessity of waiting upon God in prayer—Elijah re-ascends Carmel—Mission to his servant—The cloud as a man's hand—Rain granted—Ahab's return to Jezreel—Elijah running before his chariot—Arrival at Jezreel—Nature and power of prayer—Objection to prayer answered—Physical phenomena—Mental phenomena—Characteristics of the prayers of Elijah as mentioned by St. James—Answer expected, and not simply reflex influence—For spiritual blessings—For others—Fervency in prayer—Prayer in faith—Power of such prayers.

CHAPTER V.

ELIJAH AT HOREB (1 KINGS XIX. 1-13) 80

Feelings of Elijah at Horeb—His mistaken notions as to the character of the Almighty—His despondency—Not due to physical fatigue or loneliness, but to thought that he had failed—Injustice thus done by him to God—To himself—To the past history of his people—Evils of despondency—Reason why Elijah fled to Horeb—God reveals Himself by an angel—Horeb and Elijah's cave—Former revelation of the Almighty there—The prophet questioned—His answer—The revelation granted him—Lesson of the revelation—Divine judgment and mercy—What law can accomplish—Value and importance of law—The message of love—Its greater power.

CHAPTER VI.

REVELATION AT HOREB (*continued*) (1 KINGS XIX. 13-21) . . 99

Our right and responsibility to judge Elijah at Horeb—The prophet again questioned—His answer—Further revelation of God to him—God still a God of judgment — Hazael, Jehu, Elisha : each an instrument of judgment—Mercy of God revealed —Meaning of the 7,000—The promise contained in the words—The revelation of God thus made continues : first, in judgment ; secondly, in the preservation of a faithful remnant—General teaching of Scripture upon this point—The same truths always applicable to the Church—Elijah leaves Horeb—Abel-meholah—Call of Elisha—Meaning of Elisha's farewell salutations and feast—Spirit in which Elisha enters on his work—Close of Elijah's special mission.

CHAPTER VII.

ELIJAH AND NABOTH'S VINEYARD (1 KINGS XXI. 1-29) . . 119

Elijah disappears for a time—Naboth the Jezreelite—Ahab desires possession of his vineyard—Failure of his attempt to obtain it and the effect upon him—Jezebel's plot—Its success—Naboth's

CONTENTS. vii

PAGE

trial and death—Ahab takes possession of the vineyard—Elijah appears before him there—Judgment pronounced on Ahab and Jezebel and their house—Execution of the judgment by Jehu—Fulfilment of woe uttered by Elijah—Effect on Ahab of Elijah's words—Objects of the narrative: To impress us with a deep sense of the wickedness of Ahab and Jezebel—To show the righteous retributions of God upon the sinner—To reveal God's readiness to pardon the penitent.

CHAPTER VIII.

ELIJAH AND THE COMPANIES OF AHAZIAH (2 KINGS I. 1-16) . 139

Elijah again retires from view—Importance of the interval to Ahab—To Israel—Accession of Ahaziah—His character—His illness and recourse to Baal-Zebub—Elijah appears to his messengers—His message to the king—Ahaziah s rage—He sends first captain and his fifty; their fate—Second captain and his fifty sent; their fate—Third captain and his fifty—Elijah goes to Ahaziah—His message—General character of the narrative examined—Comparison with other Scripture narratives of a similar kind—Principles upon which such destruction of life to be justified —Words of our Lord in Luke ix. 51-56—Methods of dealing with nations in different ages must be different—Teaching of Matt. v. considered—Application to state of Israel in days of Elijah—General considerations on the subject.

CHAPTER IX.

THE ASCENSION OF ELIJAH (2 KINGS II. 1-12) 159

Elijah drawing near the close of his life—Gilgal—Departure of Elijah from Gilgal—Elisha persists in accompanying him—Bethel and the sons of the prophets there—Jericho and the sons of the prophets there—Jordan—Passage opened through the river—Converse of Elijah and Elisha—The request of Elisha and its meaning—The translation of Elijah—Difficulty of the passage—No merely "natural" explanation can suffice—But not on that account are we to be indifferent to the amount of miracle involved—Modes of thought of the writer and of his age to be kept in view—Application of these principles to the narrative—The true meaning of its different parts—Elisha's cry—His return to the Jordan—River again opened—Vain search for Elijah—Concluding observations on the translation of Elijah.

CHAPTER X.

LETTER OF ELIJAH TO JEHORAM, KING OF JUDAH—CHARACTER AND WORK OF THE PROPHET (2 CHRON. XXI. 12-15). . 176

Elijah's letter to Jehoram king of Judah—Difficulties connected with it—Most probable solution—Contents of the letter—Character of Jehoram—Fulfilment of Elijah's warnings—General considerations on Elijah's character and work—The circumstances

amidst which he appeared—The school out of which he came—Prophecy in Judah and in Israel—The particular work given Elijah to do—The leading features of his character—His simplicity of faith and singleness of aim—His fearlessness of action—His sternness of spirit—Comparison with Elisha—Estimate of the prophet in after times—Book of Ecclesiasticus—New Testament references—His grandeur and uniqueness.

CHAPTER XI.

THE SECOND ELIJAH 192

Passages in the New Testament in which we read of a second Elijah—an integral part of Messianic hope—John i. 19-21; Luke ix. 7, 8; Matt. xvi. 14, xvii. 10, xi. 13, 14; Mark xv. 34, 35—Rabbinical testimonies to same belief—Founded on Malachi iv. 5, 6—Inquiry whether such passages are fulfilled in the coming of the Baptist—Alford, Moberly—Examination of Luke i. 17; Matt. xvii. 11, 12—Character of the Baptist's work—Conclusion that in the Baptist we have the second Elijah—Reference of the words in Malachi, "The great and dreadful day of the Lord"—Applicable to the beginning as well as the close of the Christian era—Jewish mode of looking at the Messianic age—Christian mode of doing so—Character of the age, not historical development, at first thought of—Judgment not less than mercy connected with it—Objection from 2 Thess. ii. 1-3—Objection answered—General conclusion that no second appearance of Elijah to be looked for.

CHAPTER I.

ISRAEL IN THE TIME OF ELIJAH, AND THE FIRST APPEARANCE OF THE PROPHET (1 KINGS XVII. 1).

State of Israel—First appearance of Elijah—Gilead—Elijah's training—Civil condition of the Northern Kingdom—Its religious condition—Ahab and Jezebel—Peculiar sinfulness of the idolatry of the time—Importance of the era—Elijah comes forth—His outward appearance—His message and its nature—Elijah withdraws from Ahab—Light from the Apocalypse—Witnessing to facts, and theology.

IT is with the suddenness of a flash of lightning and a clap of thunder out of an Eastern sky, that Elijah the prophet bursts upon us in the narrative of the Old Testament. As he was taken away, when his work was done, in a chariot of fire, with horses of fire, going up by a whirlwind into heaven, so it may be said he came. Everything was going on in Israel in its ordinary way. The people were at peace; and nothing seems to have disturbed their king as he pursued the evil courses on which he had embarked; as, not content with walking in the sins of Jeroboam, he formed his unhappy alliance with Jezebel the daughter of Ethbaal, king of the Zidonians; or as, yielding to the influence of her more wicked and powerful mind, "he reared up an altar for Baal in the house of Baal, which he had built in Samaria, and made a grove, and did more to provoke the Lord God of Israel to anger than all the kings of Israel that were before him" (chap. xvi. 32, 33). It is true that, even in the midst of all this wickedness, God still proved Himself to be the living God, and fulfilled, in dispensations of His providence well calculated to rouse the careless and to alarm the guilty the words of threatening spoken by His servants in former times, for in these days "did Hiel the Bethelite build Jericho: he laid the foundation thereof in Abiram his firstborn, and set up the gates thereof in his youngest son Segub, according to the word of the Lord, which he spake by Joshua the son of Nun" (chap. xvi. 34). No effect, however, would appear to have been produced by this upon either prince or people, and the sacred narrative leads only to one conclusion—that a flood of infidelity and idolatry, with all their attendant immoralities, was sweeping unchecked over the land.

All at once Elijah comes upon the scene. Without a word of previous information regarding him we are simply told that "Elijah the Tishbite, who was of the inhabitants of Gilead, said unto Ahab, As the Lord God of Israel liveth, before whom I stand, there shall not be dew nor rain these years, but according to my word." With the very first mention made of him, he is before us in all the fulness of his mission and in all the strength of that bold, uncompromising character which he ever afterwards displayed.

Of the early history of the prophet we know almost nothing. He is called the Tishbite, but it is uncertain what the expression means. Distinguished Oriental scholars of modern times have suggested that the word may mean simply "the stranger," and that the first clause of the chapter ought to read, "And Elijah the stranger, one of the strangers who dwelt in Gilead."[1] Could the suggestion be accepted, a fresh and even startling light would be thrown upon Elijah's history, and he would take his place beside such men as Melchizedek and Balaam, who were drawn from heathen nations to perform the part of divinely-called priests and prophets towards Abraham and the chosen people. It is better, amidst the wholly unproved character of any new proposals, to abide by the long-received interpretation, that the word "Tishbite" is properly formed from "Tishbi," the name of the town, whether the Tishbi in Gilead or in Galilee is not stated, in which Elijah was born.

It is of more importance to notice that Elijah was "of the inhabitants of Gilead," for Gilead was one of those divisions of Palestine on the eastern side of the river Jordan which possessed an entirely different character, and nurtured an entirely different population from those in Palestine proper. The land was higher, opener, and more extensive; not divided so much

[1] Smith's "Dictionary of the Bible," Tishbite.

by nature into the small patches of hill or valley or level meadow which marked the country westward between the river Jordan and the sea, but consisting of large rolling plains rising ever and again into rocky hills, and the boundaries of which were lost in the distance. No part of the world is more favourable to the habits of the roaming Arab; and the traveller who has thought himself alone in these vast solitudes is often startled by the sudden appearance of a mounted horseman coming round the base or starting up on the top of a hill, as well as by his equally sudden disappearance again. Nor this only, for that rocky nature of the country which expressed itself in the name Gilead, as well as its position on the extreme east of the Holy Land, made it the key of Palestine on that side, and fostered a warlike spirit in the tribes that had settled there. Jephthah, the most striking specimen of an undaunted, but wild and reckless captain, belonged to Gilead. It was famous for its great strategical positions; and, as in the case of Ishbosheth (2 Sam. ii. 8), and at a later time of David, when fleeing before Absalom (2 Sam. xvii. 24), its strong and precipitous fastnesses afforded shelter to the exile. Mahanaim, the place of the two hosts, and so famous throughout the whole early and middle history of the Israelites, seems to have been in Gilead, and may be taken as typical of the land. In such scenes men are nerved to the physical strength, the patient endurance, and even the moral fearlessness, by which Elijah was so strikingly distinguished. There, too, apart from the ways of men, the prophet would learn to commune with God alone; and would come to feel the full force of that relation to the Almighty which he was wont afterwards to express in his own graphic formula, "As the Lord God of Israel liveth before whom I stand."[1] We cannot fail to trace at least a correspondence between such scenes and those fits of despondency by which Elijah was at times overtaken. Of what small account was he with those vast depths of sky above his head, and that expanse of country stretching away to a horizon beyond which only the same view would be repeated. When nature presented herself to him upon such a scale he might well feel, What can the littleness of man accomplish? It may even be better for him to die (chap. xix. 4).

After all, however, we know almost nothing of the early influ-

[1] Chap. xvii. 1; xviii. 15. The formula was afterwards used by Elisha 2 Kings iii. 14; v. 16).

ences which surrounded the prophet, or which may have more or less contributed to make him what he was. It is not necessary that we should know them. Elijah's work was very different from that of Moses, of whom, as the appointed human author both of the religious and the civil polity of his people, it is well that we should be told that he "was instructed in all the wisdom of the Egyptians" (Acts vii. 22). It was no less different from that of Samuel who so long judged Israel, and whose early training in the service of the tabernacle did so much to prepare him for his task. At the hands of Elijah no new polity was needed. He had to frame no new laws. His work, it may be almost said, was to be summarized in one great act; in so far as it was done in the sight of men, it was to be begun and completed in a day. The stream of the nation's life, at the time when he appeared, was flowing in the channel cut for it; was fashioned in the outward mould prepared for it, by God. Elijah had only to heal that life by one sudden, bold, unexpected stroke, and the right constituting of the relation between his own soul and Israel's heavenly King, rather than the varied influences of an ordinary development amidst his fellows, was what he required. We do not, therefore, need to be informed as to his early training. Enough, if we know that, in communion with God and his own heart, he learned what no schools and no mere intercourse with men can teach—the greatness of the one Creator and Ruler of all; that faith in the Divine power which makes him feel, along with the deepest sense of his own weakness, that he can say to the mountain before him, "Be thou removed, and be thou cast into the sea;" and that superiority to the shows and fashions of a fleeting world which communion with the everlasting hills, and with Him who planted them or shakes them at His pleasure, is so well fitted to impart. John the Baptist, the second Elijah, "was in the deserts till the day of his showing unto Israel" (Luke i. 80). We have no reason to believe that the first Elijah was trained in any other way.

In order to understand both the meaning and the aim of Elijah's mission, we have first of all to try to form to ourselves some notion of his times. About fifty-six years had passed from the disastrous hour when the once great and firmly united kingdom of Solomon had been separated, through the revolt of the ten tribes, into its two parts, and the date—B.C. 919—when

Ahab ascended the throne of Israel as distinguished from Judah. During the whole of that half century the northern kingdom had been harassed by war without, and by bloodshed and misery within. Nadab, who succeeded Jeroboam, its first king, was, after a short reign of two years, murdered by Baasha, who seized the throne and, with the merciless policy of Eastern despotism, immediately put to death all the members of the house of Jeroboam (chap. xv. 29). After having reigned twenty-four years he was succeeded by his son Elah, who, in less than two years, was slain by Zimri, one of the captains of his chariots, while he was "drinking himself drunk in the house of Arza, which was over the household in Tirzah" (chap. xvi. 9). Zimri followed the cruel example of Elah's father, for, as soon as he took possession of the throne, he smote all the house of Baasha, leaving him not a single man child, neither of his kinsfolks, nor of his friends (chap. xvi. 11). But he enjoyed his honours only for a moment. A portion of the Israelites were then engaged at the siege of Gibbethon, in the tribe of Dan, which had been taken by the Philistines; and, no sooner did they hear of what had happened, than they broke up the siege and marched against Tirzah, the then capital of Israel, in which Zimri's court was held. The city was taken, and Zimri, setting fire to the palace (after a reign of seven days), perished in the flames (chap. xvi. 18). Omri, the leader of the attack, did not at once secure the royal honours which he coveted. Only after four years, during which a bitter internecine contest was carried on between him and Tibni, another claimant to the throne, and with half the people on his side, did Omri attain his object, and become king of Israel. Full of spirit and enterprise as a ruler, this founder of a new dynasty made himself especially famous by his conquest of Moab (2 Kings iii. 4), by his purchase of the hill Shomron from its owner Shemer, and by his building there the city of Samaria which, instead of Tirzah, became thenceforth the capital of the land. In other respects Omri's was still an evil reign. He "wrought evil in the eyes of the Lord, and did worse than all that were before him" (chap. xvi. 25). Six years he had reigned in Tirzah. Six years more he reigned in Samaria after the removal of his Court to the new city—twelve years in all. Then he died, and Ahab his son succeeded him.

Jeroboam, Nadab, Baasha, Elah, Zimri, Omri, six kings

between the date of the division of the tribes and the appearance of Elijah, with a seventh now upon the throne; and three of the six either murdered or brought to a cruel end through the usurpers by whom they were expelled;—the record is little better than one of tumult and violence and blood; while at the same time foreign wars, with the Syrians in the North and the Philistines from the South, helped to fill up the cup of national misery.

Still more fatal however to the prosperity and happiness of Israel was its religious condition. The bond which had mainly held the twelve tribes together had been a religious bond. Jerusalem was their common centre; and the temple of God there, now reared by Solomon in all its glory, was the common object of their affections and their pride. Three times a year every Jew was required to present himself at the great feasts, which were so closely associated with all the former triumphs, and all the present prosperity, of the kingdom as a whole. Three times a year they did this. From all parts of the country they collected in pilgrim bands, animated by the loftiest sentiments of patriotism to their fatherland, and of devotion to its Heavenly King. The Psalms sung by them on the way to the Holy City, glow with that poetic feeling which can spring only from the deepest emotions of the heart. The valley of mourning became a valley of rejoicing. The dry and dusty highways of that Eastern clime were changed to paths through fields covered with the blessings of the early rain. At each step, as they approached the goal of their journey, their strength increased. The courts of the Almighty were before them, and a day in His courts was better than a thousand; they would rather be doorkeepers in the house of their God than dwell in the tents of wickedness (Psa. lxxxiv. 5-10). All this time, too, it was the unity of the different tribes of the nation that was one leading object of the people's thoughts. They beheld Jerusalem builded as a city that is compact together, whither the tribes went up, the tribes of the Lord; and, when at length its towers and bulwarks rose before their delighted eyes, they cried out with one acclaim, "Pray for the peace of Jerusalem, they shall prosper that love thee. Peace be within thy walls and prosperity within thy palaces. For our brethren and companions' sakes we will now say, Peace be within thee" (Psa. cxxii).

Such was the unity of the Jewish people; and Jeroboam, king of the ten separated tribes, felt that he must break it, or see his kingdom soon wrested from his hand. Accordingly no sooner did he ascend the throne than he set himself to subvert the community of religious faith which existed between Israel and Judah. For this purpose he "made two calves of gold, and said unto his people, It is too much for you to go up to Jerusalem: behold thy gods, O Israel, which brought thee out of the land of Egypt" (1 Kings xii. 28). It was a repetition of what had already happened in an earlier age when, in the absence of Moses on Mount Sinai, Aaron, in order to appease the murmuring of the people, "made a molten calf, and the people said, These be thy gods, O Israel, which brought thee up out of the land of Egypt" (Exod. xxxii. 4.) Neither in the one case nor in the other was there any deliberate intention to deny Jehovah and His deeds. Rather, in both cases, would Israel remember them. Nevertheless, it was a dangerous thing to do this by means of images of man's devising, and He who knew the human heart had framed the second commandment of the ten for the express purpose of guarding against the idolatry which would soon degenerate into the actual worship of stocks and stones. Jeroboam either did not know this or recklessly disregarded it. He set up his golden calves at the two extremities of his kingdom, Bethel in the south, and Dan in the north, and sought to connect the memory of that great deliverance, which was the starting-point of the people's history as a nation, with a Being to be worshipped at these two places instead of Jerusalem. With the same object in view, he no longer continued the line of the priesthood in the tribe of Levi and family of Aaron, but for the sake, in all probability, of winning the popular favour, he chose his priests from the lowest of the people, and out of every tribe. Nay, he even offered sacrifice and burned incense himself; while, finally, to complete his revolution he changed the season of observing one at least of the great religious festivals, and made that which he had "devised out of his own heart" and substituted for the feast of the Almighty, a time of worldly indulgence to his subjects (1 Kings xii., xiii.). All this, too, Jeroboam carried out with a distinctness of apprehension, a clearness of vision, and a fixity of purpose which, combined with the occasion and date of his mounting the throne, made his reign one of the most memorable in the history of God's ancient people. In the strong language of the sacred writer, he "drave Israel from following the Lord, and made them sin a great sin" (2 Kings xvii. 21). As king after king is noted for his wickedness, it is with the words that he "departed not from the sins of Jeroboam the son of Nebat, wherewith he made Israel to sin" (2 Kings x. 29 ; xiii. 2, 11 ; xiv. 24 ; xv. 9, 18, 24, 28). For a period of two centuries and a half, down to the time of the Assyrian invasion, when Israel ceased to be a nation, the same direful language is continued. Jeroboam's evil example was the type and instigation of nearly all the faithlessness that followed it. He gave, indeed, a new departure to the history of Israel. Thenceforward idolatry never ceased to contend with the ancient faith until it was at last purged out by the wholesome, though painful discipline of the Captivity.

In Ahab's days, the days with which we are immediately concerned, all this evil culminated. In some respects, indeed, Ahab appears to have been a skilful ruler, and one possessed of more than common insight into the temporal necessities of a nation, as these would be judged of by mere worldly statesmanship. Following in the footsteps of his father Omri, his aim was to increase at once the internal dignity and the external prosperity of Israel. He loved peace and the arts of peace. His fame as a builder of cities and of palaces received particular notice in the Book of the Chronicles of the Kings of Israel (1 Kings xxii. 39). Among the latter was his new palace at Jezreel, which, with its extensive gardens, was to prove so fatal a spot in the history of his family ; while either there or at Samaria, he erected for himself that "ivory house" which appears to have attracted, in a greater than ordinary degree, the admiration of men (1 Kings xxii. 39). Ewald remarks that "in the time of Solomon ivory was first used for a chair of state ; Ahab decorated with it an entire house."[1] To nothing, however, does Ahab appear to have devoted himself more than to extending the commercial prosperity of Israel, and it was in connection with this that the weaker side of his character and the more evil influences of his reign appeared. He was thus led to draw closer the bonds of friendship between himself and the powerful Phœnicians in the West. His marriage with Jezebel is in no small degree to be traced to the same cause

[1] "History of Israel." Edited by Carpenter, iv. 40.

Animated by no truly religious spirit, and especially worldly in the whole tone of his mind, it was nothing to him that he thus ran the risk of strengthening any idolatrous tendencies in his subjects, as well as of defeating the purpose for the sake of which the Almighty had separated them from the other nations of the world. He envied the maritime greatness of Phœnicia. He saw the commercial advantages to be derived from sharing in its trade, and he did not scruple for a moment to sacrifice to such ends the higher and nobler destinies of Israel. Ahab was, in short, pre-eminently a weak and worldly king, thoroughly secular in his aims, destitute of all firmness even of worldly principle, ready to enjoy the rewards of wickedness which he had not strength enough to devise, and thus an easy tool in the hands of others more daring than himself. No darker account, therefore, could well be given of any king than that which is given of him by the sacred writer. "He did evil," we are told, "in the sight of the Lord, above all that were before him. And it came to pass, as if it had been a light thing for him to walk in the sins of Jeroboam the son of Nebat, that he took to wife Jezebel the daughter of Ethbaal, king of the Zidonians, and went and served Baal, and worshipped him. And he reared up an altar for Baal in the house of Baal, which he had built in Samaria. And Ahab made the Asherah : and Ahab did yet more to provoke the Lord, the God of Israel, to anger than all the kings of Israel that were before him" (1 Kings xvi. 30–33). It was the first time that a king of Israel had allied himself by marriage with a heathen princess : and the alliance was in this case of a peculiarly disastrous kind. Jezebel has stamped her name on history as the representative of all that is designing, crafty, malicious, revengeful, and cruel. She is the first great instigator of persecution against the saints of God. Guided by no principle, restrained by no fear of either God or man, passionate in her attachment to her heathen worship, she spared no pains to maintain idolatry around her in all its splendour. Four hundred and fifty prophets ministered under her care to Baal, besides four hundred prophets of the groves which ate at her table (chap. xviii. 19). The idolatry, too, was of the most debased and sensual kind. The worship of Baal was combined with that of Ashtaroth, sometimes understood to be the moon, at other times to be the planet Venus. But whichever of the two she was, there can be no doubt as to the effect produced upon the people. In the Epistle to the Church at Thyatira, contained in the Revelation of St. John, we have an inspired commentary on the character and rule of Jezebel which throws a sad and lurid light, alike upon her and upon the times of which we are now speaking. "But I have this against thee," it is there said, "that thou sufferest thy wife Jezebel which calleth herself a prophetess; and she teacheth and seduceth my servants to commit fornication and to eat things sacrificed to idols. And I gave her time that she should repent; and she willeth not to repent of her fornication" (chap. ii. 20, 21). It is the same terrible combination of idolatry and licentiousness which so often meets us in the ancient world; and with which St. Paul had to war at Corinth. We see the Zidonian queen, not perhaps licentious herself,—there is not sufficient evidence to entitle us to think that—but reckless of it as a consequence of the idolatrous practices which she fostered, and with her strong determined will forcing these by every means in her power upon her deluded subjects.

There is still another feature of this idolatry which ought not to be omitted when we would estimate aright the irreligious condition of Israel in Ahab's days. When, in another passage of his narrative, the sacred writer sums up the character of the king he does it in the words, "But there was none like unto Ahab which did sell himself to work wickedness in the sight of the Lord, whom Jezebel his wife stirred up. And he did very abominably in following idols, according to all things as did the Amorites, whom the Lord cast out before the children of Israel" (chap. xxi. 25, 26). In these words we have laid bare the crowning aggravation of the people's wickedness. They had apostatized from God to the very sins for which the ancient inhabitants of Canaan had been driven out before their fathers, and visited with such severity of punishment as to be well-nigh exterminated. The old altars were again reared, the old sacrifices again offered, the old iniquities again practised; and the worship introduced into the land defeated, in so far as it was yielded to, every end at which the theocratic people were to aim. It is a fresh start, then, in the degeneracy of Israel that we have now presented to our view. Before this time idols had been fashioned, and altars and high places built for their unholy rites. But as yet the idols had been always intended to represent the great I AM Now the gods of strange nations were introduced. The ideas of power separated from righteousness and of lust substituted for love appealed to the worst tendencies of the corrupt hearts of Israel. And in its degradation Israel answered the appeal. The narrative leads conclusively to the belief that idolatry had overspread the land. There can have been but few who had not bowed the knee to Baal, for we shall by and by see that it is only by a mistranslation that we are wont to speak of seven thousand who had remained true to the God of their fathers. Even those, again, who had stood firm in their faithfulness had been compelled to such an extent to conceal themselves that Elijah believed, in his despondency, that no worshipper of the true God was left except himself. The very prophets were become corrupt, and were for the most part ready to flatter rather than to speak the truth (2 Chron. xviii. 5). Every surviving element of good seems to have been watched by Jezebel with jealous eye; and when Obadiah, in high authority in the palace, sought to rescue some of the Lord's prophets from the cruel hands of the queen, he had been obliged to resort to stratagem, and to hide an hundred of them by fifties in a cave, where he fed them with bread and water. Baal worship had swept like a flood over Samaria, and the weak Ahab, with his strong-minded but guilty wife, had transformed the whole northern kingdom of Israel, containing a much larger population than that of Judah, into the scene of everything that was impious and vile. The day was at its very darkest, and every ray of light was threatening to perish, when Elijah appeared.

The point, therefore, at which we stand is not an ordinary point in the history of degenerate and degenerating Israel. It is one wholly by itself. It marks a new stage in the people's fall distinct from every other stage to which they had previously sunk. No era of the same character had as yet been seen. Either Israel must for ever forfeit its position among the nations, and in the religious history of the world, or the Almighty must interpose and show Himself as He was, the only living and true God, the God of holiness and righteousness. A greater crisis does not exist in the history of the Jewish people; and a more remarkable prophet does not claim our notice until we come to the days of Him in whom all men recognized a second Elijah.

Such, then, was the condition of Israel at the moment when Elijah is introduced to us. Even his outward appearance arrests our attention. We are told elsewhere that "he was an hairy man, and girt with a girdle of leather about his loins" (2 Kings i. 8). The hairiness spoken of refers not to that of his body, but of his dress. In the margin of the Revised Version the meaning is correctly given as that of "a man with a garment of hair," that is a garment made of goats' or camels' hair, at once dark and rough, and worn by him, not as a mere ascetic, but that it might be a symbol of his sorrow for the sins of the people and the Divine judgments that had been incurred by them.[1] A similar dress, and most probably for a similar purpose, was worn by the Baptist (Matt. iii. 4); and, when the writer of the Epistle to the Hebrews describes the sufferings of the saints of old, amidst which they remained faithful even unto death, he enumerates among them that "they went about in sheep-skins and goat-skins," at once the tokens of their poverty and the signs of their humiliation in a sinful world. This garb of Elijah is elsewhere called his "mantle." With it he covered his face when at the mouth of his cave in Horeb he heard the still small voice in which the glory of the Lord appeared (1 Kings xix. 13), and with it also he smote the waters of Jordan so that he and Elisha went over upon dry ground (2 Kings ii. 8). The leathern girdle again, also like that of the Baptist, was more in harmony with the garment of hair than the ordinary girdle of linen or cotton would have been. In addition to this, however, it would seem that there must have been something peculiar either about Elijah's dress or about the manner in which he wore it; for, when the messengers of Ahaziah, in reply to the inquiry of their master, what like the person was by whom the message had been sent him that he should die, referred to the dress of the man whom they had met, the king at once recognized the prophet by the description, and exclaimed, "It is Elijah the Tishbite" (2 Kings i. 8). The dress of the prophet, indeed, both told of the nature of that region of the country from which he came, and corresponded to his mission. He was no dweller in royal courts. He was nourished by no food from Jezebel's table. He did not even mingle in society; he did not eat and drink like the ordinary sons of men. He came from the solitudes of the wilderness, and what he was when he had been there he also was when he entered into the presence of kings. Ahab must have been startled by the

[1] Keil, *Comm. in loc.*

sudden and strange apparition, so startled that he could neither speak nor act, for neither speech nor action is recorded of him. In an instant Elijah was before him. In an instant he had delivered his message; and then, without any effort being made to detain him, the next instant he was gone.

If, however, even Elijah's outward appearance would startle the king, much more would his message do so: "As the Lord God of Israel liveth, before whom I stand, there shall not be dew or rain these years, but according to my word." Much in these words demands our attention.

1. The threatening uttered in them had in it nothing arbitrary. It had been one of the special characteristics by which the promised land, in comparison with Egypt, had been originally commended to the Jews that it was "a land which drank water of the rain of heaven;" and God had promised His people that, if they would hearken to the commandments of the Lord their God, and would love Him and serve Him with all their heart, He would give "the rain of their land in its season, the former rain and the latter rain, that they might gather in their corn and their wine and their oil." On the other hand, the people had been warned that, if they turned aside, and served other gods and worshipped them, "the anger of the Lord would be kindled against them, and He would shut up the heaven, that there should be no rain, and the land should not yield her fruit" (Deut. xi. 11, 13-17). The punishment now threatened was, therefore, not arbitrary. It was the theocratic penalty with which Ahab had been long familiar; and the words of the prophet must have told him, not merely of punishment, but of the particular sin for which that punishment was to be inflicted. It was not in presumption, therefore, that some unknown preacher had now entered into his presence uttering angry denunciations of his own devising, but it was one who spoke from the very heart of that Divine Economy which Ahab was bound to uphold, and who, at least, claimed to be a messenger of Him to whom both king and people owed all that they possessed.

2. The light in which God is here presented to us. He is "the living God," and the "God of Israel." As the former He stood in contrast with all those objects of idolatrous worship to which Ahab and his people had been paying homage. These were no more than "dead idols," having no life themselves,

unable to give life to others, without power or even reality, fitly represented by the stocks and stones that were worshipped in their names. But the God of Israel lived. He had life in Himself. He was from everlasting to everlasting. His eyes were upon His creatures. His ears were open to them. He took account of their actions; and, as life could only be maintained in holiness, as sin was self-destructive, He could give life to none but the obedient, and the wages of sin was death. As the God of Israel, again, He was the people's covenant God. He had not kept Himself at a distance from them. He had drawn near to them in their past history; and, as the unchangeable Jehovah, He was still drawing near to them. Not by the dread of His power only, but by the thought of His love, had He bound them to His service, and their whole past history testified to the fact. They could recall their patriarchs, their prophets, the victories that had waited upon their arms, the plenty that had crowned the labours of the year in their pleasant land. And the experience of the past was the promise of the future, for the gifts and calling of a living and covenant God could not be otherwise than without repentance. All that could either save or win the heart lay in the words, "The Lord God of Israel liveth."

3. Elijah's own personal relation to God. This finds expression in the words, "Before whom I stand;" and these words tell far more than that the prophet at that moment was in the presence of God, and that he spoke as one into whose mouth a message had been put, of the faithful delivery of which he would have to give account. An habitual attitude of the soul is pointed at in Elijah's language. To hold constant intercourse with God, to become familiar with Him, to have always an open ear for His words, to be always ready to listen to and proclaim His pleasure was the spirit of the prophet's life. Hence his authority; hence his strength. Before one who could and did so live, earthly distinctions faded. The Apostle James reminds us of this general principle when he says, "My brethren, hold not the faith of our Lord Jesus Christ, *the Lord of glory*, with respect of persons" (chap. ii. 1). The distinctions of riches and poverty fade in the light of the glory of the Lord; and thus it was with Elijah. As a king, Ahab might inspire with terror the subjects who would approach him. But there was a far greater Ruler than he, one who cuts off the spirit of princes,

and who is terrible to the kings of the earth. Before Him, before His messages and His messengers, the highest potentates of the world, when they are found in rebellion against Him, may tremble.

4. One point remains still to be noticed in what Elijah said, the manner in which he ends his threatening, "but according to my word." He does not mean that he was to send drought or rain at his pleasure; and that, as his temper or inclination varied, Ahab might expect now the one and now again the other. He had proclaimed a distinct and definite drought, to begin then and there: "There shall not be dew or rain these years." That is the threatening, the punishment. But it need not be always so. He who has withheld the rain may again send it; and, when He sends it, it will be at His servant's word. This is always the spirit of a truly Divine communication. If there is punishment for the guilty there is also pardon for the penitent. The decree that carries judgment in its bosom is not irreversible. The threatened doom may be escaped. Let Israel turn and repent, and he whose commission it is to bind has also a commission to loose. The dew and the rain will again descend. The pastures will be clothed with flocks and the valleys with corn.

Elijah's message is delivered, and the prophet does not wait to observe its effect. He knows, in all probability, that it will have none. But, whether he knows this or not, he must leave his words to vindicate themselves. Prophets, messengers, ministers of God are apt to be in every age too anxious about the immediate results of their work. There is no doubt a sense in which they ought to be so, and a sense too in which they ought to expect results. When these do not appear it may be a proof, not that the Almighty's dealings are mysterious, but that our methods are wrong. Good men have too often been blind to the imperfection of their plans or of their modes of working them, because their thoughts of God rested mainly in this, that God giveth no account of any of His matters. A juster view of the connection between wisdom and success might have led to the discovery that their failure was due to the weakness of their own human counsels rather than to the mysterious dealings of One whose footsteps are not known. But though this be an error on the one side, there is an error on the other to be equally avoided. Even the best and wisest may not succeed at once. Let them leave the issue in the hands of One who turneth the king's heart as the rivers of water. If they know that their word is His they know also that it will prosper. Paul may plant, and Apollos water, "God gave (not, will give) the increase" (1 Cor. iii. 6). Let them speak earnestly, boldly, faithfully, with no self-seeking, content to take all that comes so that God be glorified. The work is theirs: the issue is with Him.

Thus the first great step in Elijah's work is taken; and again the Revelation of St. John, a book written out of the very heart both of the Old Testament and the New, and which often elucidates the former as much as it is elucidated by it, shows us the point of view under which the prophet is to be contemplated. In that book we read of the two witnesses, "And if any man desire to hurt them, fire proceedeth out of their mouth, and devoureth their enemies: and if any man desire to hurt them, in this manner must he be killed. These have power to shut the heaven, that it rain not during the days of their prophecy" (chap. xi. 5, 6). No one will doubt for a moment that the incidents lying at the bottom of this symbolic language are to be found in the history of Elijah; and, if so, the sacred writer points out to us the nature of that light in which we are especially to regard the prophet. He is a "witness," and his prophetic work among men is "witnessing." The message which he proclaims to men is a testimony to *facts*, independent of himself and of any speculations of his own. As the apostle John says of the Baptist, so we may say of the prophet who preceded him in his spirit, "The same came for witness, that he might bear witness concerning the Light" (chap. i. 7); and the importance of the thought of "witnessing" is to be learned from the frequency with which it meets us in the writings of the beloved disciple. In various forms it occurs fifty times in his Gospel, and about thirty or forty times in his Epistles and in the Apocalypse. It is one of his most characteristic words. What could he do but catch as far as possible the rays that shone from His Divine Master, in order that, simply as a mirror, he might reflect them again for light to the world? So was it with Elijah, and herein he comes before us as the type of the true prophet in every age, of the Christian minister as well as of the messenger of God to Israel. The Christian minister, not less than the prophet of old, is to forget

ISRAEL IN THE TIME OF ELIJAH. 17

himself. Not in original speculation on Divine things; not even first in exhortation or warning or encouragement; but in a simple presentation of facts lie at once his chief sphere of action and his strength. How much has this been forgotten in later ages of the Church, and how much in consequence has the Church been weakened! For the great dogmatic systems which, in the course of the Church's history, have been prepared by the piety and genius of true messengers of God, we can never be too deeply thankful. They applied the facts of the New Covenant to the difficulties, the doubts, and the longings of the human heart in the times out of which they sprang, and they have conquered many a department of the field of truth for all time. We may honour and defend them. We may shun the ignorance which affects not to understand or the narrowness of heart which cannot sympathize with them. But, except in the presence of such errors as they met, they are not the weapons of ministerial warfare, and they ought not to be made the tests of ministerial faithfulness. There are few greater mistakes than to imagine either that theology is fixed, or that theological speculations are the aspects of Divine truth by which we are to convert the world. Theology, as distinguished from the facts that underlie it, ought to be free; and theological speculation upon these facts is not for the world at all. It is for the Church already formed, the Church that can sympathize with it, love it, and make clear to herself by means of it the height and depth and length and breadth of the facts upon which she rests. It was not by speculation about God and man and judgment and eternity that our Lord convicted the world; it was by His Divine life of love and self-sacrifice lived before its eyes; and it was by the application of that life, under the power of His Holy Spirit, that on the day of Pentecost the Church was called into existence. Then came the period of theology, but it is contained in letters to *the churches*, not in sermons to men without their pale. The example has been too much lost sight of. What has been called an orthodox theology has been substituted for an orthodox life; and practical love and self-sacrifice have given way before the harsh voices, and not less frequently the hard sentiments, of polemical divines. The remedy is to return to that witnessing to facts which is the true conception of the Church's function as she endeavours to gather into her fold the many who still wander far from the

Shepherd's tent and the green pastures. St. John teaches us that Elijah pursued his prophetic work as a "witness"; and, when we learn to pursue ours in the same spirit, then also shall the other part of the figure employed by him in the same passage be fulfilled in us. We shall be "the two olive trees and the two candlesticks standing before the Lord of the earth" (Rev. xi. 4. Comp. 1 Kings xvii. 1). Our light will burn in the tabernacle of the Lord with a bright and continuous flame; and when we send it forth as the "stars," as the "angels" of the Church, the earth will be lightened with its glory (comp. Rev xviii. 1).

CHAPTER II.

THE TRAINING AND DISCIPLINE OF ELIJAH.
(I KINGS XVII. 2-24.)

Second stage of Elijah's work and preparation for it—Lessons to be learned by the prophet—Dependence upon God, and fellowship with man in suffering—The brook Cherith—Elijah there miraculously sustained—Learns dependence upon God—The brook dries up—The prophet is sent to Zarephath—Learns fellowship with man in suffering—Second great lesson as to the wideness of God's plan and His large and universal love—Again miraculously sustained—Widow's child raised to life—Lesson of the incidents at Zarephath—The mission of God wider than we think—Need of similar lessons now—Importance of the means by which Elijah was taught—Value of action.

THE first stage in the drama of Elijah's life is over. He has begun his mission with the firmness and boldness which are to distinguish him throughout. He has met Ahab in the height of his power. In the presence of the king, perhaps in his palace at Samaria, he has announced himself as the prophet of that living God whom Israel has forsaken, and he has proclaimed the immediate approach of the most terrible of all calamities to a land so dependent upon rain as was the land of Palestine—a drought, and the famine which would inevitably accompany it. That work is over, and the people have now to be left for a time to experience the effects of the threatened judgment. Meanwhile Elijah has before him a second stage of his work, greater, more public, more imposing, more full of far-reaching issues than the first. His true work indeed, that for which he had been especially raised up as a prophet of the Lord, was still before him; and for it, as for almost all great work recorded in the Bible, preparation was needed. Public, however, as the work was to be, the preparation for it was not to be also public. The seed that is to grow into the stately tree does not seek the upper air from the moment when it is committed to the ground. It must be buried in the ground, and in the silence and darkness there must germinate for a season until its downward shoots have penetrated the soil, and have given it such a hold of its position that it shall be able to resist the scorching sun and the storms of wind and rain that would otherwise overwhelm it when it bursts into the light. So it was with Moses. It was no useless time, we may be sure, that was spent by him in Midian, when for forty years he dwelt in the desert where, at the very beginning of his retirement, God appeared to him in the bush burning but not consumed. So was it with John the Baptist, who was prepared for addressing Scribes and Pharisees, priests and people, not in the crowded city of Jerusalem, in the synagogue, or in the schools, but in those deserts of Judæa and by the Jordan where he would rarely behold a human countenance, and would seldom have an opportunity of listening to a human voice. So was it with St. Paul, whose education at the feet of Gamaliel, and in all the learning of his day, had to be supplemented by a visit of three years to Arabia, where his surroundings, whatever they may have been, were certainly widely different from the scenes in which he was afterwards to move. And so, may it not with reverence be said, was it with our Lord Himself, who not only waited till the age of thirty before He was inaugurated to His work, but who was then led up of the spirit, not to Nazareth where His first sermon was to be preached, but into the wilderness, in order that, tempted of the devil, He might overcome, as it were gathered together in one focus, all the trials that were to meet Him during His earthly ministry. Thus also was it with Elijah. No doubt he needed to wait until the effects of the famine should be felt. But the whole structure of the narrative before us forbids the thought that this was the only reason for the withdrawal of the prophet from Ahab and Jezebel, from the court and the people. A period of retirement was necessary for him that in it he might learn those lessons which an immediate public appearance would have tended to dissipate rather than enforce.

In particular, Elijah had to be taught :

1. Dependence upon God, and fellowship with man in suffering.
2. That the God of Israel who sent him had a wider plan, and

was animated by a larger and more universal love than he supposed. To the learning of those two lessons he must now devote himself.

1. The first of them is learned by the brook Cherith—"And the word of the Lord came unto Elijah, saying, Get thee hence, and turn thee eastward, and hide thyself by the brook Cherith, that is before Jordan. And it shall be that thou shalt drink of the brook; and I have commanded the ravens to feed thee there." Much uncertainty prevails as to the exact position of this brook. It is even possible that, though indicated with sufficient clearness to the prophet by circumstances not mentioned in the narrative, the sacred historian has the idea of the *nature* of the brook rather than any particular locality in view. The word "Cherith" means "cut off" or "separated," and Elijah was now to be separated from the world and to dwell for a season alone. In entire accordance with that spirit of Hebrew thought which delighted to give to places names that should express their history or character, this brook might be called the brook "Cherith," because of the use now made of it. Should this possibility be rejected we have no certain knowledge where it was. By some it is placed to the east of the Jordan in Gilead, that portion of the country from which Elijah came, and to which they think it natural that he should again be sent. By others it is found on the west side of the Jordan, but at different points, one higher up, another lower down, the stream. The question is one of entirely subordinate importance, though tradition points rather to the last of the three localities than to either of the former two. It is enough for us to know that the Cherith was one of those *wadies* or narrow defiles that are not uncommon in the Holy Land, where steep banks, often taking the form of perpendicular cliffs, confine the little stream that rushes in the rainy season down the bottom of the valley. These cliffs, composed of the limestone rock of the country, are full of caves difficult to reach, and in those by the side of the Cherith, according to the best established view of its position, not a few of the early Anchorites of the Christian Church are said to have found refuge at one time from persecution, and at another from the world. To one of these brooks or *wadies* Elijah was directed by "the word of the Lord" to flee, that he might escape the first outburst of the rage of Ahab, and that his work of preparation might begin.

Let us follow him to the Cherith. He was far from the abodes of men, or from any who could help him to obtain sustenance in what was undoubtedly a remote and desert place. But he had that promise of God to lean upon which immediately accompanied His command, "And it shall be that thou shalt drink of the brook ; and I have commanded the ravens to feed thee there." Nay, not only was the promise given. Startling as it was it was also fulfilled ; for, when he went and did according to the word of the Lord, we are immediately informed that "the ravens brought him bread and flesh in the morning and bread and flesh in the evening, and he drank of the brook." The continuance of the supply of water need occasion us no surprise. It is not spoken of as if it were miraculous; and it is perfectly conceivable that, if the stream came from the hilly country of the South, which was less affected by the drought than the territory of Israel, water might have flowed much longer there than in the northern districts of the land. Besides which we know that after a short time its supply of water failed. Elijah's dependence upon the water of the Cherith is natural and easily understood. His being fed by the ravens is the only difficulty of the passage. The miracle, indeed, is so remarkable, so much out of keeping with most even of the other miracles of Scripture, that even pious and devout minds may well be perplexed by it, and we can feel no surprise at the numerous and varied attempts which have been made to explain it in a more simple manner than that which the words taken literally suggest. Such attempts are not inconsistent with the most profound reverence for the Word of God, and the highest estimate of its practical value. They are, rather, not unfrequently, the result of a just persuasion that the Eastern mind did not express itself in forms similar to those of the West, or they are an effort to apply to the point before us the most important rule for the interpreter of the thoughts of others,—that the idea in the mind of the speaker or writer, and not the merely literal interpretation of what he says, is the meaning of his words. We must protest, therefore, at the very outset, against the harsh judgments often pronounced on those to whom the literal interpretation of this passage presents insuperable difficulties, and who would fain resort to other explanations. Those who do so cannot be fairly charged with rejecting, in this and similar cases, the plain meaning of the Bible. Their whole aim is to discover whether or not the plain meaning is the true one. In symbolical or figurative language these two meanings differ widely from one another. It may be so here; and, if it can be shown that it is so, the proof may not only relieve us of difficulties, but may enrich our knowledge of Scripture by the new rule of interpretation which is given us. Of the attempts thus made two may be noticed, but only to be rejected upon exegetical and historical grounds.

It has been proposed to translate the original word for "ravens" by "Arabians," a change easily made by altering the vowel points of the Hebrew which are of no authority. But had this meaning been intended we should certainly have no definite article prefixed to the noun, as it is impossible to think that such a charge could have been committed to a race of men at once so numerous and so widely spread. Again it has been suggested that the original, as it stands, may mean either "merchants" or inhabitants of Orbo, a small town in the neighbourhood of the Jordan, not far from Beth-shan or Scythopolis. But this solution has to face the difficulty of supposing that the Cherith was in that particular neighbourhood; besides which there is, as Rawlinson has said, "the improbability that men would come regularly, *twice a day*, to supply the prophet, thus giving themselves needless trouble and increasing the chance of detection when they might easily have left him a supply for several days."[1] In both these interpretations there is almost as much improbability as in ascribing to the ravens what was done. Other suggestions are either so trifling or so ludicrous as to be unworthy of notice.

If the miracle before us is not to be literally understood, the solution of the difficulty presented by it must be sought in some other way. So looking at it, the selection of the raven, as the bird by which Elijah was to be fed, must at once strike the mind, and the idea of that bird, as the Jews were accustomed to think of it, must be determined. There is no difficulty in coming to a conclusion on the latter point. The raven was unclean. It was one of those birds which the children of Israel were to have in abomination among the fowls (Lev. xi. 15). In the Book of Proverbs, if we adopt the marginal rendering of the Revised Version, "the ravens of the brook" are, for their carnivorous and cruel habits, classed with the young vultures.

[1] "Speaker's Commentary," *in loc.*

"The eye that mocketh at his father and despiseth to obey his mother the ravens of the brook shall pick it out, and the young vultures shall eat it" (chap. xxx. 17); while the prophet Isaiah makes use of it in order to heighten his picture of the desolation of the land of Idumæa, "And the owl and the raven shall dwell therein" (chap. xxxiv. 11). Thus, then, it is at least conceivable that an explanation of the passage before us may be found. The sacred writer may intend to express the thought that Elijah was supported in circumstances the most desperate, by means the very opposite of those likely to be helpful to him. An unclean and ravenous bird shall nourish him. The thought may be, in some degree, similar to that in St. Mark's account of the Temptation of our Lord, when the Evangelist tells us that "He was with the wild beasts." The wild beasts of the wilderness owned His presence, and submitted themselves to His sway. "When a man's ways please the Lord He maketh even his enemies to be at peace with him:" "Thou shalt tread upon the lion and the adder; the young lion and the serpent shalt thou trample under feet:" and when, in the Revelation of St. John, the triumph of the Church is celebrated, it is in the words, "Behold, I give of the synagogue of Satan, of them which say they are Jews and they are not, but do lie; behold, I will make them to come and worship before thy feet, and to know that I have loved thee" (Prov. xvi. 7; Psa. xci. 13; Rev. iii. 9).

After all, however, it may well be asked whether it is necessary to have recourse to explanations such as these. To Elijah it may have been of the utmost consequence to see that, in the very moment of his severest trial, nature and the God of nature were on his side; and nothing could more effectually convey that lesson to him than the service of these unclean and ravenous birds. If, therefore, the whole scene be not a highly poetic and figurative representation of this truth, little more can be said to meet the difficulty. The interpretation of the Old Testament has as yet made little really scientific progress. When it has made the advance so much demanded in our day, we may be better able to understand passages such as that before us. In the meantime, while we wait for light, our proper attitude is to accept the narrative as it stands. The value of the prophet's experience is neither heightened by a literal, nor diminished by a figurative, interpretation of what passed.

Thus, then, Elijah dwelt at the brook Cherith. He was not

merely alone in the wilderness, with no patch of ground to cultivate and no means of providing for himself. He was also in flight, surrounded by enemies, not daring to show himself amidst his fellow-men. Ahab, we may be sure, had already begun that search for him which, as we afterwards learn, was continued during the whole period of the drought. What was he to do? Let him trust in God. By "the word of the Lord" he had betaken himself to his present solitude (ver. 2); and He who has sent him there will provide for him. Day by day, as the sky over his head was brass, and the earth under his feet was iron, he would feel how hopeless it was to think of depending upon any resources of his own. But an unfailing supply of every want was granted him. Morning after morning, evening after evening, bread and flesh were there. Could he fail to remember the manna and the quails with which God had of old fed His people in their wanderings, or the streams of water with which in the desert He had quenched their thirst? His position was precisely analogous to theirs. They were passing through the wilderness in order to establish the Divine polity of Israel. He was in the wilderness that, after that polity had been forsaken, he might restore it to its ancient purity and vigour. In such circumstances the old histories of his nation would unquestionably come back upon him with renewed freshness and power. He would accompany his fathers at every step of their journeyings, his faith strengthening each morning as he looked forward to the trials of the day, his peace deepening each evening as he sought his nightly rest "a day's march nearer home," until at length he would think of himself as entering with his fathers into the promised land. In like manner would the living God now deal with him. There was strength, comfort, joy, hope, in the thought. The wilderness around him would become a pool of water, and the dry land springs of water (Isa. xli. 18).

But this was not all. By the brook Cherith Elijah had to learn not simply dependence upon God : he had to learn also fellowship with man. In looking at the narrative before us it seems obvious that the ministering of sustenance to the prophet, while famine was everywhere around him, is not the only fact upon which we are to dwell. For the brook dried up, although it would have been as easy for the Almighty to supply water by miracle as either flesh or bread. In addition, therefore, to the lesson of dependence upon God, the prophet was taught that, cared for as he was, he was not wholly separated from his people in their sufferings, but that, along with them, he must taste the consequences of their sin. We can easily imagine what strange questionings would arise within his breast when he first awoke to a full consciousness of the fact that the water of the Cherith was beginning to fail. For anything that appears there was no straitened supply of flesh and bread. Why then should the water fail which was yet even more necessary to life? The instrument of inflicting suffering upon others, he may have imagined that in his own case there was to be no suffering similar to theirs. The people had been faithless: let *them* suffer. He had been faithful: why should suffering fall on *him?* He had broken all social bonds with these idolaters. He had even fled from their country, and now he had no more common cause with them. He had found another home in the wilderness where bread was given him and his water was sure; and there, without having to engage further in the struggles of the world, he might think that he should be permitted to end his days in peace. The temptation was, and is, a great one. The servant of God who has fully proclaimed the message of the Divine judgment upon sin and sinners is peculiarly apt to think that he may himself escape the consequences he has denounced on others. And so he may; but worse consequences may follow. He may become selfish, indifferent, and hard; and, with neither sympathy in his heart nor tear in his eye, may fall below the level of both the prophet and the man.

The Almighty therefore deals with us upon different principles. He has so united the various classes of society together —the good and the bad, the believing and the unbelieving, the rich and the poor, the master and the servant, the pastor and his flock, the prophet and those to whom he prophesies—that none of them can suffer without the others being more or less involved in the same calamity. No one class, by attending only to its own necessities, can save itself from ruin. All classes are so bound up in the same bundle of life that what one loses or gains is to a large extent gained or lost by all. Give the laws of God free play and they will work out this conclusion for themselves; and, when they work it out, the effect will be permanent. The process may be sometimes slow. We become impatient, and we rush to legislation for an immediate cure

But legislation cannot bind the different classes of society together; and, as it is generally the legislation of the strong against the weak, whether of the aristocracy against the democracy or of the democracy against the aristocracy, it may multiply rather than diminish obstacles to the carrying out of the plans of a beneficent Creator. The true happiness of a people can only spring from what a people are in heart and life. Righteousness alone exalteth a nation, and one main part of that righteousness is the binding all its members more and more closely together in common sympathy and love. In the midst of the wickedness or sorrows of the world we may sometimes be disposed to ask, Why should we concern ourselves? We can do no good: and then, if we cannot save others, we may at least save ourselves. We may avoid their fate by shunning them, retiring from them, and nourishing a Divine life within our own souls, whatever they may do. It cannot be. The brook that has failed them will fail us also. The sources of our own life will become dry.

Elijah had been taught his first great lesson—dependence upon God and fellowship with man in suffering. His second lesson had now to be impressed upon him.

2. He must learn that the God of Israel had a wider plan, and was animated by a larger and more universal love than he supposed. Such is the point of view under which we are to regard the narrative occupying the remainder of this chapter. Our Lord has Himself given us its key. When, at the close of His first sermon in Nazareth, His hearers would have demanded of Him that, whatsoever they had heard of as done at Capernaum, He should do also in His own country, He replied, "Of truth I say unto you, There were many widows in Israel in the days of Elijah, when the heaven was shut up three years and six months, when there came a great famine over all the land; and unto none of them was Elijah sent, but only to Zarephath, in the land of Sidon, unto a woman that was a widow" (Luke iv. 25-26). These words disclose the light in which we are to look at the incident as recorded here. Not the sustenance afforded by the widow to the prophet, but that afforded through the prophet to her and to her child, is intended to occupy our thoughts. Not the lesson of dependence upon God and of fellowship with man is that now taught him whom the Almighty was preparing for his coming work, but the further lesson that,

however he may have thought of judgment only as his work, he had a mission of mercy to perform, and one too of the widest and most comprehensive kind.

The incident is connected with Zarephath, a small Phœnician town situated between Tyre and Sidon, and possessing even in Elijah's time no claims to notice, except in so far as it became associated with the history of the prophet. The inhabitants appear to have been descended from the ancient Canaanites; and we may be sure that they were worshippers of Baal, whose worship was promoted by Ethbaal, king of the Zidonians, over all that country. To this place, therefore, and into the very midst of that idolatry against which he was by and by to struggle was Elijah sent. "The word of the Lord came unto him, saying, Arise, get thee to Zarephath, which belongeth to Zidon, and dwell there: behold, I have commanded a widow there to sustain thee." Nothing is yet said of the fact that the widow was rather to be sustained through the agency of the prophet. This Elijah will learn in time. He obeyed the command thus given. He arose and went the long journey from the valley of the Cherith to Zarephath; and there is something exceedingly touching in the account given of the manner in which he fell in with the widow whom he sought. When he came to the gate of the city she was there gathering sticks; and Elijah, perhaps already divining that this was the person to whom he was commissioned, and weary with his toilsome travelling, "called to her, and said, Fetch me, I pray thee, a little water in a vessel, that I may drink." We are reminded of Abraham's servant Eliezer when he went in search of Rebekah (Gen. xxiv. 14), and of our Lord's first greeting to the woman of Samaria (John iv. 7). In readiness to help others we often best show that preparation of the heart which makes us ready for being helped ourselves. The woman at once answered the appeal, for "the fresh streams of Lebanon," the range of mountains at the base of which Zarephath lay, "would retain their life-giving power after the scantier springs of Palestine had been dried up."[1] She went away for the water, and as she went to fetch it the prophet cried after her, "Bring me, I pray thee, a morsel of bread in thine hand." Then her full misery was revealed, and Elijah knew by the very desperateness of her condition that she was the woman whom he sought, and

[1] Stanlley, "Lectures on Jewish Church," second series, lect. xxx.

that hers was the house which the Lord was to bless through him. "As the Lord thy God liveth," she replied, "I have not a cake, but an handful of meal in a barrel, and a little oil [the olive oil of the country, an important element of food] in a cruse: and, behold, I am gathering two sticks, that I may go in and dress it for me and my son, that we may eat it, and die." It was enough. The nature of the charge entrusted to him burst in all its clearness upon the prophet's mind, and the promise might now be uttered with the assurance that it applied directly to her to whom he spoke it, "Thus saith the Lord God of Israel, The barrel of meal shall not waste, neither shall the cruse of oil fail, until the day that the Lord sendeth rain upon the earth." He accompanied her home, and she, and he, and her house did " eat many days;" and the barrel of meal wasted not, and the cruse of oil failed not, "according to the word of the Lord, which He spake by Elijah."

Nothing further is told us of the manner in which the prophet employed the time spent by him in the house of the widow of Zarephath. It is not indeed necessary to suppose that during the whole interval between his entering it and his public appearance upon Carmel, a period probably not less than two years, he remained in close seclusion within its walls. In particular, we may well be permitted to imagine that he frequently crossed the small intervening space of ground separating Zarephath from Carmel, and that in the solitudes of that mountain range, which seems to have had a special attraction for him, he sought and found opportunities of converse with God. But, while within the widow's house, there can be little doubt that, both by word and by the tone and spirit of his life, he would discourage her idolatry, and guide her to the truth. Nor, as we shall immediately see, was his labour vain.

One other incident, however, of Elijah's stay at Zarephath is recorded, and must be considered before we are in a position to estimate aright the effect upon the prophet of his residence in the widow's house. "And it came to pass," we are told, "after these things, that the son of the woman, the mistress of the house, fell sick; and his sickness was so sore, that there was no breath left in him." The conjecture has been made, and even widely entertained, that the apparent death was no more than a swoon. Yet little is gained by the supposition, which is also at variance with the general spirit, as well as with some of the particular expressions of the passage. We can hardly be wrong, therefore, in accepting the commonly received interpretation, that the child had actually died. It was a sore calamity, for the boy seems, like the young man at Nain in the Gospel history, to have been the only son of his mother, and she was a widow. The mother felt all the bitterness of her loss, and it was no more than a natural outburst of maternal feeling that led her to connect it, in one way or another, with the presence of the prophet in her house. As she held the child in her bosom she turned to Elijah with the cry, " What have I to do with thee, O thou man of God? Thou art come unto me to bring my sin to remembrance, and to slay my son." There is more, however, than maternal feeling in these words. The instinct of man makes him fear that he cannot see God and live, and that if he comes into immediate contact either with God, or with any being, such as angel or man, who is truly representative of His holiness, the penalty can be nothing less than death. So deeply engraven on the human heart is the thought of the perfect righteousness of the Sovereign Ruler of the universe, and at the same time of its own desert of punishment because it has wandered from Him, that its first conception of the Divine Being is always formed in alarm, not in confidence, in terror, not in hope. Nor is it the consideration of any particular sin of which we have been guilty that produces this effect. A particular sin may be, and often is, readily enough pardoned by a fellow creature; why may it not still more be pardoned by Him who knoweth our frame and remembereth that we are dust? It is the consciousness of a sinful nature that inspires the fear; the conviction that there is a gulf between us and the Holy One to whom we owe ourselves; the feeling that we dare not stand in the presence of One who cannot look upon sin but with abhorrence. A ray of the Divine glory penetrates the soul, and the conclusion forces itself upon us that that glory can only consume the sinner as a fire. " I have heard of Thee," we cry, " with the hearing of the ear, but now mine eye seeth Thee, wherefore I abhor myself, and repent in dust and ashes" (Job xlii. 5, 6). Thus it was that Jacob beheld with astonishment his life preserved at Peniel, though he had there seen God (Gen. xxxii. 30); that, when Gideon perceived that he had seen an angel of the Lord, he exclaimed, "Alas, O Lord God! because I have seen an angel of the Lord face to face" (Judges vi. 22); and that when Manoah and his wife saw their angelic visitant ascending unto heaven in the flame of the altar, and knew that he was an angel of the Lord, Manoah "said unto his wife, We shall surely die because we have seen God" (Judges xiii. 22). Thus even was it in far later times; for, instead of starting up in joy and thankfulness when he beheld the miraculous draught of fishes, Peter fell down at Jesus' knees, saying, "Depart from me; for I am a sinful man, O Lord" (Luke v. 8); and, when the exalted Redeemer revealed Himself in His heavenly glory to the Apostle John in Patmos, the beloved disciple himself tells us that he "fell at His feet as one dead" (Rev. i. 17). Only then can we bear the glory of the Divine when our consciences have been pacified by the assurance that, not in ourselves, but in another who is the well-beloved of the Father, we are one with God. Not therefore from the thought of any particular transgression of which she had been guilty, but because the tokens of something Divine were immediately before her eyes did the widow of Zarephath turn to Elijah with the cry, "What have I to do with thee, O thou man of God? Thou art come to me to bring my sin to remembrance, and to slay my son."

Elijah immediately entered into the mother's grief, but he would act rather than speak for her in that hour of sorrow. At once he said, "Give me thy son; and he took him out of her bosom, and carried him up into the chamber where he abode, and laid him upon his own bed." Doubtless he might have done all that he was to do in the chamber occupied by the mother, and in her presence. But his own chamber was one which he must have often sanctified by prayer; his own bed one on which, like David, he must often have prevented the dawning of the morning with his cry, "Hear my voice, according to Thy loving-kindness" (Psa. cxix. 147, 149): and, familiar as he was with the power of prayer, it was natural for him now to seek the chamber and the bed where his prayers had been so often answered. If in one sense it is all the same where we pray, in another it is not. It is a good thing to have some familiar spot where we have been wont to cry to the Hearer and Answerer of prayer, and where we know that He has heard us. Thus Abram, when he returned from Egypt to Canaan, "went on his journeys from the south even unto Bethel, unto the place where his tent had been at the beginning, between Bethel and Ai, unto the place of the altar which he had made there at the first: **and** there Abram called on the name of the Lord" (Gen. xiii. 3, 4; comp. xii. 8). Thus God said to Jacob, "Go up to Bethel, and dwell there; and make there an altar unto God that appeared unto thee when thou fleddest from the face of Esau thy brother." It was to Bethel that he was to go, the place where he had previously taken the stone that had been his pillow and set it up for a pillar, and poured oil on the top of it, and consecrated it as to him "none other than the house of God and the gate of heaven" (Gen. xxxv. 1; comp. xxviii. 18). Thus, also, it was that Daniel went to his chamber with its windows open towards Jerusalem, when, in contravention to the king's command, he worshipped according to the law of his God (Dan. vi. 10): nor can we forget how often our Lord found on the Mount of Olives, and most probably on the same spot, a little sanctuary in which to pray to His Father in heaven. Yes, it is a good thing, not only to retire from the world for prayer and communion with the Father of our spirits, but to retire to some quiet retreat which we have often visited for the same purpose, and which, by that power of association of ideas so deeply planted in our nature, may do more than other places to awaken within us a holy and a joyful fervour.

Under the influence of feelings like these then it was that Elijah now took up the body of the widow's son to his own chamber; and, laying it on his bed, "stretched himself upon it three times (a number apparently intended to express the fervour and earnestness of his feelings), and cried unto the Lord, and said, O Lord my God, I pray Thee, let this child's soul come unto him again." The action was the same as that of Elisha, who, when he would restore the son of the Shunammite woman to life, "went up, and lay upon the child, and put his mouth upon his mouth, and his eyes upon his eyes, and his hands upon his hands, and he stretched himself upon the child" (2 Kings iv. 34). It was the same also as that of St. Paul with Eutychus, when the apostle "went down, and fell on him, and embracing him said, Make ye no ado, for his life is in him" (Acts xx. 10); and in all these cases the action was not intended to be curative in itself, but was for the expression and the strengthening of the faith of the supplicant. Such faith has power with God. The "supplication of a righteous man availeth much in its working" (James v. 16); and He who willeth not the death of any of His creatures answers the prayer for mercy not less than for judgment. He did so now. "The Lord hearkened unto the voice of Elijah; and the soul of the child came into him again and he revived. And Elijah took the child, and brought him down out of his chamber into the house," that is, into the lower apartment of the house, "and delivered him unto his mother."

The effect was what might have been anticipated; whatever may have been the widow's doubts before, she could resist no longer. Surely the presence and power of a far greater God than any she had ever known were there. She recognized Him of whom she had often heard, the Lord God of Elijah; and, in the spirit of the Galilean nobleman whose son Jesus restored to life, she exclaimed to the prophet, "Now I know that thou art a man of God, and that the word of the Lord in thy mouth is truth." So far as we have any information given us we have here the first-fruits of Elijah's ministry, and it will be observed that they are reaped, not amongst his kinsmen, but amongst aliens; not among God's ancient people, but among Gentiles beyond the pale of the covenant and involved in the thickest darkness.

In now endeavouring to estimate the place which these incidents at Zarephath hold in the history of Elijah, it is not necessary that we should confine ourselves to the actual effect which they produced on him. That effect may be part, but it may be only part, of the reason why they took place and are recorded by the sacred penman. That Elijah did not always comprehend the purpose of the Almighty's revelations of Himself will appear clearly when we come to consider the vision presented to him at Horeb. Here, in like manner, we have to deal with what God intends as well as with what His servant understands. We may certainly expect to find a correspondence between the two: but the correspondence may not be perfect, and the one may not be the measure of the other. The lesson may be in advance of the pupil, as indeed, to some extent at least, it ought always to be.

What, then, was the tendency of these incidents at Zarephath? It is of course easy to conceive that Elijah might have been sent there, because Zarephath was in the very heart of the idolatries of the Baal-worship; and because, like Luther at Rome, the great reformer of Israel would thus become acquainted with the worst features of the system he was to overthrow. But, even though this may have been thought of, we know, from the teaching of our Lord at Nazareth already spoken of, that it was subordinate to the higher purpose of widening the horizon and enlarging the sympathies, in the first place of the prophet himself, and then of Israel.

The most remarkable feature in the whole narrative is obviously this, that the incidents related happened in a family beyond the borders of the promised land, in a Canaanitish home, to one who by her own confession had not believed in the God of Elijah, but had rather been a worshipper of Baal, a pupil in the school of Ahab and of Jezebel. Surely there were many widows in Israel to whom the prophet might have been sent on his mission of mercy; widows as poor, as helpless, and as desolate as the widow of Zarephath, and who, perhaps, belonged to the unseen remnant of faith still existing in the land. Yet his mission had been directed to one beyond the pale of covenant privilege, an alien, and a heathen. Once again, in the life of our Lord, an incident of almost exactly the same kind happened. Jesus, too, came into these very parts, the borders of Tyre and Sidon; and there a Canaanitish woman besought Him that He would heal her daughter. The disciples regarded her with disdain. Perhaps they would even have confined the blessings bestowed by their Master to the lost sheep of the house of Israel; and they intreated Jesus to send the petitioner away. But Jesus pitied her, spoke to her, reasoned with her, and drew out what was in her heart, until at last He exclaimed, "O woman, great is thy faith, be it unto thee even as thou wilt; and her daughter was made whole from that hour" (Matt. xv. 21-28).

In both cases the lesson is essentially the same. The mission of God is wider than we think. Children of God are to be found scattered where, left to ourselves, we should hardly seek for them. There is a covenant beyond the covenant. There are those who are "of God," who are "of the truth," in scenes where we imagine that those only are to be met with who are the children of idolatry and falsehood. Jesus has " other *sheep* which are not of this fold," and He says, "Them also I must bring, and they shall hear my voice; and they shall become one flock, one shepherd" (John x. 16). Now all this we are peculiarly liable to forget, and that, in exact proportion to our earnestness. When we are most in earnest we are most in danger of identifying some narrower cause which we advocate with the cause of God. Elijah was the very embodiment of a devoted and zealous prophet; but his prophetic work had been confined to Israel, and he had so struggled and suffered in it that he had come to look upon Israel as the only object of concern to the Almighty. The disciples of our Lord in their day were again the very embodiment of faithfulness in the service of their Master, but they, too, had come to think that the chosen people alone ought to awaken interest in His heart. In neither case probably was there much reasoning upon the point. Yet they acquiesced the more cheerfully in the conclusion that it appealed at once to feeling and to sight. It appealed to feeling, because it flattered their own self-importance. That they and their people should be chosen, while others were passed by, could not fail to please rather than humble the natural exclusiveness of the heart; and, although Divine grace, allowed to operate freely, will eventually subdue that spirit, it does not gain the mastery in a moment. Narrowness of spirit appealed also to sight. The thing believed in was more visible, tangible, one may say, more material, than it would otherwise have been. Israel as an outward institution was before the eye. Its boundaries could be marked. The smoke of its offerings could be seen ascending to heaven. Its bursts of music could be heard sounding in every breeze that swept across the land. In the other case the marks of the Divine Presence were far more intangible, and could only be realized by a faith which penetrates darkness, and which can hear in "impressive silence" the song of praise. Not that this dependence upon the help of the material is in every respect wrong. The incarnation of our Lord has consecrated it for ever; and the most spiritual of the apostles has said, " That which we have heard, that which we have seen with our eyes, that which we have beheld, and our hands handled concerning the Word of life (and the life was manifested, and we have seen, and bear witness, and declare unto you the life, the eternal life, which was with the Father, and was manifested unto us); that which we have seen and heard declare we unto you also, that ye also may have fellowship with us: yea, and our fellowship is with the Father and with His Son Jesus Christ" (1 John i. 1-3). We are not, however, on this account justified in resting upon the outward Christ. "Even though we have known Christ after the flesh, yet now we know Him so no more" (2 Cor. v. 16).

Elijah in his day, the disciples of Jesus in their day, needed, and we not less in our own time need, to be trained to this spirit, for men are always prone to think that their own small vineyard is the only one in which the great Husbandman can ripen His fruits. He may there ripen them better than elsewhere. It does not follow that He ripens them only there; and it is absolutely essential that we should learn this lesson, if we are to take any effective part in promoting God's kingdom in the world. No one can rightly do the work of God, even in any limited sphere in which he may have been placed, until he has learned that there is something wider than that sphere, and that to the establishment of the wider, not the narrower, all the plans of God ultimately tend. We cannot worship truly in the temple built with hands unless we recognize the fact that there is a temple built without hands. We cannot really love our neighbour unless we own a neighbour in every child of Adam. And we cannot successfully serve the Israel of God unless we feel that those as yet beyond that Israel are also the objects of our heavenly Father's love, and that He would have all men to be saved, and to come to the knowledge of the truth.

> "There's a wideness in God's mercy
> Like the wideness of the sea;
> There's a kindness in His justice,
> Which is more than liberty.
>
> For the love of God is broader
> Than the measures of man's mind;
> And the heart of the Eternal
> Is most wonderfully kind.
>
> But we make His love too narrow
> By false limits of our own;
> And we magnify His strictness
> With a zeal He will not own." [1]

The lesson thus impressed upon Elijah by his being sent to Zarephath was one of infinite importance, and it is a part of the great truth everywhere imbedded in the Old Testament, though not clearly seen in every age, that the God of Abraham, Isaac, and Jacob, was also the God of the whole earth, and that His salvation was from the beginning designed to be universal. Israel, no doubt, did not at first apprehend this truth, and had to be educated more fully in it as it drew nearer to the age

[1] Faber.

THE TRAINING AND DISCIPLINE OF ELIJAH. 37

of Him in whom all acknowledge that there is neither Jew nor Greek, neither bond nor free, neither male nor female (Gal. iii. 28). But the point to be particularly observed is that the truth was in the Old Testament itself more than in the Old Testament people. It was not a development as time ran on and experience was gathered. To man it was so, not to God; and the simple fact that the clearest traces of it are to be met with long before it was understood by the most enlightened members of God's ancient covenant, is a testimony to the Divine idea which lies at the bottom of the Old Testament, and to the fact that Israel was guided throughout all its history by a Divine, and not a human, hand.

If the lesson thus impressed upon Elijah was important, hardly less important were the means by which the lesson was taught. The prophet was not reasoned with, but was sent to judge for himself of the sufferings of his fellow-creatures, and was instructed to relieve them. And he was to do this independently of both national and religious ties. Nay, his greatest exertions were to be made on behalf of those who were the enemies at once of Israel and of Israel's God. Thus would he learn to know the necessities of men as men, and in imitating the example, would be most likely to catch the spirit, of Him who "maketh His sun to rise on the evil and the good, and sendeth rain on the just and the unjust" (Matt. v. 45). Ministering to others was to be his great instructor, and experience teaches us that there is none more powerful, whether we would enlighten the intellect or enlarge the heart. By living only in our own thoughts we become hard, narrow, and intolerant, while others become to us like so many pieces upon a chessboard, necessary to enable us to play our part, and only valuable when they help us to beat our opponent in the game. Then, too, the difficulties of thought spring up and threaten to master us. At every step we are met by problems which we cannot solve. We become involved in a labyrinth of speculation without a clue to guide us. We rise only to fall. We hope only to sink into despair. We reach the higher world in our flight, but we find, or seem to find, that there we have no firm ground on which to tread, and that we must sink again. This lower world and its laws has, at all events, something solid amidst the airiness of loftier and nobler visions. Were it not well that, without abandoning speculation, for we cannot abandon it, we tried another way. Let us go down to men. Let us see that they are flesh and blood as we are ; that they have feelings, affections, desires, aspirations, hopes, as we have. Let us judge of their temptations by the dire reality of facts. Let us strive to benefit them, and, as we do so, let us mark how the benefit conferred, small though it may be, fills their hearts with gratitude, and touches what to them was the darkness of the world with light. This will do more to soften and enlarge our hearts than the wisest reasoning or the most urgent expostulation. It will do more also to solve our difficulties and to dispel our doubts. We cannot by the aid of the speculative reason overcome every perplexity that troubles us in the sphere of either nature or religion. Yet we must live in nature, and we live in it because we must. Action gives us a sufficient amount of certitude ; and, while we grope in the darkness that surrounds us, we hold upon our way. One generation builds upon another, each acknowledging the frailty of the foundation, yet each raising a fresh portion of the superstructure, because the instinct of life is strong. It is not otherwise in religion, and especially in the Christian faith. In its call to action, Christianity gives us a help to certitude, at least sufficient for our purpose in the meanwhile, that we shall hardly find in any other way. It appeals to our sense of the practical needs of men. It bids us relieve the wants, instruct the ignorance, and heal the sorrows, of the poor and wretched, of the fainting and dying. It shows us our Divine Master going about continually doing good, and it bids us follow in His footsteps. Then we see that, although not free from difficulties, it can effect what nothing else can for our fellow-creatures ; and, when the blind receive their sight, and the lame walk, and the lepers are cleansed, and the deaf hear, and the dead are raised up, and the poor have the gospel preached to them, we learn to exclaim with joy, "There is none occasion of stumbling in Christ" (Matt. xi. 5, 6).

Such, then, was the school to which God sent Elijah. In the widow's house at Zarephath day by day, helping the poor woman and her child ; preventing by prayer her little stock of meal from wasting and the oil in her cruse from failing ; taking the dead child from her bosom, carrying it to his chamber, wrestling in prayer for its recovery, beholding life return to it, and finally bringing it down to its mother and placing it, her living child, once more in her arms—in all this Elijah either learned, or might have learned, that human-heartedness which is so essential to the true prophet of the Lord. In all this he either gained, or might have gained, those larger views and more generous feelings which are in every age more powerful instruments in the prophet's hand than the tempest, the earthquake, or the fire.

One other lesson let us learn—a lesson for the missionary. We send our missionaries into heathen lands as lands of nothing but darkness and the shadow of death; and, no doubt, the darkness is a darkness that may be felt, the shadow of death is as deep as in the grave. But in the midst of the darkness there are rays of light; in the midst of the death there are sparks of life, needing only to be kindled into flame. We ought not to forget this. To remember it as we ought would make our missionary efforts start from a new point, and would infuse into them a fresh spirit. In order to stimulate to missionary zeal it is not necessary to think that all to whom we send the message of the gospel are without God and without hope. Such a thought rather hampers our energy, for we know that, in the inmost recesses of our hearts, we do not receive it as genuine and true. Is it not enough that we know that there are "gems of purest ray" scattered upon the mountains and in the valleys of heathenism, and that we go to gather them that they may be polished and made meet to shine in the Redeemer's crown? The argument for missions has been too much associated with the thought of simply plucking brands from the burning. There is another view of them to be taken, by which this ought at least to be always accompanied. We send our missionaries into the field of heathenism that we may there discover those who, already touched by the spirit of Christ, wait for the full revelation to their souls of the Life and the Light of men.

CHAPTER III.

ELIJAH'S WORK OF REFORMATION (I KINGS XVIII. 1-40).

Elijah enters upon his work of reformation—Effect of drought on Israel and Ahab—Difficulty of the part which Elijah had to act—Soreness of the famine—Persecution of Jezebel—Fears of Obadiah—Elijah meets Obadiah—Presents himself to Ahab—Arrangements for the contest with the prophets of Baal—Carmel—The place and its associations—The contest—The prophets of Baal and their failure—Elijah's address to the people—His arrangements for the sacrifice—His prayer—The answer—Effect upon the people—The slaughter of Baal's prophets at the Kishon—Restoration of Israel to the Covenant.

WE left Elijah at Zarephath, the small heathen village in which the house of the poor widow afforded him protection in that troubled time; where he and his hostess were miraculously sustained by the barrel of meal that wasted not and the cruse of oil that failed not; and where, both by the continued miracle and by the presence of the child whom he had raised to life, the prophet's faith must have been kept alive amidst all that might otherwise have filled him with despondency and gloom. How long he dwelt there we do not exactly know. He had been for "a while" (chap. xvii. 7) in the valley of the Cherith; and the incident upon which we are now to enter took place "after many days" (chap. xviii. 1). In the words of our Lord at Nazareth, and again in the Epistle of St. James, it is said that it had not rained for three years and six months (Luke iv. 25; James v. 17). But it may not be necessary to understand these words literally, either as to the length of the period or as to the absolute cessation of rain during the whole of it. On the one hand, in interpreting the Scriptures, so true in all their characteristics to that Eastern world from which they came, we have to make allowance for the tendency to hyperbole which prevailed there. On the other hand, we know from the Revelation of St. John that the number 3½, half of the covenant number 7, presented itself to the Jew as expressive of a period of want and suffering. Both our Lord therefore and St. James, than whom no writer of the New Testament is more marked by the impassioned spirit of Hebrew poetry, might readily enough use 3½ as a round number by which to give utterance to their thought. Yet, though thus not bound to think of three and a half years in all their literalness, the narrative will not permit us to depart far from the simple meaning of the words; and we cannot be wrong in supposing that, for a space of nearly at least three years, a terrible drought had existed in Samaria, that it had extended even to the neighbouring lands of Galilee and Phœnicia, and that during all the later part of that period it had been followed by famine, its natural and inevitable consequence. In Samaria especially the famine had been sore and the suffering great. What effect had been produced upon the people we are not informed. That they had not yet confessed and forsaken their idolatry is clear. The decisive step had yet to be taken that was to lead them to do so. But we can hardly imagine that all that long time of suffering had passed in vain. Israel had often before this been refined in the furnace of affliction. Sorrow had awakened it to repentance, and had led it to return and inquire early after God. A similar result had in all probability, to some extent, been obtained now. The cry on Mount Carmel soon to be uttered, "The Lord He is God; the Lord He is God," had been preceded by searchings of heart which helped to prepare the people for the moment when the scales of ignorance and obduracy were to fall from their eyes.

Whatever may have been the case with the people, there is every reason to believe that no salutary result had been produced in the mind of the king. None knew so well as he why the suffering had been sent; but he closed his heart against conviction, and with the vain folly of persecutors in every age, he sought to wreak his vengeance upon those who had warned him of approaching punishment instead of repenting of the sin by which the punishment had been provoked. He made every effort to discover the hiding-place of Elijah (chap. xviii. 10). Perhaps he did not try Phœnicia, for we again see Eastern hyperbole in the words of Obadiah, which we find later in the narrative, and it would hardly occur to Ahab that the prophet should have fled to the very home and centre of that worship which he had been commissioned to denounce. However this may be, Ahab failed to discover the place where Elijah was concealed, and God Himself planned their meeting.

Twice already we have read of the coming of the word of the Lord to Elijah—when he was directed to take refuge by the brook Cherith, and when he was sent to Zarephath. We now read of it again. The real drama of the prophet's life was about to begin, and the beginning was determined by Him whose servant the prophet was. "And it came to pass," we are told, "after many days that the word of the Lord came to Elijah, in the third year, saying; Go, show thyself unto Ahab, and I will send rain upon the earth." The command and the promise accompanying it are more closely connected in our minds, who know what happened, than they could be in the mind of him to whom they were addressed. To him the promise would but little diminish the danger that belonged to the command, for the first thing that he was to do was to show himself to the king, whose rage was already to such a degree excited against him, and who had been seeking him everywhere to make him the object of his vengeance. It was enough, however, that the command was given. Nothing remained for Elijah but to obey. He "went to show himself unto Ahab."

The incidents next related by which the meeting was brought about seem especially intended to illustrate the difficulty of the part which Elijah had to act, and the bold and determined spirit in which he executed his mission. Let us mark—

1. *The severity of the drought and the soreness of the famine in Samaria.* It could not indeed be otherwise. For a space of nearly three years rain had either not fallen, or had been sent only in such trifling quantities as could scarcely relieve the people's misery. Ahab had been getting more and more alarmed. The cries of his famishing subjects must have been ringing in his ears; and, though he himself and his court, with all the resources of the kingdom at their command, had probably suffered little in comparison with others, the wolf was now at length at his own door, and famine was stalking through his

own household. He determined to do more than he had yet done, and to make a tour of inspection through the land. Summoning Obadiah, the steward of his household, he said to him, "Go through the land, unto all the fountains of water, and unto all the brooks; peradventure we may find grass, and save the horses and mules alive, that we lose not all the beasts. So they divided the land between them to pass throughout it. Ahab went one way by himself; and Obadiah went another way by himself." The arrangement was well calculated to bring home to the mind of Ahab with greater impressiveness than ever the sufferings of Israel, and to make him even more determined than he had been in his pursuit of the prophet to whom he traced them.

2. *The persecution by Jezebel.* That cruel and unprincipled queen had not been content with promoting to the utmost of her power the worship of Baal and of Ashtaroth. It had not been enough for her simply to support at her own cost a large number of the prophets of her false divinities, and to maintain them at her own table. She had also instituted a persecution against the ancient faith of Israel, and had slain the prophets of the Lord. Who could doubt that what she had done before she would do again, and that even more than those who had preceded him Elijah would be the object of her rage. Her power too over the mind of Ahab must have been well known. He would certainly prove a pliant tool at her bidding, and the ready instrument of her designs.

3. *The fears of Obadiah.* There is something peculiarly graphic in the manner in which these fears are mentioned by the sacred writer. Every particular noted in the narrative is calculated to illustrate them. There is the character of Obadiah himself. As in the case of so many of the Old Testament worthies, his name is the index to what he was. He was a "servant of the Lord," for that is the meaning of his name. It is said of him "that he feared the Lord greatly," and he says of himself, "I thy servant fear the Lord from my youth." Nor is there any reason to think that he had concealed his faith, and accommodated himself outwardly to the heathenism amidst which he moved. The whole account given of him leads rather to the supposition that he was an honourable and upright man, and the simple fact that he retained his position at the court of Ahab is no evidence to the contrary. Both in sacred and

profane history there are to be found not a few instances of persons in authority who had themselves cast off the obligations of religion, but who gladly accepted and highly valued the services of pious men, when in the secret of their hearts they either despised or feared them. Thus Pharaoh prized Joseph, Saul David, and Nebuchadnezzar Daniel, and thus in later times St. Paul sent his Christian salutations to them that were of Cæsar's household. All these persons maintained the profession of their faith openly and boldly, and why may we not think the same of Obadiah when there is not the slightest intimation to the contrary? Again there is the confidence reposed in Obadiah by his master. He was "over the household" of the king, in all probability governor or chamberlain in the palace, a high and responsible office. Nay, as if even that were not enough, this confidence of Ahab in his servant is brought still more strikingly before us by the fact that, when the king desired to search the whole land for fountains of water and brooks, he divided it into two parts, himself taking one part and sending Obadiah through the other. Nothing could afford a more striking testimony to the esteem in which he held his servant, or to his feeling that the loss of such a servant would be a misfortune to his house. Still further, there is the boldness with which Obadiah could act when occasion called for it. "Was it not told my lord," he exclaims, "what I did when Jezebel slew the prophets of the Lord; how I hid an hundred men of the Lord's prophets by fifty in a cave, and fed them with bread and water?" He who could act thus could have been neither a feeble nor a cowardly man. Only at the peril of his life could he have taken such a step. Yet now, notwithstanding all this, notwithstanding the general manliness of his character, the confidence reposed in him by Ahab, and the boldness with which he had, probably at a recent date, rescued so many prophets of the Lord, he trembles when Elijah says to him, "Go, tell thy lord, Behold, Elijah is here."

The soreness of the famine, the persecution of Jezebel, the fears of Obadiah—all illustrate the danger of that position in which the prophet of the Lord was placed when, in obedience to the Divine command, he set forth from Zarephath to show himself to Ahab.

Yet he went without a moment's hesitation when the commandment came, and his first meeting was with Obadiah.

"As Obadiah was in the way, behold, Elijah met him; and he knew him, and fell on his face, and said, Is it thou, my lord Elijah?" What connection Obadiah had had with Elijah before; where he had seen him, heard him, or learned to listen to him with awe, we have no means of knowing. Perhaps it was enough to gaze upon that figure clothed in its rough garment of hair, that lofty look and determined step, to be assured that this could be no other than the dreaded prophet of the Lord. Or perhaps he may even have been in the company of Ahab at the moment when Elijah first denounced those woes upon the land which had been so signally fulfilled. We need not ask such questions. Obadiah said, as he bowed to the prophet with Oriental reverence, "Is it thou, my lord Elijah?" The answer was brief and emphatic, "It is I; go, tell thy lord, Behold, Elijah is here."

And now all the peril of the situation breaks forth in Obadiah's answer—"And he said, Wherein have I sinned, that thou wouldest deliver thy servant into the hand of Ahab to slay me? As the Lord thy God liveth, there is no nation or kingdom whither my lord hath not sent to seek thee: and when they said, He is not here, he took an oath of the kingdom and nation, that they found thee not. And now thou sayest, Go, tell thy lord, Behold, Elijah is here. And it shall come to pass, as soon as I am gone from thee, that the Spirit of the Lord shall carry thee whither I know not; and so, when I come and tell Ahab, and he cannot find thee, he shall slay me." And then the good man dwells upon those claims to Elijah's consideration that have been already spoken of, and ends with a third time repeating those words of astonishment and alarm which show so clearly what feelings were uppermost in his mind, "And now thou sayest, Go, tell thy lord, Behold, Elijah is here, and he shall slay me."

No prospect, however, of danger could arrest the prophet for a moment, and, without even attempting to combat the fears of Obadiah, he replies, "As the Lord God of hosts liveth, before whom I stand, I will surely show myself to him to-day." When Elijah first showed himself to Ahab he had said, "as the Lord God of Israel liveth." Now he says, "as the Lord God of hosts liveth." The change is not without significance. It shows that the prophet was fully alive to the dangerous position in which he stood, and to the power and hatred of the king whom he was about to meet. But it shows also that he knew in whom he believed. As in the case of Elisha, his disciple and successor, he beheld around him, though not visible to the eye of sense, the place full of chariots of fire and horses of fire. He was well aware that He who was with him was more than all they that could be against him. He had no fears therefore of what might happen. Trusting in "the Lord God of hosts" he would certainly show himself that day to Ahab.

Obadiah could no longer hesitate. He went to meet Ahab, and told him, and Ahab went to meet Elijah.

The two met—the prophet and the king—and it is almost the only moment of Ahab's life when he displays something at least of the spirit of a man. Generally in his personal, if not his public, character he was a coward; a weak, pusillanimous creature in the hands of a wife far more strong-minded than himself. At this moment, whatever the cause, he appears like one who feels that he has a part to act, and who is resolved to act it. Whether it was that Elijah's flight had given him courage, or that he was moved to the depths of his soul by the spectacles he had lately witnessed with his own eyes, or that he sought by a display of passion to conceal some inward trembling of his heart, it is difficult to say; but he has at least the appearance of being bold, and he approaches Elijah with the words, "Is it thou, thou troubler of Israel?" It does not seem to occur to him that he was himself the troubler of Israel. He followed the course taken by the world in every age, when it lays the blame of all that unsettledness of mind which so often disturbs it in the midst of its sinful ease, upon those who would awaken it to a sense of its responsibilities, and lead it to a deeper and more abiding peace. As the words of Christ go out to their fulfilment—"I came not to send peace on earth, but a sword" (Matt. x. 34)—men disturbed by the proclamation of the truth turn round upon its preachers, and charge them with unduly disquieting consciences that would otherwise be at ease, and with unreasonably condemning practices which, but for them, would be considered innocent. It is this Pharisaism, this punctiliousness, this strictness of view, and this harshness of judgment, they contend, that distract society. Let men alone, and there will be peace. Thus it was that our Lord Himself, the Prince of peace, was charged by the Jews before Pilate with stirring up the people, as He taught throughout Judæa, beginning from Galilee, even unto Jerusalem (Luke xxiii. 5). Thus it was that the uproarious Jews at Thessalonica complained, before the rulers of the city, of St. Paul and his companions. "These that have turned the world upside down are come hither also" (Acts xvii. 6). Thus it always is. Men whom misfortune has overtaken, while they dislike the truth that might have saved them, are ever ready to shift responsibility from themselves, and to charge those as the authors of their sufferings who have simply warned them that they will and must pay the penalty of their sins. In this spirit Ahab met Elijah now.

The prophet was equal to the occasion. Pointing to the nature of the wicked courses which had brought calamity upon Israel, he answered, " I have not troubled Israel ; but thou, and thy father's house, in that ye have forsaken the commandments of the Lord, and thou hast followed the Baalim." It may be well to notice for a moment in passing that the word " Baalim " is here used, as on many other occasions in the Old Testament, in the plural number, as we should say " Baals." We are not to understand by it images, but rather different and varied conceptions of the one heathen deity. Baal was properly the sun-god of Phœnician worship, "the bearer and principle of the physical life, and of the productive, propagating, power of nature, which was regarded as an efflux of his essence."[1] The idea connected with Baal became thus very comprehensive ; and, as he not only gave birth to nature in all her different aspects, but also preserved, ordered, and destroyed her, a different conception of him belonged to each aspect of his work—and there were many Baals. Against all of them did the prophet direct his anger and his scorn, or rather the indignation and the scorn of Him who had laid the foundation of true religious worship and life in the one great truth : " Know, O Israel, that the Lord thy God is one God."

Elijah was well aware, however, that he had not been sent to meet Ahab in order to exchange with him stern or angry words. A great crisis in the national history had come, and it was for each of them to act his part aright. He prepared himself for that allotted to him in the coming struggle. Let us notice the proposal.

" Now therefore," he said, " send, and gather to me all Israel

[1] Movers, "Die Phœnizien," quoted by Keil *in loc.*

unto mount Carmel, and the prophets of Baal four hundred and fifty, and the prophets of Asherah, four hundred, which eat at Jezebel's table." Whether in fear or in hope Ahab immediately complied with the request. He "sent unto all the children of Israel, and gathered the prophets together unto mount Carmel," though it would seem that, for some reason or other unknown to us, the prophets of the Asherah did not present themselves. No mention is made of them either at this point or in the subsequent narrative; but even without them the scene that follows is one of the most striking recorded in Old Testament history.

The locality was Carmel. Instead of indulging in general description, it may be well to take an account of it from the writings of one long familiar with these scenes, and who has written of them with both power and sympathy. "At the eastern extremity of the ridge, where the wooded heights of Carmel sink down into the usual bleakness of the hills of Palestine, is a terrace of natural rock. It is encompassed by dense thickets of evergreens, and upon it are the remains of an old and massive square structure, built of large hewn stones. This is *El-Muhrakah*, and here, in all probability, stood Elijah's altar. The situation and environs answer in every particular to the various incidents in the narrative. A short distance from the terrace is a fountain, whence the water may have been brought which was poured round Elijah's sacrifice and altar. The terrace commands a noble view over the whole plain of Esdraelon, from the banks of the Kishon down at the bottom of the steep declivity away to the distant hills of Gilboa, at whose base stood the royal city of Jezreel. To the eight hundred and fifty prophets, ranged doubtless on the wide upland sweep just beneath the terrace, to the multitudes of people, many of whom may have remained on the plain, the altar of Elijah would be in full view, and they could all see in the evening twilight that the fire of the Lord fell and consumed the burnt-offering and the wood and the stones and the dust, and licked up the water. The people, then, trembling with fear and indignation, seized at Elijah's bidding, the prophets of Baal; and Elijah brought them down to the brook Kishon, and slew them there. On the lower declivities of the mountain is a mound called *Tell-el-Kusis*, meaning the hill of the priests, which probably marks the very scene of the execution. May not the present name of

ELIJAH'S WORK OF REFORMATION. 49

the Kishon itself have originated in this tragic event, as it is called *Nahr-el-Mokatta*, the river of slaughter?"[1] To this description we may only add that from Carmel the eye stretches in an unbroken course along the great plain of Esdraelon (in Old Testament history, Megiddon), of which it speaks, the mountains of Galilee on the north, those of Samaria on the south, the isolated hill of Tabor, long, but erroneously, thought to be the Mount of Transfiguration, as it stands like a great sentinel at the extremity of the plain, filling the eye to the east; while the river Kishon, draining into the Mediterranean the waters which come down from the surrounding hills, and passing at times immediately below the cliffs of Carmel, at the feet of the spectator, flows winding to the sea. A more remarkable spot could not have been chosen for the purpose; for, apart from every other consideration, Elijah could see from its heights the whole of the Samaritan portion of that noble land, originally bestowed on Israel as a high tower for the light of Divine revelation, but now shrouded in the thickest darkness.

The memories of the scene were not less remarkable than the locality itself. For Elijah could recall the fact that, in past times of gloom, God had there saved His people, not so much by many as by few. In that country lying at his feet a woman had been raised up to be the deliverer of Israel in one of its darkest hours; and the Song of Deborah, the grandest perhaps of national triumphal odes, had celebrated the victory gained by the terrified Israelites over Jabin, king of Hazor, and all his host, so that "the land had rest forty years" (Judg. v. 31). There, too, Gideon had made the plain re-echo with his famous war-cry, and with his three hundred men had routed the huge army of the Midianites (Judg. vii.). Even in later ages the plain of Megiddon has never failed to be a great Eastern battlefield of the nations; and, when the Seer in the Apocalpse describes the first issues of the struggle between the conquering Redeemer and the embattled powers of "the whole world," he gathers them together "into the place which is called in Hebrew Har-Magedon," or the mountain of Megiddon (chap. xvi. 16). Such was the spot on which were transacted the events related in this chapter.

If the locality was thus famous, both in itself and in its

[1] Dr Porter, quoted in Taylor's "Elijah the Prophet," p. 108.

memories, the conflict now to be witnessed upon it was in the highest degree momentous. Israel was then wavering between the worship of the living God and that of Baal. It had not yet surrendered itself completely to the dominion of that idolatry which Ahab, and more particularly Jezebel, had been labouring to introduce. Many, indeed, had probably done so, but not the people as a whole. The God of Israel may still have been acknowledged, but side by side with Him Baal was acknowledged too. This, however, was entirely to defeat the purpose of God's revelation of Himself to His chosen people. He was the one living and true God, and no idol divinity could be permitted to share that throne which was solely and exclusively His. Let Baal be honoured along with Him, even although not substituted for Him, and not only would the foundation of Israel's existence as a nation be overthrown, but the mission assigned to that people in the religious training of the world would be defeated. In such circumstances were the events now before us to be enacted.

Ahab's command for the gathering together of Israel has been issued and obeyed. Elijah is on the one side of the mountain hollow: four hundred and fifty prophets of Baal are on the other,—one man, poor, wild, shaggy, apparently without a friend in the great assembly that has been collected there, over against four hundred and fifty, well-clad, sleek, prosperous, and popular; while around them stand the king and a great multitude of his people watching the issue with strained eyes and eager expectations. Similar scenes have been not unfrequently witnessed in the history of the world, for in the contests of truth with error, and righteousness with unrighteousness, the few have generally stood against the many. *Athanasius contra mundum* has even passed into a proverb; and the example of Him who before Pontius Pilate witnessed a good confession will ever be the chief stay of those who feel that they have a prophet's message to deliver to men. In that chosen group Elijah may certainly take his place. One against four hundred and fifty: his tone, his bearing, his gestures show that he was not afraid.

The contest is about to begin, and Elijah proposes the conditions. But first of all he appeals to the people as to the unworthiness of their present state of mind: "How long halt ye between two opinions? If the Lord be God, follow Him; but if Baal, then follow him." It would seem that all were not so entirely given up to idolatry as Jezebel and Ahab. They simply hesitated as to the being whom they were to worship and obey. On the one hand they remembered the past. On the other they were tempted by the present. They could not forget what the Almighty had done for their fathers; yet they could not steel themselves against the allurements of the sensuous idolatry into which their king and his queen would lead them. They halted between two opinions, incapable of determining, or unwilling to determine, what it were best to do. No state of mind could be more utterly at variance with the claims of truth or the possession of that truthfulness of character without which we cannot hear God's voice. Again and again does the Bible protest against this divided service, against the idea that we can listen to both God and Mammon, against our being neither cold nor hot: while St. James, always ready with his rich poetical allusions, exclaims, "He that doubteth is like the surge of the sea driven by the wind and tossed. For let not that man think that he shall receive anything of the Lord, a double-minded man, unstable in all his ways" (chap. i. 6–8). The human conscience acknowledges the force of such an appeal; and "the people answered Elijah not a word."

Things were now ready for the contest, and little remained but to see that the method and the terms of it should be clearly understood. To this, therefore, the prophet next devoted himself. But first he would have Israel own how much, according to human calculation, the balance was against him. "I, even I only," he said, "am left a prophet of the Lord; but Baal's prophets are four hundred and fifty men." It is not necessary to take the first words literally, or to suppose that all the other prophets, whom Obadiah had hid in a cave, had been before this time massacred in one of Jezebel's bloody persecutions. Enough that Elijah was alone now. No other prophet was there to stand by him or to afford him encouragement in the trying position which he occupied. As far as mere human strength went what was he against four hundred and fifty? We need not doubt that the people saw it, and that in the bold attitude of that solitary man they may even have beheld some token that would prepare them for his coming victory. Solitary as he was Elijah asks no favour. There is no thought of weakness in his mind, no idea of eliciting the sympathy of the multitude, and thus fighting his battle with weapons which, if mainly Divine, shall also be partly human. He will give every advantage to his adversaries, that so it may more clearly appear that the excellency of the power is not his but God's. "Let them give us two bullocks," he said; "and let them choose one bullock for themselves, and cut it in pieces, and lay it on the wood, and put no fire under; and I will dress the other bullock, and lay it on the wood, and put no fire under. And call ye on the name of your god, and I will call on the name of the Lord; and the God that answereth by fire, let him be God." Nothing could be fairer than the proposal; or, if there was any inequality in the parties, it was wholly against Elijah. Not only did he stand there alone, but Baal was the sun-god, the god of fire. It would thus be easy for him to answer the demands of his votaries if he were able or disposed to do it, for he would only exert a power which flowed from his very nature, and which he was supposed to possess in an eminent degree. The people were alive to this, and when the prophet's proposals had been made they answered with one voice, "It is well spoken."

The conditions of the contest had been laid down, and the contest itself was now to begin. It is described at length, yet in a manner only corresponding to its importance, by the sacred writer. It began with the prophets of Baal, for to them Elijah said, "Choose you one bullock for yourselves, and dress it first; for ye are many; and call on the name of your god, but put no fire under." The prophets, like the people, obeyed: and from morning even until noon they cried, "O Baal, hear us." The words are simple; but, repeated as they were, they are sufficient to convey to us a graphic picture of the melancholy scene. Here for six hours was undoubtedly that "much speaking" of which our Lord complains when He warns His disciples against resorting in prayer to the "vain repetitions" of the Gentiles (Matt. vi. 7). Now perhaps from larger, now from smaller, groups; and yet again from the whole company of the prophets, went forth hour after hour the same continuous, earnest, eager cry, "O Baal, hear us." And, as time went on and their excitement began to increase, they "leaped about the altar which was made." "But there was no voice, neither any that answered." No fire descended from the burning sky. The sacrifice lay unconsumed, untouched, before the eyes of all.

Then followed what the most brilliant writer of modern times upon the history of the Old Testament has spoken of as if it displayed "a savage humour, a biting sarcasm in the tone of Elijah which forms an exception alike to the general humanity of the New Testament and the general seriousness of the Old."[1] The language is scarcely just. It is true that there is biting sarcasm, but their is no want of humanity or seriousness. The most cutting irony is not inconsistent either with the one or with the other; and here we may be assured that the prophet's words produced no "burst of laughter," but only a deepened sense of the disastrous nature of the issue that was at hand. "And it came to pass," we are told, "at noon, that Elijah mocked them, and said unto them, Cry aloud: for he is a god; either he is musing, or he is gone aside, or he is in a journey, or peradventure he sleepeth, and must be awaked."

The irony went to the heart of those to whom it was addressed, and stimulated them to still greater efforts. They cried aloud, and cut themselves after their manner with knives and lances, "until the blood gushed out upon them." The phenomenon may appear at first sight extraordinary, but it was by no means uncommon in that Phœnician worship of Baal, which had now been transferred to Palestine. "Many ancient writers notice the custom, from whose statements the processions of the strolling bands that wander about with the Syrian goddess may be thus described. 'A discordant howling opens the scene. Then they fly wildly through one another, with the head sunk down to the ground, but turning round in circles, so that the loose flowing hair drags through the mire; thereupon they first bite themselves on the arms, and at last cut themselves with two-edged swords which they are wont to carry. Then begins a new scene. One of them, who surpasses all the rest in frenzy, begins to prophesy with sighs and groans, openly accuses himself of his past sins which he now wishes to punish by the mortifying of the flesh, takes a knotted whip which the *Galli* are wont to bear, lashes his back, cuts himself with swords, until the blood trickles down from his mangled body.'"[2] But it was not only in Phœnicia, or in the time of which we are speaking, that these cruel rites existed. The commandment in Deut. xiv. 1,2, though having direct reference to another point, shows at once the practices of the surrounding nations, and the tendency of Israel to imitate them: "Ye are the children of the

[1] Stanley, "Jewish Church," lect. xxx.
[2] Keil, on 1 Kings xviii. 26–29, quoting Movers, "Die Phoenizien."

Lord your God; ye shall not cut yourselves, nor make any baldness between your eyes for the dead. For thou art an holy people unto the Lord thy God, and the Lord hath chosen thee to be a peculiar people unto Himself, above all peoples that are upon the face of the earth." It was well, therefore, that heathenism should now be manifested, not only in its most revolting forms, but in forms in which the assembled people might see it as it really was, and which they had been expressly forbidden to imitate.

All this lasted for hours. At midday Elijah had addressed the prophets with his words of burning scorn. From midday onwards till the time of the offering of the evening oblation there was no pause in the excitement. But, as in the earlier, so in the later part of the day it was unattended by the slightest tokens of success. From noon till towards sunset the terrible scene continued: but "there was neither voice, nor any to answer, nor any that regarded." The cries, the shouts of despair, the leapings about the altar, the cuttings with knives, and the wounds inflicted upon themselves by the maddened worshippers had been spent without effect. The bullock lay untouched upon the altar. The wood of the sacrifice was as cold and dead as it had been when it was first heaped upon the pile. Exhausted nature could no longer stand it; and, with the gathering shades of evening, stillness fell upon the prophets of Baal and the multitude—a strange expectant stillness, more full of meaning than all the noise and shouting of the day.

Then Elijah stepped forth, and his words and actions alike betoken the calm and determined resolution with which he did so. There is neither scorn nor irony in his tones. He has a great work to do, and he will do it with the quietness, the deliberateness, and the firmness which the work demands.

In the first place, he called the people to come near to him, that they might see in the clearest manner that there was no deception in what he was about to do; and the people came.

In the second place, he repaired the altar of God that had been thrown down in the past idolatrous days of Jezebel. It was a striking feature of his proceedings. He built no new altar. His object was not to introduce a new worship, but to restore the old. Like all true reformers he would connect himself with the past and not obliterate it. He felt, as we ought to feel, at the very time when we are most sensible of the insufficiency of the past, of its shortcomings and of its sins, that that past has in great measure made us what we are. It has formed the largest portion of our lives. It has trained and disciplined the powers by which we are able to correct it. At no point in the whole progress of the race is it possible to say that there a great gulf divides it into two distinct and separate stages, and that across that gulf there is no bridge. The Christian Dispensation itself, the mightiest revolution that ever occurred in the history of man, was a fulfilling, not a destroying, of the past At the moment when it superseded that of the Old Testament, acknowledging its weakness and announcing its vanishing away, it paid it honour; and if, in one sense, it may be said that, when our Lord introduced Christianity with all its exalted privileges its higher life, and its glorious hopes into the world, He introduced a new thing, in another and still more important sense it must be added, that it was only new because it was the fulfilment of the old. "I am not come," said the Saviour, "to destroy, but to fulfil;" and in that single sentence He has given us a principle of universal range and of inestimable value. It is a lesson for the politician, telling him that in all wise change he must take up those threads of the past which have interwoven themselves with a nation's life, and that only in so far as he does so can the measures by which he would promote the progress of a people possess true adaptation to their wants, secure a firm hold of their minds, gain that stability for the time which is necessary to all real advance, and become in their own turn a foundation upon which at some future day a still higher fabric of national welfare may be reared. It is a lesson for the rulers and guides of the Church, impressing upon them that, in their efforts to carry the Church onward to the perfection which they anticipate and long for, over-hastiness will defeat their end; and that if they grasp too suddenly at the coming glory they will only unsettle instead of deepening conviction, and will plunge us into confusion and darkness instead of bringing us nearer to the perfect day. It is a lesson for the Christian thinker, bidding him be careful that in all developments of truth and life he recognize what has been true in days which may have been less enlightened than his own, and that his developments are certainly false if, in their loftier concep tions of belief and duty, they do not embrace the more imperfect views of the generations that are gone. Finally, it is a lesson for any man who would "forget what is behind and reach on to what is before;" reminding him that however he may be dissatisfied with the present, there is yet a glory in the earth even as it is; that there is a light on the land and on the sea; that an entirely new world is not needed to accomplish either the patriot's or the poet's dream, but that the arrangements of society, the bonds that unite men in the family, in the neighbourhood, in the state, have a long and valuable history behind them, and that to begin with subverting them would be to cut down the very tree into whose stem and branches he would introduce the sweeter sap of which he boasts.

"I am not come to destroy, but to fulfil;" what words both for the desponding and the hopeful, for those whose affections linger in the past, and for those who press forward to the future! The old is not despised while the value of the new is felt. The one does not die, while yet the other springs up in power and beauty. By that single principle our Lord places Himself upon a platform from which He commands the progress of the race; and we, if we imbibe His spirit, become "the heirs of all the ages." We see that they have an inheritance to bestow on us; and, when we receive it, we learn to lay it out in such a way that our children shall be richer and more favoured than ourselves.

Thus, then, it was that Elijah acted now. That old altar, the stones of which were lying neglected upon the mountain side, had its history, its associations, and its memories. It told of better days when the true God had been worshipped there, and had there answered the prayers of His worshippers by the blessings which He bestowed. It had a connection with the most faithful and prosperous times of the Theocracy, and it could appeal to Israel as no erection fashioned at the moment could. A Divine wisdom guided Elijah when, instead of building a new altar, he repaired the altar that had been broken down.

In the third place, the prophet repaired the altar of God in the way best fitted to remind the people of the brightest period of their past, and of the high destiny to which the Almighty had appointed them. There was a time when twelve stones had been used before as a memorial of the signal favour which they had enjoyed at the hands of Him who had delivered them from Egyptian bondage, had led them through the wilderness, and had opened for them a passage through the river Jordan into the Promised Land. For "it came to pass, when all the nation were clean passed over Jordan, that the Lord spake unto Joshua, saying, Take you twelve men out of the people, out of every tribe a man, and command ye them, saying, Take you hence out of the midst of Jordan, out of the place where the priests feet stood firm, twelve stones, and carry them over with you, and lay them down in the lodging place, where ye shall lodge this night." And Joshua did so, and explained the reason of the act: "That this may be a sign among you that, when your children ask in time to come, saying, What mean ye by these stones? then ye shall say unto them, Because the waters of Jordan were cut off before the Ark of the Covenant of the Lord; when it passed over Jordan, the waters of Jordan were cut off: and these stones shall be for a memorial unto the children of Israel for ever" (Joshua iv. 1-3, 7). These twelve stones could never be forgotten by the people: nor could they ever fail to remind them of those manifestations of Divine power and grace which had accompanied their settlement in Canaan. So also was it now, for Elijah "took twelve stones, according to the number of the tribes of the sons of Jacob, unto whom the word of the Lord came, saying, Israel shall be thy name, and with the stones he built an altar in the name of the Lord." From the disordered condition of Israel at the moment when it had separated from Judah he turned to its still deeper national and religious feelings. The Jewish people could never forget that the twelve tribes had been originally one nation. They had been *the twelve* tribes. They were destined, in spirit at least if not in the letter, to be the twelve tribes again. Abraham was the father of them all. In Isaac their covenant history began. The sons of Jacob, whom God had surnamed Israel on that memorable night when as a prince he had wrestled with God and had prevailed, were the heads of its different sections; and the one living God had made them all in Himself one family. Elijah had now to restore no separatist worship in which Judah should vex Ephraim or Ephraim envy Judah. He had to bear witness for the true worship of the united parts of Israel as a whole; and only in twelve not ten stones, or in any other number, could that idea be expressed.

The altar was built; but the prophet deemed it necessary to take every precaution to convince the multitude around him of the reality of that miraculous interposition of God upon which he counted with so much confidence. His other arrangements were directed to that end. "He made a trench about the altar, as great as would contain two measures of seed. And he put the wood in order, and cut the bullock in pieces, and laid it on the wood." Then, calling others to aid him, he said, "Fill four barrels with water, and pour it on the burnt-offering, and on the wood," and it was done. "He said, Do it the second time; and they did it the second time. He said, Do it the third time; and they did it the third time. And the water ran round about the altar; and he filled the trench also with water."

All was now ready, and in the midst of the still multitude Elijah raised his voice. He "came near, and said, O Lord, the God of Abraham, of Isaac, and of Israel, let it be known this day that Thou art God in Israel, and that I am Thy servant, and that I have done all these things at Thy word. Hear me, O Lord, hear me, that this people may know that Thou, Lord, art God, and that Thou hast turned their heart back again." The prayer was calm, simple, and touching; and it presents a striking contrast to the frantic cries and self-lacerations of the prophets of Baal. The contrast is indeed so striking as almost of itself to vindicate the truthfulness of the narrative. No painter from the fancy could well have imagined, in the midst of a scene so full of tumult and excitement, a prayer so sober, and so free from exaggeration either of manner or of speech.

But, if even outwardly remarkable, Elijah's prayer was still more remarkable in its contents. He addresses God as the "God of Abraham, of Isaac, and of Israel," a formula taking us back to the moment when, at the burning bush, God had first revealed Himself to Moses as Israel's covenant God : "And God said moreover unto Moses, Thus shalt thou say unto the children of Israel, The Lord, the God of your fathers, the God of Abraham, the God of Isaac, and the God of Jacob, hath sent me unto you : this is My name for ever, and this is My memorial unto all generations" (Exod. iii. 15). Again, in this formula Elijah designedly changes the name Jacob into that of "Israel," not so much, apparently, for the sake of bringing out the fact that all the twelve tribes were one, as for the sake of giving expression to the thought that the word "Israel" was peculiarly fitted to remind them of that all-prevailing power of prayer which was now to be so strikingly exhibited. Once more, it may be noticed that the very essence of the relationship between God and His people finds utterance in the petition, "Let it be known this day that Thou art God in Israel, . . . that this people may know that Thou, Lord, art God, and that Thou hast turned their heart back again." Not the simple welfare of Israel, and certainly not the glory of God's servant, except in so far as represented through him, but the glory of God, is the main object of the prophet's desire.

To the prayer thus offered the answer was immediately given. "The fire of the Lord fell and consumed the burnt sacrifice, and the wood, and the stones, and the dust, and licked up the water that was in the trench." Nothing could be more complete, and Elijah needed only to be silent, and to let the Lord work.

The effect upon the people corresponded to the sight which they had witnessed. When they saw it, "they fell on their faces and said, The Lord, He is the God; the Lord, He is the God." Their words were a reply to the alternative which had been put before them by the prophet at the beginning of the contest, "How long halt ye between two opinions? If the Lord be God follow Him; but if Baal, then follow him." There was no hesitation; there was no halting; there were no two opinions now. The worship of Baal was at once renounced, and the God of Israel was acknowledged to be the only God.

One thing yet remained to be done, and it may be said that it was imposed upon both Elijah and the people by the necessities of the case. Of these prophets of Baal we form an altogether inaccurate idea if we imagine that any wholesome impression would be produced upon them by the proceedings of the day. No miracle, however great or striking, will convince one who has resolved not to be convinced; and there can be little doubt that the prophets of Baal were in that condition. They were interested in the degradation of the people. They were the deceivers rather than the deceived; and they must have been marked by peculiar obduracy, when for the three years during which the drought lasted, they still made, as they must have made, every effort to prevent the eyes of Israel being opened. Nothing, too, could be more terribly explicit than the law of Moses on the question of dealing with those who endeavoured to seduce the people to idolatry: "If thy brother, the son of thy mother, or thy son or thy daughter, or the wife of thy bosom, or thy friend which is as thine own soul, entice thee secretly, saying, Let us go and serve other gods, which thou hast not known, thou, nor thy fathers ; of the gods of the peoples which are round about you, nigh unto thee, or far off from thee, from the one end of the earth even unto the other end of the earth ; thou shalt not consent unto him, nor hearken unto him ; neither shall thine eye pity him, neither shalt thou conceal him ; but thou shalt surely kill him ; thine hand shall be first upon him to put him to death, and afterwards the hand of all the people" (Deut. xiii. 6–9). It cannot surprise us, therefore, that at a supremely critical moment, when the spirit of the old Theocracy was being restored in all its sternness and vigour, Elijah should have cried to the people, after all that had happened, "Take the prophets of Baal, let not one of them escape." Nor was it less natural that, when the command was given, it should be instantly obeyed ; and that, in the first paroxysm of the popular rage against those prophets who had proved themselves so weak, the people should have laid hold of them, and hurried them down the sides of Carmel to the Kishon, and slain them there. It would almost appear, indeed, from the words of the sacred narrative, that Elijah slew them with his own hand ; but it may be doubted if such an interpretation is necessary. No more may be intended than that he was the adviser and guide of the slaughter that took place. What was done by his instructions may be spoken of as if done by himself.

Consideration of the principles upon which such a destruction of human life took place may be delayed till we can speak more fully than could be done at the close of a chapter, of the sterner aspects of Elijah's work. In the meantime we must be content with noticing the fact that, before the sun went down that day behind the range of Carmel, Israel had, for the time at least, been restored to the covenant which it had dishonoured and forsaken.

CHAPTER IV.

ELIJAH AND THE BREAKING UP OF THE DROUGHT
(1 KINGS XVIII. 41-46).

Delay in the fulfilment of the promise—Necessity of waiting upon God in prayer—Elijah re-ascends Carmel—Mission to his servant—The cloud as a man's hand—Rain granted—Ahab's return to Jezreel—Elijah running before his chariot—Arrival at Jezreel—Nature and power of prayer—Objection to prayer answered—Physical phenomena—Mental phenomena—Characteristics of the prayers of Elijah as mentioned by St. James—Answer expected, and not simply reflex influence—For spiritual blessings—For others—Fervency in prayer—Prayer in faith—Power of such prayers.

WITH the events recorded in our last chapter the great work of Elijah's ministry was already accomplished. He had been raised up as the prophet of Restoration, as the healer of that breach which Israel had made of the Covenant of God, as the recaller of an apostate people to their allegiance to Jehovah. They who, but a little before, had owned the deities of the heathen nations around them, and been sunk in all the abominations of their worship, had now cried, with one simultaneous shout, "The Lord, He is God," "The Lord, He is God;" and, inspired by a just indignation towards those who had misled and betrayed them, had seized the prophets of Baal, hurried them down the side of Carmel to the river Kishon, which flows at the foot of the mountain; and, in the spirit of the old dispensation, slain them there. Not one of them escaped. The land was cleansed, and it remained only that the people should return to their homes, sweep away what still remained of the provision made for the rites of the heathen divinity for whom they had forsaken the God of their fathers, and wait for the blessings of which they had been so long deprived—the early and the latter rain.

It is a significant circumstance that the blessing was not immediately bestowed. Already clouds might have gathered in the sky, the heavens been black with tempest, and, instead of the fire which but a little before had descended upon Carmel, the showers been now pouring down refreshment and life upon the parched and desolated ground. As yet, however, there were no signs of change. The sun still burned in the heavens which were stretched over the land like a molten looking-glass : the eye was still pained by the fierce glare which there was no "shadow of a cloud" to soften ; and the brown, withered grass stretched away to the horizon, recalling past misery, emblem as much as it had long been of hopelessness, heartlessness, and despair. Why should it have been so ? Are the people to be dealt with on the principle enunciated by our Lord, when after the miracle of the feeding of the five thousand they followed Jesus, "not because they had seen signs, but because they had eaten of the loaves, and had been filled" (John vi. 26)? Had they felt the power of the miracle, but not understood the "sign"? Was the reality of their new convictions, the sincerity of their new devotion, to be further tested? Must they show that they no longer follow Baal but God, because of what He is in Himself, and even at the time when He may further try them? He has chosen them in the furnace of affliction. In that furnace is their dross to be finally separated from the gold?

Not, it would seem, for any of these reasons was the coming of the rain delayed, but that the people, perhaps that Elijah himself, might see, that even blessings promised must still be sought for, until they are given, in continual prayer. It is not enough, at any particular moment, to cast ourselves upon the word of promise ; and, having received the assurance that it will be fulfilled, to dismiss the subject from our minds until the fulfilment comes. We must wait upon the Lord until He answer us. We must not cease to "put Him in remembrance" until He actually bestows what we require. We must cultivate the spirit of the patriarch as he wrestled with God at Peniel, "I will not let Thee go except Thou bless me." How much Elijah acted in this spirit upon the present occasion we may

ELIJAH AND THE BREAKING UP OF THE DROUGHT. 63

learn from more than one particular in the narrative. For he knew that the drought was to be suspended at his word. "There shall not be dew nor rain these years, but *according to my word*" had been his language to Ahab at the first, and there can be no doubt that that language was the reasonable interpretation of what had been communicated to him by the Almighty. Yet he felt that he could not speak the "word" without prayer to Him who would show him the precise moment at which to do so. And again, although he heard even now, with the ear of faith, the coming storm, he was convinced that he must continue to pray. Not till the windows of heaven are opened, and the longed-for treasures are discharged upon the earth, may he desist from presenting his petitions before God.

For this, then, the prophet now makes preparation. He cannot pray effectually where he is. Surrounded by the excited multitude his thoughts would have been diverted from the duty, and he would have been unable to concentrate upon it all the energy of his soul. Then, too, at the spot where he stood by the river Kishon, he was not in the most favourable position for marking the first symptom of a favourable answer to his prayer. The storm we know was to come from the west; from that quarter of the heavens he had no doubt heard the "sound" of which he speaks; but between the west and him the range of Carmel lay. Two points therefore were to be gained—solitude, and a station whence the eye might stretch over the wide range of that Western sea across which the rain-clouds were to travel to the Holy Land. These two points Elijah proceeded to secure.

First, he addressed himself to Ahab, who had gone down with the multitude from the place of sacrifice to witness the slaughter of the prophets of Baal, "Get thee up, eat and drink; for there is the sound of abundance of rain." The word used in the original implies that Ahab was so far at least again to ascend Mount Carmel from those banks of the Kishon, to which a little before he had gone down. But it is by no means necessary to think that he was either to ascend to the top of the mountain, or to return to the spot on which the fire had recently descended from heaven. All the conditions of the narrative are satisfied by the supposition, that he was to leave the spot where the slaughter had taken place, and to seek one more suitable to the new thoughts that filled his mind and the new duties that were before him. Owing to the nature of the ground he could hardly do this without going up the side of Carmel, unless he were to proceed immediately on his journey to Jezreel, and it was not desirable that he should do this until the events of the day had been brought to a conclusion by the bursting forth of the expected rain. Much ingenuity has also been expended on the sense to be attached to the words "eat and drink," some supposing that they were spoken simply with a view to that fatigue by which Ahab must by this time have been oppressed; others that they were uttered in derision; while the conjecture has been made by one of the highest authorities in Old Testament criticism (Ewald) that the king was now invited to that meal which usually followed the completion of an offering. The suppositions are improbable or far-fetched. Worn out with hunger, excitement, and anxiety the king might indeed well be; but it was hardly in keeping with the solemnity of the moment, or with the thought of what still remained to be done, that Elijah should have given so much attention to his mere bodily necessities. To bring in the thought of derision, again, is to introduce an element entirely out of harmony with what must have been the tone of the prophet's spirit, to say nothing of the fact that, had Ahab been thus addressed in scorn, he would hardly have complied with the injunction so readily as he is reported to have done. The last supposition, that of Ewald, is not more tenable than these. The materials of a sacrificial feast consisted mainly of those parts of the victim which had not been used in the sacrifice. Here no such parts remained, for the bullock sacrificed by Elijah had been entirely consumed. The meaning of the command, therefore, can only have been, that Ahab might now look upon his own trials and those of his land as over. The drought was about to end. The anxieties of the three past years, which might well have disturbed the ordinary tenour of his life, might give place to confidence and hope. He might eat and drink at peace; and he did eat and drink, because there was a sound of abundance of rain.

Elijah's own anxieties, however, were not yet past. While Ahab ate and drank he went up to the top of Carmel, not indeed the very top, for he afterwards sent his servant to a point still higher than that occupied by himself, but to some retired spot near the top where he might give himself to prayer. There he

ELIJAH AND THE BREAKING UP OF THE DROUGHT. 65

'bowed himself down upon the earth, and put his face between his knees." The act was at once an act of prostration before the majesty of God, and of such separation from all around him as might leave undisturbed the singleness of his mind and the fervour of his spirit of devotion. That he went to pray, and that he prayed, we know (Jas. v. 18); but he not only prayed, he looked for an answer to his prayer. To his servant who was with him he said, "Go up now, look toward the sea." It may seem at first sight strange that he did not himself go up to the point from which the earliest symptom of the approaching storm could be discerned. But he was probably aware that the moment for that sight was not yet come. The same spirit of God, through whose working in his soul he had heard the sound of the abundance of rain, probably also taught him that before the distant sound changed into the present reality God was still in some way to ratify His covenant or to set His seal upon the covenant long ago made and now renewed. By abstaining, therefore, from going to the point whence he could see, he could the better continue, in prayer, to keep alive his faith. It was not a view of the distant approach of the blessing, it was the blessing itself, that he desired.

The servant went, and looked, and came back with the tidings. "There is nothing." Elijah said to him, "Go again seven times;" and in the number of visits thus referred to lies the Divine seal of the covenant. It would occupy far too much space were we now to endeavour to point out the singular use of this number both in the Old Testament and in the New. Everywhere throughout Scripture it is the number of the covenant between God and man, the pledge of the close and intimate relation which God has introduced between Himself and those who were formerly estranged from Him. This meaning the number seven has here, and only at the seventh mission does the promise begin to be fulfilled. "And it came to pass at the seventh time that he said, Behold, there ariseth a cloud out of the sea, as small as a man's hand." Geographers and travellers often tell us of those great storms of wind and rain which are thus indicated in the Levant, so that, while all around their ship there is calm and sunshine, that little speck in the sky near the horizon is so sure a symptom of the coming gale that, as quickly as possible, the sails are furled and every preparation made for the tempest that is at hand. Such a speck, small as a man's hand, may in the natural course of things have been witnessed now, and Elijah may have known well what it portended. The supposition, however, is of little use so far as the miraculous element in the narrative is concerned. The finger of God, if not traced in each individual detail of the scene before us, cannot be excluded from the combination of details, or from their adaptation to one another, in such a way as to produce the final result. In the plagues of Egypt, and even in the miracles of Christ, natural phenomena were supernaturally magnified and brought into action ; and it may have been so here. There is nothing to prevent those who wish to think of a Levantine storm from introducing it. But they cannot thus banish the working of Him who sent the storm at the precise instant when it was needed. That little cloud in the distant sky told Elijah that the moment for which he had waited upon God in all the eagerness and the constancy of fervent prayer was come. He said to his servant, " Go up, say unto Ahab, Make ready thy chariot, and get thee down, that the rain stop thee not." What a moment must that have been for the prophet, for Ahab, for the land ! Suspense was over. The startling events of the day were closed. The prophet of God whose life had so long been sought was vindicated in all that he had said and done. Ahab himself, if not convinced and converted, was silenced. The land was about to realize its covenant blessings. The thirsty soil was about to drink of the water of the rain of heaven. The fields would soon be covered with flocks, and the valleys with corn. " And it came to pass in a little while, that the heaven grew black with clouds and wind, and there was a great rain."

In the meantime " Ahab rode, and went to Jezreel." It was the place where he had built a summer palace for himself, and where Jezebel seems to have been living at the time (chap. xix. 1). The distance from Carmel was not less than fourteen or fifteen miles. Of the feelings with which he thus returned from Carmel we are not informed. The first words indeed of the next chapter, where it is said that " Ahab told Jezebel all that Elijah had done, and withal how he had slain all the prophets with the sword," make it too probable that his heart was yet untouched. We may speak of miracles. Miracles have no power either to convince or to convert. There is not a reflecting man who cannot satisfy himself that the most stupendous miracle might be performed under his own eyes without producing upon him any moral or religious impression. He would find a hundred ways of escape from a conclusion he was determined to reject. "If they hear not Moses and the prophets, neither will they be persuaded if one rise from the dead" (Luke xvi. 31). Ahab may have gone home astonished, perplexed, confounded. It is quite natural, and much more in consonance with his character as it afterwards displayed itself, to think that he went home not less steeled than ever against the truth.

One remarkable incident is still related of Elijah. "And the hand of the Lord," it is said, "was on Elijah; and he girded up his loins, and ran before Ahab to the entrance of Jezreel." "The hand of the Lord was upon him," words indicating that he acted under a Divine impulse, and that he was upheld by Divine power. Animated by this spirit he girded up his loins, so that he might be unhampered by the long dress which would otherwise have impeded his course, and ran before the chariot of the king. There is no need to think that any extraordinary speed was demanded. No doubt Ahab would drive with all the haste with which his horses could carry him along; but the nature of the road was such that a quick runner would without great difficulty be able to keep pace with him, while the prophet's training amidst the hills of Gilead, and the physical discipline by which his whole previous life had been marked, would now stand him in good stead.

The action itself has been variously interpreted. Yet, as the feelings and actions of the East change but little in the course of centuries, the customs of the present may probably best explain the customs of Elijah's time, and the interpretation that would be put by the people on his act. There, then, even now, when the ruler of the people drives abroad, he has his two couriers before him, who run in one continuous race to clear his way. So Elijah ran. He was as a courier to the king. The contest between them was at an end. Ahab to all appearance had, with his people, that day bowed in submission to Jehovah, and the prophet might well entertain the hope that the submission was real. Ahab was once more the covenanted king of a covenant nation. Why should he not receive every mark of respect and honour? It was the more necessary to pay this because it might have been thought that Elijah was the victor in the struggle that had taken place. In one sense he was; in another and a higher *he* was not. God was victor: Elijah was His servant; and, giving the glory to Him to whom it was due, Elijah could only disclaim, in the most emphatic manner, all personal aggrandizement, and show, in a way which no one could misunderstand, that he returned to his old relations towards his king and country.

With these feelings we are told that he ran to the "entrance of Jezreel," but we are not informed why he stopped there, instead of accompanying Ahab into his city and palace. It could not be from any fear of Jezebel, for the suddenness of his flight into the wilderness, recorded in the following chapter, can hardly be explained, unless we suppose that the thought of the vengeance of the queen came upon him as an unexpected blow. The probability is that he acted still in the same spirit as that which led him to run before Ahab's chariot. He was a servant, an attendant, with no claim to honour. Why, though he might run before the king, should he stand in his presence? "They that wear soft raiment are in kings' houses" (Matt. xi. 8). A royal palace was no place for him, the plain rough prophet of the truth. He stopped at the entrance of Jezreel, and Ahab went his way to Jezebel.

At this point of his history the mission of Elijah may be said to have been accomplished. In the face of every difficulty and trial he had successfully vindicated the honour of the God of Israel, had brought back His people to His covenant, and had been the instrument of securing for them a restoration of the blessings promised them while they continued faithful to Him who had chosen them out of all nations for His name. It had been part of the prayer of Solomon when the temple at Jerusalem was dedicated to the Lord, "When the heaven is shut up, and there is no rain, because they have sinned against Thee; if they pray towards this place, and confess Thy name, and turn from their sin, when Thou dost afflict them; then hear Thou in heaven, and forgive the sin of Thy servants, and of Thy people Israel, when Thou teachest them the good way wherein they should walk, and send rain upon Thy land which Thou hast given to Thy people for an inheritance" (1 Kings viii. 35, 36). That prayer had just been answered. In his public capacity and in his relation to the people Elijah had little more to do. We have still indeed to follow him through important details of his personal history. He is still to be the recipient of revelations of the Lord, full of lessons for the Church in every age. But in its most prominent aspect his work is done. From this time forward he never again met assembled Israel, and the carrying forward of his work was to be handed over immediately to other agencies and other men.

We have still, however, to look back upon the scene which has been passing before our eyes ; for it is full of the most instructive lessons. In doing so, it is unnecessary to dwell upon the fact that many of the wonderful characteristics of the prophet appear in it in as striking a light as in the events which the earlier part of the same day had witnessed. In the one, not less than in the other, we see his faith, his boldness, his complete forgetfulness of self. Reference to these, however, may at least for the present be omitted. One great lesson, for which the narrative has been appealed to by an inspired writer in the New Testament, may more properly engage, and may at the same time be sufficient to occupy, our thoughts. It is the narrative by which the apostle James illustrates the nature and efficacy of prayer. That apostle might have found illustrations of his theme in many another hero of the ancient faith, in Abraham, or Isaac, or Jacob, or Moses, or Samuel, or David. He names none of these, but he turns to Elijah. "Pray for one another," he says, that ye may be healed. "The supplication of a righteous man availeth much in its working" (chap. v. 16), and then follow those words as to Elijah's prayer, first, that it might not, and secondly, that it might, rain, which are familiar to all. The circumstance that Elijah, rather than any other saint of old, is thus appealed to, affords of itself a striking proof how deeply this part of the prophet's history had impressed itself upon the mind of the Jewish people. But more than this : we have in the fact a Divine commentary on the nature and power of prayer.

In this light, therefore, and guided by the language of the apostle, we may now consider the prayer which was offered by Elijah, and answered by the Almighty, at Carmel. What characteristics of that prayer presented themselves to the mind of St. James when he spoke of it in the language already quoted?

Before answering the question, it is impossible to forget that, at the very threshold of the subject, an objection meets us which, if well founded, at once disposes of the whole matter, and makes further inquiry needless. The very idea of prayer, we are told, is unscientific. Whatever earlier ages and rude philosophies may have permitted men to believe, all modern inquiry has demonstrated, with constantly increasing clearness, the absurdity of supposing that, in compliance with any entreaties of His creatures, the Creator of the universe will, or even can, interpose to avert consequences flowing from the operation of the known or discoverable rules by which He works. It is maintained that the world is, and always has been, governed by immutable laws; that these laws are inextricably interwoven with the whole constitution of nature; that events are so related to one another that, at every point in their eternal evolution, each is absolutely dependent upon all the members of the series which for the moment we may think of them as closing; that each could not be other than it is unless the members of the series had been also other than they were; that herein lies the grandeur of the present system of things as it stands in silent majesty before us from age to age; and that to think of the interposition of God at any particular instant is to reflect upon the wisdom with which the system was originally planned. Not, therefore, with any conscious intention of dishonouring God does the disciple of this school come to his conclusion. Rather, he would urge, with the intention of saving Him from all possibility of being charged with the wilfulness, the caprices, and the arbitrary actings of His creatures. He removes God, no doubt, from all interference in the affairs of men after the great machine of the universe has been put in motion; but, by the very fact that He does not need to interfere; that away, we know not where, occupied, we know not how, He can leave the infinite variety of events continually happening to the control of His eternal and unchangeable laws, does He impress us with the loftiest conceptions of His greatness. Here is no wilfulness, no caprice, no arbitrary acting, but a majesty of unchanging order before which we can only bow in admiration, and to which it is our highest duty to conform ourselves.

The answer to the difficulty thus proposed to us depends upon our conception of the Being of God. If God be only a blind, unintelligent, and uninterested force; if He possess nothing of what we mean by personality; if He have no constantly active and operative will; and if, after creating us as we are, He limited Himself by laying aside all those affections and emotions without which there can be no intercourse between Himself and the creatures of affection and emotion that He has formed, then certainly we must accept the conclusion offered us. But the moment we conceive of Him as One who is to maintain fellowship with us, and we with Him, that moment we must also conceive of Him as One who may alter His relations to us, and whose feelings towards us cannot but be affected by our obedience or disobedience, by our love to Him or alienation from Him. With a human brother in whom we recognize nothing more than an automaton, incapable of any exercise of will, and the victim only of immovable law, it would be out of the question to speak of forming any intimate relation, and any emotion that we might experience towards him would die in disappointment when it was seen that there was no response. It is not otherwise in our relation to God ; and if He be simply a force, without an eye to see, an ear to hear, or a hand to save, not only all positive prayer, but all possibility of communion with Him is at once destroyed.

It is no reply to this to say that the possibility of effecting any change in the Divine purposes by prayer is denied only with reference to physical phenomena, and that the field of our spiritual relations with the Divine Being is left untouched. If, because of the idea of law and the dependence of phenomena on one another, we may not pray for sunshine or rain, or a good harvest, or safety in the midst of pestilence, or success in any undertaking, no principle is left upon which we may pray for spiritual blessings such as the enlightening of the intellect, the softening of the affections, the subduing of the will, or the strengthening within us of the graces of faith and hope and love. The former, indeed, it is alleged, are the result of law which has been operating throughout all past time and with universal influence. Are the latter not so too, at least on the supposition with which in this matter we have to deal? Let us imagine that, when we pray, our intellects are darkened or our affections cold, that our wills refuse to bend in submission to what has befallen us, or that our faith and hope and love are weak and fitful. This state of things is not the result of some arbitrary dealing on the part of God. We did not become what we are, in these spiritual aspects of our nature, by some random appointment of His Providence, or by some withdrawal of His grace without a reason, and simply because He willed it. We sank into a spiritual condition needing revival and improvement because we had sinned against those principles of the Divine government of men which would have preserved us in a more perfect state. In other words, we sinned against law, against laws as real, as true, as powerful in the spiritual sphere as are physical laws in the sphere appropriate to them. Every step taken by us in our downward course was the consequence of the non-fulfilment in our experience of some spiritual law which we had violated; and the consequences can only be escaped by an interference of the Divine law of mercy with the Divine law of retributive judgment. If a new law, a new order, may come in in spiritual, why may it not also come in in physical, things? The distinction attempted to be drawn between these two spheres of the Divine action is altogether futile; and, if we are compelled to admit into the spiritual sphere that limitation, though it be self-limitation, of the Almighty which is alleged to exist in the physical sphere, to what a result are we reduced! To an unmitigated fatalism, destroying all the dignity of man's nature, doing violence to our dearest convictions as to our own powers, and extinguishing the very idea of human responsibility. Such indeed is logically, as well as actually, the issue of that conception of God which denies the possibility of His being the answerer of prayer. Everywhere hard, material, physical laws, laws in virtue of which nothing could have been different from what it is, all distinction between mind and matter destroyed at one fell swoop, all the glory of human labour and suffering in the past resolved into necessity which can merit no praise, and all hope of our being able to quicken the wheels of the world's progress into the brighter future for which we long, proclaimed a "pious imagination," the fantastic delusion of a fevered dream! Are we prepared for this? Better not to be than to believe that our being is a delusion. We believe that man can modify the effect of many a law by that power of will which God has given him; and surely what man may do is within the power of God.

It is forgotten too by those who urge the fixed course of all events as an objection to the possibility of obtaining an answer to prayer, that the very prayer, the efficiency of which they deny, may be a part of the predetermined series. Elijah prayed and there came drought: he prayed again and there came rain. How do they know that the prophet's prayer had not been foreseen and foreordained as well as its result? and that in the original plan of the Almighty the one was not in some way dependent on the other? or, if it be replied that this is to make the prophet as much automatic as the rain, the answer is, that the difficulty is thus transferred to the insoluble problem of reconciling the absolute predestination of God with the free action of man. Even if Elijah's prayer was in one sense the result of necessity, in another and equally important sense the prophet was free. Judged of according to his own feeling of responsibility he was absolutely and entirely free. No theory of the Divine predestination could have saved him from pronouncing judgment upon himself; and on the great day of account the judgment of the Eternal God will be in harmony with that of our own hearts, "Out of thine own mouth will I condemn thee."

Prayer, then, may be answered; and we turn again to the language of St. James in order to learn from it what those characteristics of Elijah's prayers on the present occasion were which made the apostle behold in them an illustrious example of the power of prayer.

1. They were prayers to which a positive answer conveying the things asked for was anticipated. There is a mode of looking at prayer to which not the slightest countenance is given in the scene before us. Alive to the inextinguishable nature of the instinct that leads men to pray, and fully convinced that without prayer religion must perish; yet at the same time unable to see how the eternal series of causes and effects constituting the history of the world can be infringed without the destruction of all order, there are not a few who rest their defence of prayer only upon its reflex influence. It does us good to pray. It is the acknowledgment of our dependence upon God. It brings us into communion and fellowship with Him. It teaches us to acquiesce in His wise and well-ordered government; and, in this result produced upon ourselves, not from any expectation of obtaining what we ask for, lies the benefit of prayer. Let us acknowledge the value of the reflex influence thus spoken of; but what is it that it really springs from? Is it not most of all from this that, in prayer, we approach One who will consider our wants with infinite love and wisdom, and who will judge for us better than we can ourselves? In order to the reflex good it is obviously necessary that the process through which we pass to the obtain-

ing of it shall be genuine, shall be at least real and true. But there is no reality or truth in asking what we know beforehand can neither be granted nor obtained, or what, if it is to come, will come whether we ask or not. With what profit to himself shall a son ask a father to change plans, which, by the very necessity of his nature he cannot change; or how long, with this conviction in his mind, will he continue his petitions? The falseness of his attitude will force itself upon him in every request he makes; and, so far from either honouring his father or benefiting himself in continuing to make it, he will soon discover that he is destroying the moral fibre of his own nature, and that he is seeking an honest result by dishonest means. The reflex benefit of prayer is wholly dependent upon our confidence that a direct benefit may be secured. Like all indirect blessings it is made ours when we are not thinking of it. To think of it changes it at once to a blessing that is direct, and lands us in the very dilemma from which we had been endeavouring to escape. Let us suppose that we have but one petition to present at the throne of the Almighty—that we may learn to acquiesce in the unchangeable order of things of which we are a part. Is not this as direct a petition as any other that we can offer? Does it not involve the idea that our wills may be rebellious, and that we desire to have them subdued into conformity with the Divine will? If the order of the universe be unchangeable we have as much attempted to violate it as though we had asked for any other blessing of which we had felt our need. To direct us to the reflex benefit of prayer, and to bid us find in it our encouragement to pray, is thus as inconsistent with reason and the lessons of human experience as it is with the teaching of Scripture, or with the example of the saints. It was not thus that Elijah prayed. When he prayed for drought it was in expectation that the drought would come; when he prayed for rain it was in the belief that rain would follow. In like manner must we pray, believing that we may receive the blessing that we ask, or we shall soon cease to pray. No thought of a reflex influence upon ourselves will ever maintain within us the habit or the attitude of prayer.

2. The prayers of Elijah were for spiritual blessings. It is true that he prayed for rain and that the earth might again give forth her fruit. But it is impossible not to see that, as his prayer for drought had been connected with the people's sin,

and had been intended to awaken them to repentance, so his prayer for rain was connected mainly with their spiritual recovery, and the ratification of a spiritual covenant. It was not mere rain for which he prayed; it was the rain of the covenant, the rain promised to the land so long as its inhabitants were faithful to Him who had given them it in possession, that they might fulfil His purpose in the history of the race. Nor is it otherwise with St. James when he quotes Elijah in illustration of his argument. He is not speaking only of the supply of bodily wants, or the healing of bodily ills. At first sight it might seem as if he confined himself to these things. "Is any among you sick? Let him call for the elders of the church; and let them pray over him, anointing him with oil in the name of the Lord: and the prayer of faith shall save him that is sick, and the Lord shall raise him up." Temporal blessing, recovery from sickness, is spoken of; but the apostle immediately adds, "And if he have committed sins it shall be forgiven him" (Jas. v. 14, 15). The addition shows that bodily sickness was not the only thing of which the apostle thought. He thought also of sin, which, whether the direct cause of the sickness or not, was yet inseparably connected with it. Had he been able to separate the two, recovery from bodily ailment would probably have seemed to him a point of subordinate importance. He shared the feeling of the New Testament, that body and spirit cannot be looked at apart from one another, that the body is the expression of the spirit, and that the welfare of both is indispensable to that welfare of the man which is contemplated in the purposes of God.

Nor was it otherwise with our Lord Himself, who in many passages associates salvation with the restoration to health or soundness of the sick or the lame who came to Him; while the central petition of that prayer which He taught His disciples, "Give us this day our daily bread," cannot well be regarded as a petition for mere bodily sustenance. It certainly points also to that spiritual support which is ministered to us by "the bread of life."

This conjunction of the spiritual and the temporal corresponds indeed with the whole tone and genius of the gospel dispensation. We are not forbidden to ask for temporal blessings; but, if we are to receive them, our asking must never be separated from the thought of God's kingdom in ourselves and others. In the advancement of that kingdom lies our main interest. All else is subordinate to it. Its progress regulates the fate of empires, and much more the history of individual lives. Christ is not only Head over all things, but He is over them for His Church (Ephes. i. 22). No prayer therefore can be agreeable to Him which does not flow from this as the paramount consideration in our minds; and we have no ground to expect an answer to our prayers if, here as well as elsewhere, we are not of the same mind with Him who presents our supplications to the Father, and whom the Father heareth always.

3. The prayers of Elijah were for others rather than himself. This aspect of his prayers seems to be especially present to the mind of St. James when he refers to his example. "Confess your sins one to another," he says, "and pray one for another, that ye may be healed." "One for another" is thus the key-note of his words. He had, indeed, in an earlier part of his Epistle, exhorted and encouraged Christians to pray for themselves, "But if any of you lack wisdom, let him ask of God who giveth to all liberally, and upbraideth not, and it shall be given him." When he refers to the case of Elijah, however, he refers to prayer for others, and it is not unimportant to remember this. For in what way, it is often asked, in spirit if not in words, can others be affected by our prayers? "Supplications, prayers, intercessions, thanksgivings made for all men" (1 Tim. ii. 1) may procure blessings for ourselves, but how is it possible that they should procure blessings for others? The persons for whom we pray are what they are by influences coming down for many generations, as well as by those surroundings of their own, which, whatever be our prayers on their behalf, will remain the same as they have been. How can they be affected by prayers of which they have probably never heard? It is conceivable that our interest in them and longing for their welfare, when seen by them or told them, may soften their hearts or awaken their sympathy with our designs on their behalf. But what good can be done when they neither see us nor hear us, nor know of our existence? How can our prayers turn the stream of tendency which courses through their veins, or the disposition of those molecules which, with every new thought that they cherish and every new resolution that they make, must change their relation to one another? We have already replied to such an argument, and need say no more of

it. Enough for our present purpose that the Apostle repeats his words, "one to another," "one for another."

And he is right, for he is speaking not of prayer only but of effective prayer ; and one of the most important elements of effective prayer is that we pray for others. In family, or even in private, prayer, there can be no greater mistake than that of confining our petitions to our own necessities. Interest in others enlarges the heart, and brings us nearer to the mind of God. Our Lord Himself has taught us to say "our" Father which art in heaven. We cannot approach the Father without being interested in His children. We cannot love God whom we have not seen unless we love our brother whom we have seen : and the expression of the heart in both cases is inseparably connected with its expansion in either case. Let men test themselves, or examine the record of their own experience. They will find that prayer from which intercession for others has been excluded speedily languishes or becomes formal : and they will equally find that, when they have been most importunate in entreating for the good of their brethren, they have also been enabled to rise into the deepest earnestness of supplication for themselves.

4. The prayers of Elijah were fervent. We have already seen this in the very attitude which he assumed in prayer. That stretching himself out upon the earth and that bowing of his head between his knees were evidently more than the expression of reverence. They were to secure to the prophet freedom from the distraction of surrounding objects, and opportunity for giving himself with all the earnestness of his heart to the task in which he was engaged. The same spirit of fervency appears in his prayer in the earlier part of the day, " Hear me, O Lord, hear me." How strikingly does a similar spirit show itself in the prayers of Daniel and of St. Paul ; or, if we turn to the highest example of all, what shall we say of the prayers of Jesus, of whom we are told that, during His agony in the garden, He three times retired to pray saying the same words, "O my Father, if it be possible, let this cup pass away from me" (Matt. xxvi. 44), and of whom the writer of the Epistle to the Hebrews tells us that, in the days of His flesh, He offered up prayers and supplications "with strong crying and tears," and that He was heard for His "godly fear" (Heb. v. 7)? Thus St. James says of Elijah that he " prayed fervently " (Jas. v. 17).

Without such fervency, indeed, prayer is little else than a profession, a pretence, a form of words. What we really desire we must ask for with an earnestness and importunity that will not be denied. Because of this, the man in the parable of our Lord who came seeking bread from his friend in the dead hours of the night was heard. Because of this, the widow in the parable, spoken for the express purpose of teaching us that we ought always to pray "and not to faint," received an answer from the unjust judge; and when God's elect cry unto Him to vindicate His own cause they do so "day and night" (Luke xviii. 7). Want of fervency in prayer shows that we take no real interest in the blessing asked; and how, in these circumstances, shall we expect to be heard and answered?

5. Once more the prayer of Elijah was a prayer of faith, and again this characteristic of it is present to the mind of St. James, when he turns to the prophet for an illustration of the fact that "the prayer of faith shall save him that is sick" (chap. v. 15). In the very opening of his Epistle he had taught the same lesson, "But if any of you lacketh wisdom, let him ask of God who giveth to all liberally and upbraideth not, and it shall be given him. But let him ask in faith, nothing doubting: for he that doubteth is like the surge of the sea driven by the wind and tossed. For let not that man think that he shall receive anything of the Lord; a double-minded man, unstable in all his ways" (chap. i. 5–8). Without faith it is indeed impossible to be well-pleasing unto God; "for he that cometh to God must believe that He is, and that He is a rewarder of them that seek after Him" (Heb. xi. 6). Such faith is an unwavering conviction that God has promised, and that what He has promised He is "able also to perform" (Rom. iv. 21),—not, as so often quoted, "both able and willing to perform," but simply "able." The will is already there. It is found in the very utterance of the promise. Faith grasps not only the will, but the power of God; and, knowing that His power is irresistible, it asks in full assurance that the blessing promised will be obtained.

How mighty then is such prayer as Elijah's was! It moves the arm of the Omnipotent Creator and Governor of the universe, who speaks and it is done, who commands and all things stand fast (Psa. xxxiii. 9). It secures for us "in everything" either what we suppose that we stand in need of, or that "peace of

God" which makes us feel that it is better to have our requests denied than granted. It is one of the mightiest weapons of our Christian warfare—

"We conquer heaven by prayer."

In the history of Elijah we see one of the most striking instances of what it can accomplish, and he was "a man of like passions with us." Let no one ever hesitate to cry to Him who heareth and answereth prayer, and no one will fail to find that "the supplication **of a** righteous **man a**vaileth much **in its work·ing**" (**Jas. v. 16**).

CHAPTER V.

ELIJAH AT HOREB (I KINGS XIX. 1-13).

Feelings of Elijah at Horeb—His mistaken notions as to the character of the Almighty—His despondency—Not due to physical fatigue or loneliness, but to thought that he had failed—Injustice thus done by him to God—To himself—To the past history of his people—Evils of despondency—Reason why Elijah fled to Horeb—God reveals Himself by an angel—Horeb and Elijah's cave—Former revelation of the Almighty there—The prophet questioned—His answer—The revelation granted him—Lesson of the revelation—Divine judgment and mercy—What law can accomplish—Value and importance of law—The message of love—Its greater power.

OF all the sudden and startling changes presented to us in the life of the great prophet of what we may call the second Reformation in Israel, none is more striking than that recorded after the events of the last chapter. It might have seemed that Elijah had then attained the summit of his prosperity and the main object of his mission. In the presence of the king and assembled Israel he had vindicated the honour of the true God against all the forces of a magnificent and popular idolatry. He had been the means of leading Israel to abandon its false worship and to return to its early faith. He had destroyed the priests of Baal in the terrible slaughter at the river Kishon; and, finally, at his word [1] the long-continued drought had been brought to an end, a great rain had fallen, the hearts of the people as well as the parched soil were rejoicing in the prospect of plenty in the land; and, as we see shortly after this in the case of Elisha,[2] the husbandman had returned to the plough.

[1] Compare Jas. v. 18. [2] 1 Kings xix. 19.

ELIJAH AT HOREB.

Every expectation of the prophet seems to have been fulfilled. He could desire nothing more.

Suddenly there is a change. Neither from his present nor his future action is there any reason to believe that Ahab, though silenced, had been converted. His weak, cowardly nature was incapable of receiving any deep impression. He was still the same as he had all along been, a man unable to rise to the height of a pure and lofty monotheism, the victim of his own guilty passions, and a tool in the hands of Jezebel. His first care was to report to the queen "all that Elijah had done, and withal how he had slain all the prophets with the sword." The words forbid the supposition that Ahab told this with any humble acknowledgment of the nature of that Divine intervention which he had so lately witnessed. The sacred writer, in describing his action, does not speak of the prophets of Baal He does not even say that Ahab told Jezebel that Elijah had slain all her prophets in particular. He speaks simply of "all the prophets," and by so speaking he appears still to identify Ahab with them, as if they were the prophets whom the king honoured and obeyed.

The burst of rage which Jezebel's nature might have led us to anticipate immediately followed, and a messenger was sent by her to Elijah, saying, "So let the gods do to me, and more also, if I make not thy life as the life of one of them by to-morrow at this time." It was a firm and determined message uttered by a woman of firm and determined character, who would undoubtedly leave no stone unturned that might help her to execute her threats But what should all that have been to the prophet of the Lord ? Surely the God who at his word had sent down fire from heaven upon Mount Carmel to consume the sacrifice, had given him the victory over four hundred and fifty prophets of Baal, and in answer to his prayer had brought the famine to an end, will enable him to prevail over a woman, however powerful and cruel. Surely he might have been satisfied that He who was with him was far more than all that could be against him. It is easy to reason thus, but the experience of life refutes our reasoning. Strong and passionate natures are peculiarly liable to reaction. Depression follows close upon exultation, and despair upon hope. It was so with Moses in a crisis of his life very similar to that here before us, when "he said unto the Lord, See, Thou sayest unto me, Bring up this people; and Thou hast not let me know whom Thou wilt send with me."[1] It was so with the Baptist when his heart failed him in his prison; and when, notwithstanding all that he had witnessed of the glory of Jesus, and all the testimony that he had borne to Him, he yet sent to Him two of his disciples saying, "Art Thou He that cometh, or look we for another?"[2] And it was so with the Apostle Peter, when, bold as he had been in walking upon the waters to come to Jesus, he no sooner saw the wind than he was afraid, and, beginning to sink, cried out, "Lord, save me."[3] In like manner was it now with Elijah. His nature had been too intensely strung during the last few hours, and it could no longer bear the strain.

But more than this. We learn, from what follows, that the education of Elijah was not yet completed. He had mistaken one special manifestation of the Almighty for a revelation of His essential nature; and he had to learn that not by fire and storm such as he had beheld, but in calmer, gentler ways, does God accomplish His purposes and train the race for its final destiny.

The message of Jezebel delivered to Elijah terrified him, and his terror was obviously deep and unfeigned. He immediately arose, and went for his life to Beersheba, far beyond the boundary of Samaria, at the most southern extremity of Judah, where the cultivated land begins to sink into the desert. Not content with this, he left there the servant who had accompanied him, and went a day's journey into the wilderness, and sat down under a juniper tree, one of those bushes of broom, rising at times to a height of many feet, which are so grateful to the weary traveller in his journeys over the scorching sand. There he requested for himself that he might die; and said, "It is enough, now, O Lord, take away my life; for I am not better than my fathers;" and, having said this, he fell asleep.

What a change, we may well exclaim, is here! A few days only have passed since Elijah stood on Carmel, the victorious prophet of God, and Israel bowed in submission at his feet. Now he is alone in the wilderness, wearied in body, depressed in spirit, as weak as the generations that, one after another, had disappeared before him. Whither, he, as it were, exclaims, are

[1] Exod. xxxiii. 12, compare chap. xxxiv.
[2] Matt. xi. 2, 3.   [3] Matt. xiv. 30.

these generations gone? Their name and their memorial are as completely blotted out as footprints are blotted out that have been left upon the sand within reach of the rising tide. And, notwithstanding all that has happened, it is to be the same with me. In this lay the secret of his despondency. We are not to seek it mainly in the exhaustion of his physical frame. Elijah was a hardy son of the desert who had long been accustomed to privation and toil, to scanty food, and the fatigue and exposure of a desert life. But a day or two previous he had run before the chariot of Ahab sixteen miles from Carmel to Jezreel, and, even after he was strengthened by food miraculously supplied from heaven, he continued as despondent as before. Nor was loneliness and want of sympathy the cause. He had all his life lived alone. No wife, no companion, had cheered him in his desert solitude. On Carmel he had stood one man against four hundred and fifty, and he had rather gloried in his solitary strength. Even on the present occasion he need not have been alone. His servant had accompanied him when he fled from Samaria, but he had left him behind at Beersheba that he might be alone. Men are to be met with who in such circumstances are strongest. It is not desirable that it should be so, but it is a fact. As a general rule the prophet, the minister, the missionary, ought never to be alone. And our Lord proceeded upon His deep knowledge of human nature when, in sending forth his disciples, he sent them two by two. Without Silas or Timothy St. Paul would have been weaker than he was; and so would St. Peter without St. John or St. Mark. But it does not seem to have been so with Elijah. He did not "faint or fear to live alone." In solitude he braced his soul for the warfare he had to maintain and the trials he had to endure. It was his apparent want of success that troubled him. He thought that he had failed, that his mission had been fruitless, and that the reformation he had effected at Carmel was but a momentary burst of enthusiasm without reality, without depth, to be forgotten in a moment and for ever. The trial is one often experienced by the eager and passionate reformer, and the more, the more eager and passionate he is. Strong in his own belief of the truth he has proclaimed, in the power of his arguments, and in the unselfishness of his motives, the reformer will not doubt for an instant that he shall prevail. The minds of all who hear him will open to his summons They will see themselves and their true interests as he sees them. They will yield to the higher order of things he would introduce. The shout of applause with which he is at first welcomed is the proof that he is right; and before it, continued, repeated, redoubled, as before the shout of assembled Israel, he seems to behold the walls of Jericho fall flat. Alas! how often is he quickly undeceived. Sin is not thus at once forsaken. Prejudices are not thus at once dispelled. Old habits are not thus at once thrown off. The tide of error which had been driven back to its furthest verge sweeps in again with a mightier than its usual volume, and more than had been apparently gained is lost. Then comes the trial of faith, the weakness despondency and despair.

But such despondency, whatever it may spring from, is entirely wrong. Mark how it affected Elijah in the present instance. It led him to do injustice

1. To God. He thought that God was failing to vindicate His own truth. He had himself been "very jealous for the Lord, the God of hosts," but his language implies the doubt whether God had been so. Had He continued to exert the power which He had manifested on Carmel His prophet would not have been where he was that day. Could not He who had sent down fire from heaven to consume the sacrifice, have also by a similar fire consumed Ahab and Jezebel and every obstinate worshipper of Baal in the land? Then why had He not done it? Why was Jezebel in all probability again triumphing in her palace at Jezreel, setting up fresh altars, appointing new prophets of Baal, persecuting the faithful, sweeping before her every trace of the reformation he had accomplished? It seemed to him that there was only one explanation. The Almighty had been less zealous than His servant, had forsaken His own cause, and was either unable or unwilling to secure for it the victory which it deserved. Here was faithlessness, distrust of God, a presumptuous pronouncing upon plans that he did not comprehend. He would be wiser than his Maker. The short-sighted child of the dust would direct Him who sees the end from the beginning, and who best knows how to further His own kingdom among men.

2. It led him to do injustice to himself. "He requested for himself that he might die, and said, It is enough: now, O Lord, take away my life." We are reminded of a moment, in one

respect at least similar, in the life of the Apostle of the Gentiles. He was a prisoner at Rome, in the hands of a tyrant who, in any moment of unregulated passion, might send him forth to execution without pity and without remorse. Nay more, his opponents were taking advantage of his absence from the field, were preaching Christ out of contention, and were striving to alienate the affections of his converts from him. St. Paul felt the pangs which these things caused, and he exclaimed, "I am in a strait betwixt the two, having a desire to depart and be with Christ, for it is very far better;" "to die is gain." Yet no sooner had he said this than he cried out, "Yet to abide in the flesh is more needful for your sake. And having this confidence, I know that I shall abide, yea, and abide with you all, for your progress and joy in the faith" (Phil. i. 23–25). And so he returned to his work, and went on preaching, warring, conquering, until in God's own time the end came, and he entered into his rest. So ought it to have been with Elijah, but it was not. Similar temptation, indeed, often comes to an earnest but disappointed labourer in the Lord's vineyard—the wish that he may die, that he may have no more experience of disappointment and sorrow, that he may at length find rest. We have no right to wish this. Our times are in God's hands, and not in our own. He gave us our being, He appointed our labours at the first; and it is His alone to bring either the one or the other to a close. So long as we have strength to work we are to work. So long as life is ours we are to look upon it as a talent committed to our care, and to listen to the command, "Trade ye herewith till I come" (Luke xix. 13). It may be hard, it may be disappointing; but it is the only path of duty. Anything else is injustice to ourselves as well as God.

3. It led him to do injustice to the past. "Take away my life," he said, "for I am not better than my fathers." The reflection is indeed a sad one for him who would reform and renew the world, but who appears to fail in his attempt, that it has been to some extent at least the same in every age. "Our fathers where are they, and the prophets do they live for ever?" They are gone, and of most of them the very names have perished. A few names live. The heroism, the genius, the intellectual grandeur, the moral and religious worth of those who bore them are not forgotten. But what of the mass of those who, before they fell asleep, served God and their generation

without a thought beyond this, that God might be honoured and their generation helped? Look at the shelves of a great library. Read name after name of the authors crowded there, and you shall find that of most of them you have never heard. Turn over page after page of their huge volumes and you shall see that they relate to questions the very terms of which it is now difficult to understand, that they are devoted to controversies which, though they once separated the world into opposing camps, now sleep side by side as quietly as the combatants in their graves. It will be the same in time to come. Future generations may take into their hands most of the books written now that shall have survived the storms of time, may gaze at them for an instant, and may wonder who the writers were. Some curious student may wish to know more of those who thus denied themselves the pleasures of the world and lived "laborious days and nights devoid of ease;" and, with all his searching, he may be able to discover nothing but the fact that they lived—and died. Then we are apt to cry, What does it all come to? Why should we perplex ourselves? Why trim the midnight lamp? Why tax the already wearied brain? No long period hence, and it will be all the same. There is an unquestionable sadness in the thought that one generation goeth and another generation cometh, and that the last is as rapidly forgotten as the first.

But Elijah was not entitled to speak of the past in the way he did. Had he forgotten Abraham and Isaac and Jacob, Moses and Aaron, Samuel and David? Had he completely lost sight of men who had brightened the history of his people with many a deed of patriotism and religious zeal? He had much better have asked whether he was as good as his fathers, and whether he was now doing his work as well as they did theirs. They met the demands of their own day. Not a few of them found their place, if not in the perishable records of human fame, yet in the imperishable records of Him who is from everlasting to everlasting. Their names might have faded from the memories of men, but many of them, at least, were written in that book of life from which no name, once entered in it, shall ever again be blotted out. Although what they did in faith or suffered in patience might have found none to tell its story, it was enough if it were preserved there where neither rust corrupts nor moth consumes.

Nor did their work perish when they themselves died and were forgotten. Was it really good, it became a part of the inheritance of the race. The seed they sowed sprang up into a harvest, to be sown again over a wider area and with more enlarged results. Being dead, they speak; and the voices that come to us, and most entwine themselves with all the fibres of our being; the voices that swell up in our hearts, impelling us to action as no others do, have often their deepest hold over us from this, that we know not whence they come. They have glided down to us from bygone ages. We have breathed them in the atmosphere. We have listened to them in the silence. They have taken root within us, and have grown with our growth and strengthened with our strength. They have become a part of ourselves, and when they now influence our conduct they are no longer from without but from within. They are thus a far more intimate part of our being than any lesson that may be suddenly forced upon us by some solitary and exceptional incident of our lives. Not less in this then was Elijah unjust to the past than when his despondency led him to be unjust both to God and to himself. Let us never think lightly of our fathers. They did their work; let us do ours. Well for us if we are only as true, as honest, and as brave as they.

Such then were the evil consequences of that spirit of despondency which took possession of Elijah at this crisis of his history. It is always so. Nothing throws a darker light over both the present and the past, over both ourselves and others. "Why art thou cast down, O my soul?" is a question that we may well ask whenever we feel despondency beginning to steal upon us. If we are unable to subdue it, it will take all the spirit out of life, and will make us think that everything that has ever been, as well as everything that is, is vanity.

We have seen that Elijah was despondent, and that the cause of his despondency is to be found in his impression that, notwithstanding everything that had happened, his mission to Israel had been a failure. It is not enough, however, to say this. There must have been something else to account for his present flight to Horeb. High as his expectations had been a day or two before, even he must have known well that no time had yet been given to show whether the effect produced by him at Carmel was to be fleeting or permanent. We must look still farther, therefore, into his feelings if we would comprehend his state of mind as he lay under the juniper tree in the wilderness. Why, then, we have to ask, was he here rather than in some other place which he might have reached more easily? Why should he have fled in this particular direction to the south? If his sole object was to escape the wrath of Jezebel, he might have fled to Phœnicia, which had already for three years afforded him a secure shelter against the efforts of Ahab to discover him. Or, if Phœnicia, for some reason or other unknown to us, gave no promise of a safe retreat, he might have tried Gilead, with the passes of which he was doubtless intimately acquainted. If we attend to the spirit of the narrative, we shall have little difficulty in accounting for the course which he actually took. Elijah fled southward, notwithstanding the long tract of inhabited country through which he would have to pass before he reached the wilderness, because southward lay the way to Horeb. It was to Horeb, to Sinai, to the scene of the terrors amidst which the law had been given to Israel that he naturally turned. He was himself the embodiment of the law in its sternest aspects, and he seems now to have been drawn by an irresistible impulse to the spot where that sternness had been most strikingly revealed, and where he might best hope to see the indignation of the Almighty once more burn against the sinner. The savage grandeur of the spot, together with the memories connected with it, made it, of all other places, that most congenial to his present state of mind. There he could most feel strengthened by the thought that the God whom he served was still a God of vengeance.

It would thus appear that the prophet had misunderstood God's character. He imagined that a revelation by avenging fire was the only way by which the Almighty could make Himself known to men, the only way by which He could either begin a reformation in Israel or confirm it after it had begun. The fire that had come down on Carmel was to him the only symbol of the Divine presence, the only instrument by which stubborn wills could be subdued and hard hearts broken. In these circumstances he needed other teaching than he had yet received.

That teaching shall not be wanting. However Elijah might be mistaken, his heart was sound, and to the upright God maketh light to arise in the darkness.

He did so now, for He saw the truth that was beneath Elijah's gloomy view of his position: and, as the prophet slept, an angel, we are told, touched him, and said unto him, "Arise and eat." He arose and found a cake baked on the coals and a cruse of water ; and he ate and drank and laid him down again. The meaning of the provision made for his wants was not yet clear. A second time he slept, and a second time an angel of the Lord touched him, saying, "Arise and eat, because the journey is too great for thee." That journey was a deeper plunge into the wilderness, a wild and solitary way, until he should come to those mountains at the extremity of the desert of the wanderings which had been hallowed by the descent of the God of Israel at the giving of the law.

Elijah arose and ate ; and, comprehending now the meaning of that supply of food which had been miraculously granted him, "he went in the strength of that meat forty days and forty nights unto Horeb, the mount of God." To a traveller in ordinary circumstances the journey ought to have occupied a much shorter time. It is therefore necessary to think either that the prophet was to make a circuit until that number of days and nights was fulfilled, or that the number forty is not to be literally understood. We have already seen that this is most probably the case with the number three-and-a-half, and that these figures may be intended to express not so much the actual number which they indicate to us as a broken and trying time. A similar remark may be made now. Israel had wandered forty years in the wilderness, and to the Jewish mind the number forty may thus have come to express the idea of want and sorrow, of temptation and suffering. To travel forty days and forty nights may therefore, when faithfully interpreted, mean no more than to make amidst many privations the journey spoken of. In this manner then Elijah travelled until he reached the spot upon which his thoughts had all along been bent, and found a cave in which to rest. Let us pause for a moment to behold him there.

The probable spot is thus described by a competent traveller who himself has visited it. "A pathway starting from the convent of St. Katherine conducts the traveller to the summits of Jebel-Mousa, the southern-most peak of Sinai, and 7,000 feet in height. About half way in the ascent the place is reached. A few notes, made on the spot, may describe it as it now is. The second of two archways constructed for levying toll on pilgrims opens upon a secluded little plain, forming a singular amphitheatre, in the very heart of Sinai, surrounded by magnificent peaks and walls of granite, in the centre of which is a little enclosed garden, with a solitary cypress standing at its entrance, and near it a spring and a little pool of water. A few paces from the cypress is a chapel, said to be built over the place of the prophet's abode in Horeb, one compartment of which covers the so-called Cave of the Vision. It is a hole only just large enough to contain the body of a man, and into which he might creep. It is 'a temple not made with hands,' into which, through a stupendous granite screen, which shuts out even the Bedouin world, God's priests may enter to commune with Him."[1]

The scenery of the spot, however, is comparatively of little moment. It is of more consequence to remember that on some one or other of those peaks which mark the solemn and awe-inspiring surroundings of the neighbourhood the Almighty God once before appeared at the first giving of the law; and that if not exactly to the same spot, at least to one in all respects similar, Joshua and the elders had accompanied Moses at the time when, in reply to the prayer of their great leader, "Show me Thy glory," the Lord said, "Behold there is a place by Me, and thou shalt stand upon the rock; and it shall come to pass, while My glory passeth by, that I will put thee in a cleft of the rock, and will cover thee with My hand until I have passed by; and I will take away Mine hand, and thou shalt see My back; but My face shall not be seen" (Exod. xxxiii. 31–33). Recollections of these great events could not fail to be present to the prophet's mind on this occasion; while, apart altogether from his feelings, it was a fitting thing that the lesson now to be enforced, and which was to present so striking a contrast to that of the first promulgation of the law, should be taught amidst those very scenes where the peculiar glory of the law had been so strikingly revealed.

Here, then, Elijah lodged in the cave; and, as he did so, "the Word of the Lord came to him, and He said unto him, What doest thou here, Elijah?" Often as it has been doubted, it seems impossible to deny that there is censure in these words. Nor does the fact that God had fed the prophet, and cared for him, and strengthened him on his flight, make it improbable that He would now address him in the language of reproof,

[1] Dr. Allon, Elijah in "Biblical Educator," vol. iii. p. 155.

Elijah was still His servant, and a servant full of earnestness and zeal for the cause of God in Israel. His mission was not yet accomplished. His work was not yet done. He has indeed taken alarm too soon. He has failed to apprehend the real nature and purposes of Him whom he served. But not for such reasons only shall he be cast away; and, although he needs reproof, he is still a chosen instrument in the Almighty's hand to execute His purposes, and to be the medium of another and higher revelation of Himself than had yet been granted to the world. We need have no hesitation, therefore, in taking the words before us in the meaning which they naturally bear, and in beholding in them the Divine censure of that spirit of despondency which had for the moment betrayed a prophet generally so strong, and of that want of knowledge which, though it might plead much in its behalf, did not, on that account, need the less to be corrected. Yet, after all, it is not necessary to think that reproof is the chief characteristic of the words. They are rather a summons to reflection, a call to Elijah to enter into his own heart and to make clear to himself the nature of those feelings that had brought him there. We are never ready for any higher and fuller revelation of God until we have thoroughly appropriated the lower stage of revelation upon which we stand. "What doest thou here, Elijah? What is that impression of My nature and aims that has led thee to this spot? What mistake is this that thou hast made in thinking that then only I am with thee when I send down fire from heaven on Mount Carmel, or when thou art in the midst of scenes which once so blazed with My lightnings and echoed to My thunders that the whole camp of Israel trembled? Search thee, and know thy heart; try thee, and know thy thoughts; and see if there be any way of wickedness [in margin of Revised Version, 'grief,' Psa. cxxxix. 24] in thee, and I will lead thee in the way everlasting."

To the words thus addressed to him Elijah replied, "I have been very jealous for the Lord, the God of hosts; for the children of Israel have forsaken Thy covenant, thrown down Thine altars, and slain Thy prophets with the sword: and I, even I only, am left; and they seek my life to take it away." The appellation by which Elijah here addresses the Almighty betrays, as on a former occasion, the feelings of his heart. God is not so much the God of Abraham, of Isaac, and of

Jacob, not so much the God of Israel, as the "God of hosts." But He has not been proving Himself to be so. He has permitted His people to forsake His covenant and to throw down His altars, and to slay His prophets, till it would appear that only one true prophet was left; and even he was compelled to flee for his life to these distant wilds. Was this to be "the God of hosts;" to be the God of whom it might be said in the language of the psalmist that, when the cry of His people came into His ears, "the earth shook and trembled; . . . there went up a smoke in His wrath; and fire out of His mouth devoured; coals were kindled by it" (Psa. xviii. 7, 8. Revised Version, margin)? Where now were all His terrors? Was He unable to execute His purposes, or to fulfil His threatenings?

This, however, was not all. Elijah's words show still further that he identified the cause of God so completely with himself and his own manner of proceeding as to believe that it was lost, because he was no longer upon the scene to carry it forward as he had done. That cry of his, "I, even I only, am left, and they seek my life to take it away," when taken in connection with the answer of God properly translated—" Yet *will I leave Me seven thousand in Israel*"[1]—is a proof that he not only mourned over the past, but that he was hopeless as to the future. There was but one way, it appeared to him, in which God could work, the way to which he had been at first called, but which had failed. He imagined not only that there was no better, but that there was no other, method by which the Divine kingdom could be established in the world, than that which had ended in his flight from Samaria and in the prospect of an early and violent death. And then, when he is gone, after him the deluge; altars again overthrown; prophets, if any were left, killed by the sword; Ahab and Jezebel triumphantly spreading idolatry in Israel; and, it might be, a new assembly gathered upon Carmel to shout "Baal, he is the god; Baal, he is the god." To this state of mind the answer of God is given.

"And He said, Go forth, and stand upon the mount before the Lord." The manifestation of the Divine glory followed. First, a great and strong wind rent the mountains and brake in pieces the rocks,—but the Lord was not in the wind. After the wind an earthquake followed,—but the Lord was not in the earthquake: and after the earthquake a fire,—but the Lord was

[1] Comp. p. 108.

not in the fire. The most tremendous powers of nature, the whirlwind, the earthquake, and the lightning had been summoned into play, and, under their operation, the rocks had been rent from what had seemed to be their everlasting resting-places, the solid mountains had reeled to and fro, and the gloom of the dark cave in which Elijah stood (comp. 1 Kings xix. 13) had been lightened with those fearful bursts of fire which make the strongest quake, followed by the long and ever-renewed roar of thunder as it reverberated from peak to peak and valley to valley;—all terrible, all far beyond human power to summon into action, all calculated to leave upon the mind a profound impression of the littleness of man and of the majesty of Him who sitteth alike above the floods and the tumult of the people; yet something told the prophet that not in any one of them was the Lord. They ceased, and a deep silence followed. Then in the silence was heard a still small voice, and something again told the prophet that this was the Lord; and he wrapped his face in his mantle and went out and stood in the entering in of the cave, awed, humbled, meek, ready to listen. He hears the same words addressed to him as before, "What doest thou here, Elijah?" And he answers in precisely the same language that he had previously used. The fact is startling. Has he learned nothing from all that he has seen and heard? No intimation is given us that he has. It has indeed been often imagined that, although the words are the same as formerly, the tone in which they were spoken must have been different. And, so long as we apply this to the prophet's personal relation to the Almighty, so long as we ascribe to him only deeper humility, awe, and reverence, we may accept the statement. We know too that he will learn as every true and honest heart will learn. Nay, we know, from a more wonderful incident in his history than any that occurred while he was upon earth, his appearance on the Mount of Transfiguration, that he did learn. But there is no evidence that he has as yet done so. The lesson was too deep, too vast in its far-reaching influence, to be apprehended in a moment. It includes in it the history of those principles upon which God deals with a sinful world, and which thousands of years were needed to unfold in the perfection in which we know them now. The thought of this lesson gives its main interest to the scene at Horeb; and we may well endeavour to understand it.

That lesson then is this, that not in the law, but in the Gospel, not in the revelation of Divine wrath, but in that of Divine love and mercy, we are to find the great instrument for renewing the hearts of men, and for establishing in the world that kingdom of righteousness for which it waits and longs. There is a sense, indeed, in which the law precedes the Gospel, but the order in which they follow one another arises less from the nature of God than from the sinfulness of man. In the third chapter of his Epistle to the Galatians, St. Paul has taught us, with a clearness leaving nothing to be desired, both that the Gospel is before the law; the covenant of promise, the covenant of God's grace with Abraham, before the covenant at Sinai; and that the latter cannot disannul the former. There was no thought, indeed, of disannulling the covenant with Abraham when the law was given. The law was simply an intermediate step on the part of God, designed not to make void the earlier promise, but to shut men up to the promise yet to be revealed in fulness. The deepest foundation, the very essence, of the Divine character is not wrath, but love. "God is love," and there is a breadth and length and depth and height in His love as it is revealed to us in Christ without the knowledge of which we cannot be filled with all the fulness of God (Ephes. iii. 18, 19). Had man never fallen we should have experienced nothing but those communications of Divine grace which would have filled our hearts with constant rejoicing and our lips with uninterrupted song. But the fall took place. We know that we have sinned, and by that fact our whole relation to God is changed. We know that sin deserves wrath; and, as the inextinguishable voice of our own nature testifies to what we ought to be, we feel that a revelation of the Divine holiness is what is chiefly needed by us. A revelation of mercy alone will never satisfy the thoughtfully awakened soul. "A God all mercy were a God unjust." It is not the fact that, when we are brought to a true sense of our condition, mercy is what we chiefly long for. Our modern theology, founded so much upon the personal experience of Luther and the special requirements of the period of the Reformation, has no doubt gone far to impress upon us a different lesson. It has taught us that the cry for pardon is the deepest cry of the human spirit, and that it is the great glory of the Gospel to meet and still that cry by the proclamation, "Son, daughter, be of good cheer, thy sins are forgiven thee, go in peace." The teaching is not correct. The deepest cry of the human heart is the cry for holiness, for conformity to that original type of our nature, the consciousness of which, amidst all our sinfulness, has not been lost, and to the possession of which we long to be restored. The holiness of God, therefore, is that which first starts up before the mind of the awakened sinner, and from the thought of holiness it is impossible to separate the thought of wrath against sin. In so far, accordingly, as Christian teaching speaks of the wrath of God, keeping it at the same time in it proper place, it speaks the truth. It has no pleasure in cruel pictures. It would form no unduly harsh estimate of man. It would only recognize that fact of sin the existence of which in human nature the student of human nature, however he may turn away from it, finds himself unable to deny. The law, then, must precede the Gospel; the tempest, the earthquake, and the fire must precede the still, small voice.

Such however is, after all, not the main lesson of the vision which passed before Elijah at Horeb. There is a still deeper and more important lesson connected with that scene, and one which, we cannot doubt for a moment, it was especially designed to teach—that the Gospel not the law, that the proclamation of mercy not the denunciation of wrath, is at once the final and the most effective means to which the Almighty trusts for the establishing of His kingdom among men.

It is not to be denied that law can accomplish much. Apart altogether from the well-deserved punishment which it inflicts upon the transgressor who falls under its sentence, it can remove temptation. It can make indulgence in vice less easy. It can support the weak against the strong. It can place a limit to the demands made by selfish power upon those who are practically unable to resist its bidding It can improve a vast number of material relations which, though at first sight connected only with the body, have the closest bearing upon the moral and religious welfare of society. Nay more, law has a direct educative and training influence upon many who are not yet ready for higher things. A wise and good law is like the hand of a grown up man laid upon the head of a wayward child. The child is checked, calmed, awed, by the thought of a power greater than itself: and, as it looks into the countenance of the man the pressure of whose hand it feels, it gains an impression of the dignity, of the majesty of something which it ought to obey. The writer of these pages had once a striking illustration of this, when complaining to a member of the London School Board of what seemed to him the tendency of the time to depend too much, in all circumstances, upon law as an educational force. It could not be spoken of as a mistake, he was answered, in the East-end of London, for the effect of compulsion there had been to create a belief that there must be value in what the law took pains to compel. The remark was interesting in itself; but it was doubly interesting as a fresh illustration of the wisdom of Him who had of old prepared His people by law for the higher dispensation of the Gospel. Yes, law can do much. It is a noble thing for a statesman to have his name associated with the passing of a wise law. It is a blessing for a country to have judges who can administer wise laws wisely.

Let us never undervalue law. Let us rather magnify it and make it honourable. "Of law," said one whose words cannot be too often quoted, "there can be no less acknowledged than that her seat is the bosom of God, her voice the harmony of the world. All things in heaven and earth do her homage, the very least as feeling her care, and the greatest as not exempted from her power; both angels and men and creatures of what condition soever, though each in different sort and manner, admiring her as the mother of their peace and joy."[1] Scripture confirms such a view. Our Lord honoured the Mosaic law at the very time when He expanded and perfected it; and, at the moment when the apostle of the Gentiles proclaimed with all his energy and zeal that "the righteousness of God without the law is manifested," and that "we are saved by faith," he cries, "Do we then make void law through faith? God forbid. Yea, we establish law" (Rom. iii. 31 : Revised Version, margin). There is no worse sign of a community, of a corporation, of an individual, than lawlessness. Let parents beware how they allow their children to grow up without a due respect for law. Let them teach their children to obey not for the sake of pleasing only, or of obtaining a reward from those who love them; but because right is right and law is law.

All this is to be at once and cheerfully acknowledged. But it is not the less necessary to remember that law, with its striking accompaniments, with its tempest, its earthquake, and

---

* Hooker's Works, vol. i. p. 240.

its fire, can never cure the world's ills. Such healing is to be found in the Lord Jesus Christ alone, and in the Christian dispensation introduced by Him in all the brightness of its light and in all the fulness of its power. "What the law could not do," says the apostle, "in that it was weak through the flesh, God, sending His own Son in the likeness of sinful flesh, and as an offering for sin, condemned sin in the flesh, that the ordinance of the law might be fulfilled in us who walk not after the flesh, but after the Spirit" (Rom. viii. 3, 4). By that one fact, Jesus Christ come in the flesh, our whole relation alike to God and to goodness is changed. We see that the Almighty is reconciled to us. We hear His voice of pardon. We believe in His eternal and unchanging love. Then it becomes a pleasure to us to walk in His ways, to maintain communion with Him, to behold Him in every department of nature, in every arrangement of society, in the circle of the family, in the privacy of our most secret and solitary hours. "Perfect love casteth out fear." We have the confidence of children, the spirit of adoption, the desire to do a Father's will, and to drink every cup which a Father puts into our hands. Thus we feel that we are reaching onward to the end of our being, and that we may grow up into the holiness which shall be a reflection of the holiness of God.

Nor is this all; for in the Lord Jesus we obtain also constantly fresh supplies of strength for the life thus begun, so difficult to pursue. He bestows His spirit upon us. He strengthens us with all needful grace, so that we can overcome the world, and be more than conquerors through Him that loved us. This is true healing; and it is due not so much to Christ the Lawgiver as to Christ the Saviour. The secret of the Redeemer's power over men has not been so much the moral precepts which He uttered, not even the Sermon on the Mount interpreted as a system of practical morality, although it is really far more than that, but words like these, "Come unto Me all ye that labour and are heavy laden, and I will give you rest. Take My yoke upon you, and learn of Me, for I am meek and lowly in heart, and ye shall find rest unto your souls." Under the influence of such words morality lives, enlarges, deepens; but the words themselves, and the spirit which they awaken, precede it, mould it, beautify it. To them the eye turns amidst surrounding darkness; the ear listens amidst the cries of misery of which earth is full; the heart clings when in the desperation of perplexity one is tempted to wish for death rather than life. In them, and other words like them, rest has been found for the weary, comfort for the sorrowful, a softening grace for the hardened, and an attractive power which has made the publican and the sinner draw near in awakened sensibility not only to the thought of what Jesus is, but of what they themselves may be. Take such words out of the New Testament, and out of the mouths of Christian ministers, and experience says that you have taken away what in every age has made the teaching of the New Testament "the wisdom of God and the power of God unto salvation." This was the main lesson taught Elijah at Horeb, and never was a time in the history of our own country when the same lesson was more needed than it is now.

CHAPTER VI.

REVELATION AT HOREB (*continued*) (1 KINGS XIX. 13-21).

Our right and responsibility to judge Elijah at Horeb—The prophet again questioned—His answer—Further revelation of God to him—God still a God of judgment—Hazael, Jehu, Elisha: each an instrument of judgment—Mercy of God revealed—Meaning of the 7,000—The promise contained in the words—The revelation of God thus made continues: first, in judgment; secondly, in the preservation of a faithful remnant — General teaching of Scripture upon this point—The same truths always applicable to the Church—Elijah leaves Horeb—Abel-Meholah—Call of Elisha—Meaning of Elisha's farewell salutations and feast—Spirit in which Elisha enters on his work—Close of Elijah's special mission.

THE vision to Elijah at Horeb considered in the last chapter contained a revelation of the Almighty for which the prophet had been entirely unprepared. After the wonderful events at Carmel, in which he had borne so prominent a part, the signal manifestation of God's presence which had been granted to him there, the complete revolution in the feelings of the people which he had been the instrument of producing, and the slaughter of the prophets of Baal at the brook Kishon, by which the land had been thoroughly cleansed from those who were leading it astray, Elijah had looked for nothing but the immediate and complete triumph of his cause. It is possible even that earthly elements may have mingled with his devotion to the service of God, and his zeal for the restoration of His worship. He may have been unable altogether to avoid thinking of himself and of his own glory. He may have forgotten that weakness of the earthly instrument which the Apostle Paul so vividly remembered, when, in the very midst of all the success of his mission to the Gentiles, he exclaimed, "By the grace of God I am what I am; and His grace which was bestowed upon me was not found vain; but I laboured more abundantly than they all; yet not I, but the grace of God which was with me" (1 Cor. xv. 10). He may have counted upon a continued pouring out of the Divine wrath, until not only the prophets of Baal but all his worshippers had been rooted out of Israel. When, accordingly, instead of this, Jezebel at once rose against *him* with all the authority of the kingdom at her command; and when, instead of taking the lives of others, he was compelled to flee for his own life, he was overwhelmed with disappointment, and with despondency even approaching to despair. Nay, more. A feeling of indignation and doubt took possession of his mind, and he hastened all the way to Horeb, that, amidst those awful peaks upon which the fires of God once burned, and in those wild valleys which once re-echoed with the sound of God's thunders and with the voice of the trumpet "exceeding loud," he might hold communion with the God of hosts, and learn whether He had ceased to be what He had formerly been. The spirit in which Elijah thus fled to Horeb was undoubtedly wrong, and we need have no hesitation in condemning it. We are not called upon to defend all the thoughts and words and actions recorded of even the most famous prophets. Elevated above us as they may seem to be, we must judge them, not indeed precisely as we would judge men now, for their age and circumstances were different from ours, but in the main by the application of the same great principles, modified only by the remembrance of the historical position which they occupied. When St. James tells us that Elijah was "a man of like passions with us" (chap. v. 17), he must be understood to say this, not only as the result of general reasoning, but because he saw, in what was told of the prophet in the Old Testament, tokens of ordinary human frailty and human sin. Nothing has done more harm in the past, or does more harm still, than to look upon the saints of God whose lives are recorded in Scripture as beyond the range of our judgment or our criticism. God has not left us, in our estimate of right and wrong, to be guided only by what, notwithstanding the power of Divine grace in its subjects, must always be the varying standard of human excellence. He has taught us that "the saints shall judge the world," and that "we shall judge angels" (1 Cor. vi. 2, 3) ; and we cannot be fitted for the exercise of such judgment if we do not learn both to distinguish and to pronounce upon the distinction between the true and the false in religious character. It is even with a special view to the drawing of such distinctions that St. Paul reminds Timothy that God has not given us a spirit of fearfulness, but " of power and love and soberness " (2 Tim. i. 7, Revised Version, margin). We may err in our judgments, but we can only be corrected by further enlightenment, or by those to whom, through the operation of the same spirit by which we judge, such further enlightenment has already come. The work of the Spirit in our maturer age must supply what is wanting, and correct what is defective in our reception of the same Spirit in our earlier years. In the fact that it should be so lies one of the greatest elements of our responsibility ; and of that responsibility we cannot rid ourselves without injury to our Christian manhood. As, therefore, the narrative now before us cannot be rightly understood without our judging Elijah, we must judge him ; and when we do so we cannot fail to see how much there was of earth to mar the purity of his zeal, and to dim the singleness of his vision when he fled to Horeb.

Nor was it otherwise even after God had revealed Himself to him there, not in the stormwind or the thunder or the fire, but in the "still, small voice" which told him that it, and not the manifestations which preceded it, was the voice of God. For no sooner was that vision over than " there came a voice unto him, and said, What doest thou here, Elijah ?" The very same question had been asked before, though it is not introduced in exactly the same way by the sacred writer. In the ninth verse of the chapter it is said, " Behold, the word of the Lord came to him, and He said to him." Here we read, " There came a voice unto him and said." Perhaps there is no difference between the two expressions. Yet, when we consider the general carefulness of the sacred writers in their choice of words, and the fact that the mention of " a voice " instead of " the Word of the Lord " in the latter passage follows immediately the mention of the "still small voice," it does not seem altogether improbable that there was at least a difference of tone in the way in which the question was asked upon the two occasions spoken of. In the first instance, there may have been more of the terrible, in the second, of the tender. If it were so it illustrates still more strikingly the degree to which the prophet had misunderstood or declined the teaching of the vision, for his reply was in the same words as before : " I have been very jealous for the Lord, the God of hosts, for the children of Israel have forsaken Thy covenant, thrown down Thine altars, and slain Thy prophets with the sword ; and I, even I only, am left ; and they seek my life to take it away."

Yet let us not blame him more than the circumstances of his position absolutely demand. He could not enter in a moment into those merciful purposes of God which had just been revealed to him. All his own previous experiences had led him to an opposite conclusion. The long continued drought and the unchecked slaughter of Baal's prophets had made him familiar with the thought of wrath rather than of love. His sense of the sin of Israel, too, was as deep as ever ; and, with the exception of what might perhaps yet prove to have been a mere momentary outburst of rage at the foot of Carmel, he had had no time to see any reformation among his people. Even the very sadness of his cry, " I, even I only, am left," is not unnatural. It is the cry which comes down from not a few of God's most faithful and zealous servants in every age of Christian history, and that alike from the crowded city, and the desert or the mountain solitude. Because everything does not fall out exactly as we had planned ; because religious institutions are not arranged precisely as we would have them ; because piety does not assume the garb, and appear in the forms, most pleasing to us, we are ever ready to think that things are in a far more hopeless condition than they are. We limit the extent of the Divine goodness, and the operation of the Divine Spirit in the hearts of men. We forget that the freedom of the God of nature is only equalled by the freedom of the God of grace. Hence, like Elijah, we are ever ready to complain that there are none serving God truly but ourselves. The mistake needs correction, and it was corrected here by a further revelation to Elijah. This revelation may be most naturally divided into two parts.

1. The manifestation of Divine mercy is not inconsistent with the manifestation of Divine judgment. Such is the explanation of the first part of the reply given to the prophet, "And the Lord said unto him, Go, return on thy way by the wilderness to Damascus (Revised Version, margin) ; and, when thou comest,

thou shalt anoint Hazael to be king over Syria: and Jehu the son of Nimshi shalt thou anoint to be king over Israel: and Elisha the son of Shaphat of Abel-meholah shalt thou anoint to be prophet in thy room. And it shall come to pass, that him that escapeth from the sword of Hazael shall Jehu slay; and him that escapeth from the sword of Jehu shall Elisha slay." The general meaning of these words cannot be misunderstood, and it is with the general meaning alone that we have to do. No where is the great rule of interpretation more necessary than here, that not only the words themselves, but all the circumstances connected with them must be taken into account when we would determine the idea in the speaker's mind; and that that idea, and not simply the literal rendering of the words, is the meaning of which we are in search. For, in the first place, it is to be noticed that Hazael does not appear to have been anointed at all to the kingship that is here spoken of. The record of the Old Testament rather seems distinctly to exclude that thought. In the second place, it was not Elijah but Elisha who carried out the command of God now given with regard to both Hazael and Jehu. In 2 Kings viii. 7-15, we have an account of the one transaction, and in the same book, chap. ix. 1-10, an account of the other. From the first of these accounts we learn that Benhadad, king of Syria, at a time when he was sick, heard that Elisha had come to Damascus, and sent Hazael, an officer in high position at his court, to inquire of the prophet whether he should recover from his sickness. Elisha answered the question, and then settled his countenance steadfastly upon Hazael until the latter was ashamed, and "the man of God wept." Whereupon, in reply to Hazael's question why he wept, he told him of all the evil that he would do to the children of Israel, and that he would himself be king over Syria. The communication recorded here did not take place between Hazael and Elijah, but between that officer of Benhadad and Elisha. A similar remark applies, though still more strongly, to the case of Jehu. Neither Elijah nor Elisha anointed Jehu. One of the sons of the prophets was sent by the latter for the purpose. In the third place, in no literal sense of the words could it be said that Elisha slew any of the Israelites. No doubt he seems to be the instrument of destroying the forty-two children at Bethel mentioned in 2 Kings ii. 24. But this incident can no more be regarded as a fulfilment of the words here spoken to Elijah than any of the other acts of Elisha's life. That prophet used no sword like Hazael or like Jehu against the idolatrous worshippers of Baal; and the writer of this history, whoever he was, could not but have known the fact. It follows that, in the interpretation of the words before us, two principles must be kept in view; first, that Elijah may be justly considered as responsible for acts done by any of his disciples in the spirit which they had imbibed from their master; and secondly, that the words are not intended to be understood in their most literal sense, but rather as expressive of the general truth, that He from whom they came, marked as He may be by mercy rather than wrath, by the still, small voice rather than the tempest, the earthquake, and the fire, is still a God of judgment.

The execution of such judgment against sinful Israel may be clearly traced in the case of each of the three persons named.

For after Hazael succeeded to the throne of Syria he was a constant thorn in the side of Israel. We read that in these days "the Lord began to cut Israel short," and that "Hazael smote them in all the coasts of Israel" (2 Kings x. 32); that a little later "the anger of the Lord was kindled against Israel, and he delivered them into the hand of Hazael, king of Syria, and into the hand of Benhadad, son of Hazael, all their days;" while it is even said in yet stronger language, that the king of Syria had "made them like the dust by threshing" (2 Kings xiii. 3, 7).

If Hazael thus scourged Israel as a people, still more did Jehu scourge Ahab and Jezebel and all their house. So terrible was the work of extermination upon which he entered when he took possession of the throne, that it has been justly described as one "hitherto unparalleled in the history of the Jewish monarchy."[1] He slew Jehoram the reigning king, one of the sons of Ahab, with his own hand on that day when he drove furiously to Jezreel; and, remembering the word of the Lord which he had heard when he accompanied Ahab to the vineyard of Naboth, he ordered the body of the king to be cast into the plat of ground that his father had so cruelly acquired (1 Kings xxi. 19; 2 Kings ix. 26). He was the chief instrument also in the death of Jezebel; for, when he hastened to Jezreel after the

[1] Stanley, in Smith's "Dictionary of the Bible," Jehu.

despatch of Jehoram, that fierce and haughty queen painted her eyes and tired her head, and looked out at a window as he passed, and cried to him, "Is it peace, thou Zimri, thy master's murderer?" Then Jehu "lifted up his face to the window, and said, Who is on my side? Who? and there looked out to him two or three eunuchs. And he said, Throw her down. So they threw her down, and some of her blood was sprinkled on the wall, and on the horses; and he trode her under foot." Even this was not all, for, touched in some degree by the thought that, whatever she had been, she was a king's daughter, he afterwards sent to bury her. But the messengers "found no more of her than the skull and the feet and the palms of her hands. Wherefore they came again, and told him. And he said, This is the word of the Lord, which he spake by His servant Elijah the Tishbite, saying, In the portion of Jezreel shall the dogs eat the flesh of Jezebel: and the carcase of Jezebel shall be as dung upon the face of the field in the portion of Jezreel; so that they shall not say, This is Jezebel" (2 Kings ix. 30–37).

Nor was even this all. By still more terrible measures did Jehu prove himself to be the scourge of Ahab and of his house; for he did not rest until he had secured the destruction of all the surviving members of the old royal family. He terrified the rulers and elders of Samaria into slaying seventy of the sons of Ahab who had fled to them for refuge; and, when their heads were sent to him, he piled them in two heaps at the entering in of the gate of Jezreel, and said, "Know now that there shall fall unto the earth nothing of the word of the Lord, which the Lord spake concerning the house of Ahab; for the Lord hath done that which He spake by His servant Elijah" (2 Kings x. 10). Even the more distant relatives of Ahab did not escape his vengeance; for, as he travelled on one occasion from Jezreel to Samaria, he met, at the binding house of the shepherds, forty and two princes of the house of Ahaziah, king of Judah, who had married a daughter of Ahab, and slew them there (2 Kings x. 14). Thus the house of Ahab was finally extinguished. Of all his great men and his kinsfolks and his priests Jehu left him none remaining (2 Kings x. 11).

Not only, however, did Jehu prove himself the scourge of Ahab, he was not less the scourge of those worshippers of Baal with whom that house had been so closely identified. Uniting fierceness, hypocrisy, and cunning to a degree which, but for the recorded facts, it would have been almost impossible for us to conceive, he plotted and accomplished their extinction at a single blow. "Ahab," he said, "served Baal a little, but Jehu shall serve him much." He proclaimed a solemn assembly for Baal in the great temple which Ahab had built in Samaria to that false divinity. Thither he summoned, under the penalty of death to any who should absent themselves, all Baal's prophets and servants and priests; and all the worshippers of Baal came, so that there was not a man left that came not; and the house of Baal was filled from one end to another. The gorgeous vestments were brought out, the worshippers were clothed with them, and went into the temple to offer sacrifices and burnt offerings. Then the fatal moment arrived. As soon as the offerings were over Jehu gave the command, to those whom he had provided for the purpose, to fall upon them, letting none of them escape. "And they smote them with the edge of the sword, and the guard and the captains cast them out, and went into the city of the house of Baal (or the inner sanctuary of the temple). And they brought forth the obelisks that were in the house of Baal, and burned them. And they brake down the pillar of Baal, and made it a draught-house unto this day. Thus Jehu destroyed Baal out of Israel" (2 Kings x. 18–27).

Finally, Elisha was also in like manner a warning and a scourge to the idolaters of his time. An entirely different idea has indeed been entertained with regard both to the work of Elisha and to the relation in which he stands to Elijah. It has been supposed that between the two prophets there was a contrast rather than a similarity of character; that, while the one was the child of the desert, rough, impetuous, and harsh, the other was the child of the family and the home, full of gentleness of disposition and kindness of heart. Then, as to the flight in which Elisha is presented to us in Elijah's vision, it has been urged that, comparing it with that to Moses at Sinai, Hazael and Jehu illustrate the fact that God "will by no means clear the guilty," while Elisha illustrates the other aspect of the Divine character in which God is "merciful and gracious, long-suffering and slow to anger." It is most difficult to accept such an interpretation. The words, "Him that escapeth from the sword of Hazael shall Jehu slay; and him that escapeth from the sword of Jehu shall Elisha slay," appear to describe all the three men spoken of as if they were animated by the same spirit and summoned to the same task. Besides which, the acts recorded of Elisha reveal something wholly different from the soft and gentle spirit thus ascribed to him. If he was less severe than the prophet of the wilderness, if he moved more among the abodes of men, and if he exhibited in a larger degree human sympathy and pity, the difference arose from the fact that he was less single and powerful in the essential elements of his character, and that he less fully embodied the sternness of the Law. But he belonged to the same school of prophecy. The mantle of Elijah, and with his mantle his spirit in so far as he was capable of receiving it, had descended upon him. He had the same contest to maintain, and the same work to do. "After Elijah's decease," says one of the most eloquent historians of Israel, Elisha was known as the one who "had poured water on the hands of Elijah. And certainly Elijah could scarcely have chosen a more powerful servant. Recognized and honoured as the most intimate and trusted disciple of the great prophet, he lived in the exercise of a constantly increasing influence till the beginning of the reign of the grandson of Jehu. . . . But, although he had inherited Elijah's mantle, and many might esteem him equally great, yet it was always an essential feature of the representation of him that he had only received two-thirds of Elijah's spirit, and had with difficulty obtained even that. . . . He is great only so far as he continues, and carries out with more force than any other man of his time, the work which Elijah had begun with new and wonderful power, namely, of defending the ancient religion with a courage which nothing could shake. . . . But he was still less capable than Elijah of inaugurating a purely benign and constructive mode of action, since at that time the whole spirit of the ancient religion was still unprepared for it."[1] Dean Stanley has indeed taken an entirely different view of Elisha's character and work,[2] but it may well be doubted if it is as true to the facts of the case as that of his German predecessor. In Elisha there is indeed a greater mingling of the gentle with the harsh, of the tender with the severe, than there was in Elijah, but the lines on which he wrought were in no wise different, and his prophetic

[1] Ewald, "History of Israel," edited by Carpenter, iv. 81, 82.
[2] "Lectures on the Jewish Church," lect. xxxi.

work was in the main a protest against the idolatrous tendencies of Israel, and a condemnation of its sins. Looking, therefore, at the words we have been examining in the light of Elisha's life taken as a whole, it cannot surprise us that he should be described, in language similar to that employed with regard to Hazael and Jehu, as a scourge of Israel. The translation into the future history of Elijah's people of the still, small voice which at the entrance of his cave he had recognized as the immediate emblem of the Divine presence has not yet been given.

Hazael, Jehu, Elisha—all the three were to be instruments of the Divine wrath, and ministers of the Divine vengeance upon degenerate Israel. They were to be the great and strong "wind" which was to rend the mountains and break in pieces the rocks before the Lord, the "earthquake," and the "fire." They were to reveal the character and attributes of that God of Israel who was a God of judgment; and who, whatever might be the fortunes of His servants, would be the same in His dealings with sin as He had been when He answered the prayer of His prophet upon the heights of Carmel. The words "before the Lord," used in connection with the great and strong wind at Horeb, and belonging by analogy also to the earthquake and the fire, are to be particularly marked. As he apprehended the meaning of the thought which they express, Elijah would see that these terrible visitations were directed by the same Divine hand that had been so signally revealed to him a day or two before, that he was still in the presence of the unchangeable Jehovah, and that, whatever might be the manifestation of Divine mercy which was given him, it was not inconsistent with the manifestation of Divine judgment. Thus he was prepared for the second part of the words addressed to him.

2. These words immediately follow: "Yet will I leave me seven thousand in Israel, all the knees which have not bowed unto Baal, and every mouth which hath not kissed him." The words, it will be observed, as they are correctly given in the Revised, though not in the Authorized Version, contain more than an intimation that, though Elijah had thought himself alone, there were seven thousand in Israel still faithful to the truth. They are also a promise that, amidst all the judgments that were to follow, seven thousand would be found worthy to escape them, because they would refuse to yield to the general

apostasy of the people. Nor are we again to understand the number seven thousand literally. Seven is the number of the covenant; and, as may be seen more fully in the Apocalypse, thousands were associated in the mind of a Jew with what was heavenly and Divine, while hundreds belonged rather to what was earthly and devilish. Seven thousand, therefore, is a sacred, a rounded, a covenant, an ideal number; and, while it might perhaps indicate a smaller, it indicates in all probability a larger number of persons than the figures naturally denote. These figures are indeed obviously symbolical, expressive of steadfast adherence to the covenant, and of the continued enjoyment of its privileges. The promise, when correctly interpreted, thus implies more than it is generally supposed to include—not merely that at that moment there was a remnant according to the election of grace, and that Elijah did not stand alone in his allegiance to the Almighty, but that that election would be preserved through all the judgments that were to follow. There were times of heavy trial in store for the Church of God in Israel, in the midst of which many would fall and be overwhelmed. Yet, whatever might happen to the merely outward members of the body, the Lord knew them that were His, and to them the promise long afterwards made to the Church of Philadelphia would be fulfilled, "Because thou didst keep the word of My patience, I also will keep thee from the hour of trial, that hour which is to come upon the whole world, to try them that dwell upon the earth" (Rev. iii. 10).

If the words formerly considered by us were a translation into speech of the *whirlwind*, the *earthquake*, and the *fire*, those of which we now speak are thus a similar translation of the *still, small voice*. In the three agents of the destructive powers of nature we hear the utterance, "Him that escapeth the sword of Hazael shall Jehu slay, and him that escapeth the sword of Jehu shall Elisha slay." In the soft whisper which followed, and which told of human sympathy, we hear the utterance, "Yet will I leave me seven thousand in Israel, all the knees which have not bowed unto Baal, and every mouth which hath not kissed him." First in deed and then in word is the prophet spoken to.

It ought to be hardly necessary to say that the revelation thus made by the Almighty of Himself to Elijah has always been continued, and is still continued, to His Church and people. For,

1. The element of judgment never ceases to mark the course of history, and never fails, as it is traced there by the eye of faith, to elevate and sustain the heart. Neither vindictiveness nor a spirit of vengeance, in the sense in which that word is commonly understood, marks those who believe that, whatever may be the appearances to the contrary, the Lord God omnipotent reigneth. Their feeling is simply one of joy that everything is under the control of Him who, as Judge of all the earth, does right, who weighs the actions of men in the balances of His own unswerving rectitude, and the course of whose providence will sooner or later show that justice and judgment are the habitation of His throne. We may at times be disposed to exclaim, not so much "Hath God forgotten to be gracious, hath He in anger shut up His tender mercies?" as, Hath God forgotten to be righteous, hath He in anger withheld the thunderbolts of His wrath against transgression? On the one hand, we see the wicked in great power, the selfish schemers around us attaining the ends of their ambition, the unscrupulous apparently prosperous and happy; on the other hand, we see humble piety trodden upon, overreached, and oppressed, its very goodness, its weakness, its simplicity the temptation to the daring and unprincipled.

And, when we see this, what can we do but cry for the speedy coming of the time when God shall make bare His holy arm in the sight of the nations, visit wrong-doing with the punishment which it deserves, and bring forth the righteousness of those who wait upon Him as the light and their judgment as the noon-day? Or with what other sentiments than those of satisfaction and of triumph can we listen to the words, "Shall not God avenge His elect which cry to Him day and night, and He is long-suffering over them, I say unto you that He will avenge them speedily" (Luke xviii. 7, 8). Throughout the whole of Scripture the same thought runs, that we are in the midst of a righteous order, and throughout the whole of history that thought has lifted up the Church's head, as she has felt that the hour of her redemption was drawing nigh. Not only, however, does the Almighty constantly keep this hope before His people, He assures them

2. That He will never fail to preserve His own elect amidst the trials which encompass them. The consolation afforded to Elijah is indeed the very consolation afforded to the

Church throughout the whole both of the Old Testament and the New—not so much that the Church shall attain the completeness of her victory before the end, as that the faithful remnant within her shall be preserved for the end, not one of those who compose that remnant being lost. We are too apt to imagine that it is the purpose of God to establish even in this world a Church which shall be outwardly triumphant over the world, which shall gradually spread from sea to sea, and which shall by degrees leaven the whole world with its heavenly principles. We console ourselves with the reflection that, slow as the progress of the Church was during the times of the Old Testament dispensation, and slow as it has been during the eighteen centuries of the Christian era, there has yet been perceptible advance. And we anticipate, it may be at no distant period in the future, the sudden breaking up of winter before the rushing in of spring, and nations "born in a day." It may well be doubted whether Scripture gives countenance to such ideas. Rather would it seem as if the purpose of God's gracious dealings with men were to call out of the nations a people for His name, to rescue from surrounding darkness those who are there waiting for the light, and to bring to the knowledge of Himself those who, more or less " of the truth," are ready to hear His voice, and to come to that eternal Son of whom it is said, " Neither doth any man know the Father save the Son, and he to whomsoever the Son willeth to reveal Him " (Matt. xi. 27). The conception, in short, of the Church of God which runs throughout the Bible is more that of a remnant to be preserved than of an army of the redeemed marching forward to new and ever-extending conquests.

In this spirit it is that Isaiah cries, " Except the Lord of hosts had left unto us a very small remnant, we should have been as Sodom, we should have been like unto Gomorrah ; " and again, speaking of the day when "the glory of Jacob shall be made thin," " Yet there shall be left therein gleanings, as the shaking of an olive tree, two or three berries in the top of the uttermost bough, four or five in the outmost branches of a fruitful tree, saith the Lord, the God of Israel ; " and once more, " Thus saith the Lord, As the new wine is found in the cluster, and one saith, Destroy it not, for a blessing is in it : so will I do for My servants' sakes, that I may not destroy them all. And I will bring forth a seed out of Jacob, and out of Judah an inheritor of My mountains: and My chosen shall inherit it, and My servants shall dwell there" (Isa. i. 9; xvii. 4; lxv. 8, 9). In a similar spirit our Lord Himself, referring in His great discourse upon the Last Things to the fortunes of His Church throughout all her pilgrimage, exclaims, "And except those days had been shortened, no flesh should have been saved; but for the elect's sake those days shall be shortened" (Matt. xxiv. 22). It is not otherwise with St. Paul when, in the midst of that unbelief and hardness of heart by which the Jews of his time were characterized, he fell back upon this very revelation of the Almighty to His prophet: "Wot ye not what the Scripture saith of Elijah? how he pleadeth with God against Israel, Lord, they have killed Thy prophets; they have digged down Thine altars; and I am left alone, and they seek my life. But what saith the answer of God unto him? I have left for Myself seven thousand men, who have not bowed the knee to Baal. Even so, then, at this present time also there is a remnant according to the election of grace" (Rom. xi. 2–5). The same thought also lies at the bottom of the representation given us by the Seer in the Apocalypse when he beheld an "angel ascend from the sunrising, having the seal of the living God; and he cried with a great voice to the four angels, to whom it was given to hurt the earth and the sea, saying, Hurt not the earth, neither the sea, nor the trees, till we shall have sealed the servants of our God on their foreheads," and when there were sealed one hundred and forty-four thousand out of the twelve tribes of God's spiritual Israel (Rev. vii. 1–8). These hundred and forty-four thousand "were purchased from among men to be the firstfruits unto God and unto the Lamb" (Rev. xiv. 4). They are that faithful remnant which in every age is kept safe amidst the revolutions of the world and the trials of its pilgrimage until it is crowned with glory.

The two truths, then, thus spoken to Elijah in the last words addressed to him before he left Horeb to go on his way to Damascus, were not spoken to him alone, nor were they adapted only to his peculiar circumstances. They are always applicable and always of value to the Church of Christ. That Church may often fear that she shall never be able to escape the malice and hatred of her enemies. Her position in this world is constantly presented to her as one of difficulty and trial and persecution. Our Lord compared His disciples to sheep in the midst of wolves. He spoke of tribulation as their natural and appropriate portion. He told them that without taking up their cross and following Him they could not be His disciples. And He represented drinking of the cup that He drank of, and being baptized with the baptism with which He was baptized, as necessary to their being made ready for any honours in His kingdom. The same lesson is taught, in passages far too numerous to quote, by His apostles in their letters to the Churches, and by St. John in the Apocalypse. We are particularly to observe, too, that in all this teaching the main reference is not to such suffering as might be produced by poverty, sickness, or bereavement. It is opposition at the hands of the world, opposition to the Church on the ground that she is the Church, opposition to her doctrines and demands as in themselves essentially distasteful to men, that is constantly in view. Hence also the permanency of this opposition. It was not, as so many would fain persuade themselves, confined to the first ages of Christianity, because the world was so evil, while it may be hoped that it has for ever vanished through the growth of knowledge and civilization. Rather is the saying of our Lord always true: "If ye were of the world the world would love its own, but because ye are not of the world, but I chose you out of the world, therefore the world hateth you" (John xv. 19). There is no prospect, so far as Scripture teaches, of something like a millennial peace and rest for the Church before the end. Down to the very close of this dispensation the same enmity and opposition will continue on the one side, and the same suffering from it on the other; or, should it at any time be otherwise, it will be found that the ease arises not from the world's being less hostile to the Church, but from the Church's having become more conformed to the world. The Church of the Lord Jesus Christ, when faithful to her high calling, can never fail to be in the position of the boat in which, as described in the Fourth Gospel, the disciples were when they were overtaken by the storm on the Sea of Galilee. It is dark; the sea has risen by reason of a great wind: it would seem for the moment that Jesus has not come to them; yet all the while the Saviour marks them from the mountain-top, where He has remained to pray to His heavenly Father. He knows their danger: He notices their alarm: He will come to them walking upon the waters which arouse their fears: and when they take

Him into the boat it will be "straightway at the land whither they were going" (John vi. 21) That is our encouragement and our hope. The seven thousand shall be always found, and not one of them shall be lost. Against them the gates of Hades shall never prevail. They may prevail against the world. They may prevail against the outward Church, the great community calling itself by the name of Israel. Nay, they may even find there the smoothest hinges upon which to turn. But there will never be wanting those who listen to the words, " Come forth, my people, out of her, that ye have no fellowship with her sins, and that ye receive not of her plagues" (Rev. xviii. 4); and these at least will keep the lamp of truth burning until the Bridegroom comes, and His whole redeemed Church enters in with Him into the marriage feast.

In that hope, that confidence, let Elijah, let ourselves rejoice. "Let the sea roar, and the fulness thereof; the world, and they that dwell therein. Let the floods clap their hands; let the hills be joyful together before the Lord: for He cometh to judge the earth; with righteousness shall He judge the world, and the people with His truth" (Psa. xcviii. 7–9).

The revelation to the prophet was over, and it remained for him only to return by the wilderness to Damascus, that he might execute the commission with which he had been charged. He set out from Horeb northward, and pursued his way, apparently without interruption, towards the upper part of the valley of the Jordan. There he reached a small place called Abel-meholah, or the meadow of the dance. The name would seem to indicate that it was a fertile plain near the river, well adapted for the purposes either of pasture or of agriculture, and at the present moment used for the latter. The field was under the plough, and twelve men, each with a yoke of oxen before him, were engaged in cultivating it. The last of the twelve was Elisha, the son of Shaphat; and Elijah, whether he had known him before or not, at once recognized the man whom he was to anoint as prophet in his room. Obedient to the heavenly vision, he did not hesitate an instant as to the course he was to follow, but "passed over unto him, and cast his mantle upon him." Not a word would appear to have been spoken. On the part of the one actor in the scene the action was symbolical; on the part of the other it was understood. And no sooner had it been performed than Elijah, in all probability resuming his mantle, strode on upon his way. The feelings of Elisha are sufficiently indicated by the course which he pursued. His first impression may well have been one of bewilderment. What was the precise nature of his call? Must he at that very instant leave his plough standing in the furrow? Must he quit that field upon which he had often laboured, the oxen which he had often guided, and the prospect of even a more abundant crop, from the newly fallen rain, than he had often gathered? Must he leave father and mother, and relations and home, to enter upon a life so different from that which he had previously led? And there before him is the gaunt figure of Elijah already disappearing in the distance. Questions like these could hardly fail to pass rapidly through his mind, but they were as rapidly answered. There was no possibility of mistaking the nature of the Divine commission. He must leave all and follow him by whom it had been given. And so he did. "He left the oxen," we are told, "and ran after Elijah, and said, 'Let me, I pray thee, kiss my father and my mother, and then I will follow thee.'"

There is difficulty in interpreting these words; but, before endeavouring to interpret them, it may be well to take the rest of the narrative into account. Elijah answered the request, "Go back again; for what have I done unto thee?" The permission was embraced. Elisha "returned from following him, and took the yoke of oxen and slew them, and roasted their flesh with the instruments of the oxen, and gave unto the people, and they did eat. Then he arose, and went after Elijah, and ministered unto him."

In what light then are we to understand the events which are thus described? Have we before us in Elisha a man of gentle nature and family affections, who cannot bear to part suddenly with those whom he has loved, who must give them a final embrace before he goes, and who, in the exercise of a kind and generous hospitality, must afford proof to his old friends and neighbours that, even in the new and important sphere upon which he is entering, he will not forget the pleasant days they had spent together in the village or in the fields? Have we, in short, here a sweet idyll of the country upon which the eye may rest with fond delight, amidst those stern and rugged sights, those sights even of bloodshed and of slaughter, with which the rest of the narrative is filled?

Such is the light in which the passage is generally regarded, but it is not easy to think that it is correct.

(1) There is a remarkable incident in the life of Christ, in which the language of our Lord can scarcely be separated from remembrances of the scene before us. When Jesus was upon His last journey from Galilee to Jerusalem, there came to Him a man who said, "I will follow Thee, Lord; but first suffer me to bid farewell to them that are at my house. But Jesus said unto him, No man, having put his hand to the plough, and looking back, is fit for the kingdom of God" (Luke ix. 61, 62). Our Lord had immediately before been alluding to the history of Elijah (ver. 54), and in the words now quoted it is hardly possible to mistake an allusion to that of Elisha. But, if so, we cannot imagine that Elisha is referred to as one who, by looking back, had proved himself unfit for the kingdom of God. That history, therefore, cannot be intended to describe looking back in the ordinary sense. It was rather the history of one who did not look back, but who obeyed the Divine call with singleness and with earnest promptitude.

(2) It is by no means necessary to interpret the "kiss" which Elisha proposed to give to his father and mother as a mere kiss of affection, the giving of which may be supposed to betray a heart still clinging to earthly relationships and ties. It was probably no more than that kiss of farewell with which Orientals are in the habit of saluting one another when they part. To give it was perfectly consistent with the most absolute abandonment of earthly goods, and the most devoted submission to the new life upon which the prophet was to enter. The going back to say farewell may, when looked at in this light, be the clearest proof of the strength of his determination to enter at once upon the prophetic life, and to make every sacrifice for its sake.

(3) The killing of the oxen and the mode in which they were prepared for food indicate something altogether different from an ordinary feast. The Hebrew word rendered killed means properly to kill in sacrifice, and is constantly used in that sense throughout the Old Testament Scriptures. Again, the "instruments of the oxen" would never have been thus used to prepare an ordinary festive meal. It is impossible to think that there could have been any necessity for such a course, or that fuel could not easily have been obtained in some other way. Besides

which there is at least one other instance in the Bible in which a similar course was resorted to, and by which, therefore, light is shed upon the action now taken by Elisha. When David told Araunah that he was come to buy his threshing-floor of him in order to build thereon an altar to the Lord, Araunah at once offered to make a free gift of the spot to the king, and added, "Let my lord the king take and offer up what seemeth good unto him : behold, the oxen for the burnt-offering, and the threshing instruments and the furniture of the oxen for the wood " (2 Sam. xxiv. 22). Here was undoubtedly a sacrifice to the value of which it must have been thought that the consuming of the oxen and of their harness contributed. And so now. Not because other oxen and other firewood could not have been obtained were these resorted to by Elisha, but because, in surrendering them, he surrendered all that he esteemed most useful and valuable to himself.

(4) Lastly, the peculiar character of the feast here partaken of may be noticed. It was not an ordinary festival, but a feast after a sacrifice ; and it had thus a sacred meaning. It was the pledge that those who partook of it were in covenant with God, that they had surrendered themselves to His service, and that they were at peace with Him.

Looked at in this light, the whole transaction now recorded assumes an aspect wholly different from that in which we commonly regard it. Instead of supplying evidence of even momentary hesitation upon Elisha's part, it supplies the clearest evidence that there was nothing of the kind. Instead of indicating some remains of attachment to the world, it indicates that the future prophet not only renounced the world, but that he was desirous to tell the world that he did so. And, if it shows that he had tender affections and friendly feelings, it shows also that he had learned from the moment when Elijah cast his mantle upon him to count all things but loss for the excellency of the service to which he had then been summoned. The force and vigour of Elisha's character appear as conspicuously in this scene as they do in every other action of his life.

The revelation of God to Elijah at Horeb was now over, and with the calling of his successor the chief part of his activity closed. He has, indeed, yet to come before us in one or two striking scenes ; but his main work was done. Little more than three years had passed since he first in the presence of Ahab announced the judgments coming upon the land. By far the larger portion even of these years had been spent in the obscurity of a poor woman's house in a heathen land. Only for a few weeks would it seem that he was in the field, and but two or three days out of that time in presence of the foe. Yet in that brief season he fought his fight and gained his victory.

CHAPTER VII.

ELIJAH AND NABOTH'S VINEYARD (I KINGS XXI. 1-29).

Elijah disappears for a time—Naboth the Jezreelite—Ahab desires possession of his vineyard—Failure of his attempt to obtain it and the effec upon him—Jezebel's plot—Its success—Naboth's trial and death—Ahab takes possession of the vineyard—Elijah appears before him there—Judgment pronounced on Ahab and Jezebel and their house—Execution of the judgment by Jehu—Fulfilment of woe uttered by Elijah—Effect on Ahab of Elijah's words—Objects of the narrative: To impress us with a deep sense of the wickedness of Ahab and Jezebel—To show the righteous retributions of God upon the sinner—To reveal God's readiness to pardon the penitent.

WITH the departure of Elijah from Abel-meholah at the time when he cast his mantle upon Elisha, the public career of the prophet may be said to have come to an end. It had been short, but decisive. Elijah had fulfilled the work which had been given him to do. He had vindicated in the sight of assembled Israel the honour of the only living and true God. He had drawn from the people assembled at Mount Carmel the loud acclaim of praise, "The Lord, He is the God; the Lord, He is the God." He had been the instrument of effecting the destruction of the priests of Baal at the river Kishon. He had received that revelation at Horeb of the nature of God's character and government, which was to lead Israel to higher thoughts of the Divine Being, and to prepare the way for the introduction of a better dispensation in the fulness of the times. Finally, he had been guided to the selection of one who was to succeed him in the prophetic office and to carry on his work in Israel. His great task, therefore, was accomplished.

But, as illustrated by numerous instances in the sacred narrative, public work is not all that is demanded of the prophets of God. They have to apply the principles of the Divine government to private life; and partly to bring out this truth, partly to throw further light upon the characters of Ahab and Jezebel, so that we may better understand all the particulars of the terrible fate that was in store for them, we are made acquainted with the tragical story of Naboth and his vineyard.

Of Naboth himself, apart from his connection with this vineyard, we know almost nothing. He is called "Naboth the Jezreelite," so that we may positively conclude that he was an inhabitant of Jezreel. In that city we further know that Ahab had erected a royal palace to which he was particularly attached, and which he had surrounded with terraces and gardens. Naboth must thus have been a constant witness of the idolatry and corruption of the Court. But his feelings and language in reference to his vineyard entitle us to infer that, like Lot in Sodom, he had remained unaffected by the profligacy around him, and that he was one of that remnant in Israel which had not bowed the knee to Baal. His possession of land in the neighbourhood of the city must have lent him some importance; and this impression will be confirmed if, with Dean Stanley, we adopt the idea of Josephus that, when an assembly was convened to judge him, he was placed *in virtue of his position*, at its head.[1] There is little, however, to warrant this conclusion. And the probabilities are rather in favour of the generally received opinion that, with the exception of possessing a small "plat of ground" (2 Kings ix. 26) near the city, he was poor. This plat of ground was his own. He had inherited it from his fathers, and he was attached to it by all the ties which everywhere bind men to the land that has come down to them, and which were even peculiarly strong amongst the Jews.

The vineyard thus spoken of was "hard by the palace of Ahab, king of Samaria." It would seem even to have run like a tongue into the rest of the ground which Ahab possessed in the neighbourhood of his palace, and to have thus interfered with his privacy and the full carrying out of the plans of improvement that he had in view. He desired, accordingly, to obtain it; and, unless it be that he already knew the sentiments of Naboth, there was no unfairness in the steps taken by him to

[1] Smith's "Dictionary of the Bible," Naboth, note 6.

effect his end. He had been dwelling in Samaria at the time,[1] but he came personally to Jezreel to see Naboth on the point, and the fact that he did so could hardly fail to impress the Jezreelite with a sense of the king's earnestness in the matter. In Jezreel he found Naboth, "and he spake unto him saying, Give me thy vineyard that I may have it for a garden of herbs, because it is near unto my house: and I will give thee for it a better vineyard than it: or, if it seems good to thee, I will give thee the worth of it in money." In the mouth of an idolatrous king, who had forsaken the God of Israel, it may be said that there was nothing wrong in the proposal thus submitted to Naboth. But there was a wrong, and it lay in this, that Ahab was king of God's people Israel; that he had been taught in the most striking manner, and had probably in words at least acknowledged, the sovereignty of Jehovah; and that the Divine law expressly forbade such a transaction as he now contemplated. No Israelite was entitled thus to part with or to sell his property. The land really belonged to God, and not to him. Jehovah Himself was the proprietor of the whole soil of Palestine, and He had originally divided it among the people on the condition that it should always remain in the families to which it had been assigned. Even in the case of poverty it could only be sold for a sum of money calculated by the number of years that were to run between the time of sale and the date of the next celebration of the jubilee. After being sold it might at any moment, if the old owner could afford it, be redeemed: and, if this could not be done, it returned in the year of jubilee to the first possessor or his family (Lev. xxv. 13-28). Such was the distinct provision of the Mosaic law—"The land shall not be sold for ever, for the land is Mine" (Lev. xxv. 23). Ahab must have known this. If he did not he ought to have known it. In either case he was equally to blame. His proposal to Naboth was one involving a direct infringement of the Divine law; and, when we take into account his character as it appears in all the other actions of his life, we shall hardly be doing him injustice if we suppose that his apparent fairness may have been in some degree due to his knowledge that he was tempting Naboth to be guilty of sin. It is no uncommon thing thus to trick out in the fairest colours any temptation to wrong-doing that we present to others.

[1] Keil, *in loc.*

Whatever may have been the case with Ahab there can be no doubt as to the spirit that animated Naboth. "The Lord forbid it me," he replied, "that I should give the inheritance of my fathers unto thee." There is no reason to doubt that the scruple thus expressed was thoroughly conscientious, or that, though Naboth may at the same time have been influenced by other motives, he was guided mainly by his conviction that to transfer his inheritance to another, as he was now asked to do, was directly contrary to the law of God. The bar, too, thus presented to the accomplishment of the demands of Ahab was insuperable. No promise of a larger piece of ground, or of more money than he may at first have been willing to spend upon the purchase, could be of the smallest use. Ahab had not to deal with an avaricious proprietor, desirous to raise the price of his commodity, but with a pious Israelite, who knew the Divine law and was determined to obey it. All hope of accomplishing his object had to be abandoned by the king.

The effect, accordingly, produced on him is next described. ". He came into his house heavy and displeased because of the word which Naboth the Jezreelite had spoken to him And he laid him down upon his bed, and turned away his face, and would eat no bread." It is difficult to think that the sacred writer, in penning such a description, could have failed to be alive to the almost ludicrous weakness of the man of whom he speaks. A king acting like a spoilt child; prevented from accomplishing his purpose by causes the force of which he was secretly compelled to own, yet not straightforward enough to confess them openly; standing before an iron gate, which he is well aware cannot be opened, and yet injuring himself by kicking against it in an impotence as petulant as it was absurd—such is the picture that is here presented to us. Ahab was not only wicked; he was weak. He was not only morally, but, intellectually, a fool.

A stronger than he was not far off to solve the difficulty. We have met her before as she displayed a marked contrast to her husband; for, when, after the slaughter of the priests of Baal, the latter drove home consenting to what had been done, and permitting Elijah, the instrument of effecting it, to run as one of his company before his chariot, she, on the other hand, no sooner heard of it than she was up in arms, bent upon immediate vengeance. "So let the gods do to me, and more also," had then been her instant message to the prophet, "if I make not thy life as the life of one of them by to-morrow about this time." We see the same spirit now, a spirit to be commended for its strength had it not been at the same time marked by such impious contempt of principle. As it was, she came to Ahab and asked the cause of his sadness. The explanation given, she was at no loss to make immediate reply, "Dost thou not govern the kingdom of Israel? Arise, and eat bread, and let thine heart be merry; I will give thee the vineyard of Naboth the Jezreelite." The wife, and not the husband, was after all the monarch.

Nor did Jezebel content herself with words. She took immediate steps to effect her purpose, and these were worthy of the craft and cruelty which have ever since been associated with her name. She wrote letters in the king's name, and sealed them with his seal, and sent them to the elders and nobles of Jezreel. In these letters she commanded them to proclaim a fast, that the feelings of the people might be excited by the thought that something of far more than ordinary importance had occurred, and that the wicked deed which she proposed might be clothed with all the solemnities of a religious act. In the midst of the impression thus produced, an assembly of the people was to be called; Naboth was to be placed at the head of it, in order that a deeper horror might be awakened by the charge of impiety brought against one who occupied so exalted a position; and then, two false witnesses having been suborned for the purpose, these witnesses were to testify that the unhappy owner of the coveted vineyard had cursed God and the king. By the law of Moses the two offences were essentially connected (Exod. xxii. 28); and, as the law further ordained that idolatry should be punished with stoning (Deut. xiii. 10), it was considered that blasphemy should be visited with no lighter punishment.[1] In bold confidence in her iniquity, Jezebel did not hesitate a moment in her calculation as to what the result would be. "Then carry him forth," were the words of her letter, "and stone him that he die." Everything fell out according to her plot. The assembly was convened; Naboth was placed at its head; the false witnesses appeared; their testimony was given; no denial of the charge was listened to; Naboth was carried forth out of the city, for no execution was permitted within the

---

[1] Michaelis.

walls, and there stoned with stones that he died, and the very dogs of the city were permitted to lick up his blood that had been shed. His sons, we elsewhere learn, shared his fate (2 Kings ix. 26). It was a dreadful deed, having its only parallel in the Bible in the false accusations brought against Jesus of Nazareth, when He, too, was led forth out of the city, and crucified on Calvary.

No compunction seems to have touched the heart of the fierce Sidonian queen. In her palace at Samaria she received her messengers when they returned, and, as we may well suppose, without either pallor on her cheek or tear in her eye, she listened to their words, "Naboth is stoned, and is dead." She went in immediately to Ahab. The prize was gained, for the property of any one condemned for treason came into the possessions of the Crown. "Arise," she said, "take possession of the vineyard of Naboth the Jezreelite, which he refused to give thee for money; for Naboth is not alive, but dead." No explanation is given by her of the manner of his death. Ahab may have had his own suspicions that there must have been foul play somewhere. But, when men see that at last an object has been reached upon which their hearts have been long bent, they have a wonderful power of silencing their own doubts as to the means by which it may have been attained. These hands, they say to themselves, at all events are clean. If some crime has been committed, we at least have had no part in it. Thus it was that Pilate washed his hands before the assembled multitude when Jesus was at his bar, and said, "I am innocent of the blood of this righteous man; see ye to it" (Matt. xxvii. 24). He did not choose to own, what his very defence of himself shows to have been the verdict of his own hardened and hardening conscience, that he who permits, and reaps the fruit of, crime that he could have prevented, is as guilty as the actual criminal. Ahab, when he heard from the message of Jezebel that Naboth was dead, asked no questions. He "rose up to go down to the vineyard of Naboth the Jezreelite to take possession of it."

The deed is accomplished, and Ahab possesses what he has so long desired. As we behold him in that garden on the slopes of Jezreel, we feel that we have passed through one of those scenes of human life which have troubled the hearts of good men in every age. Man believes that righteousness is right, and that iniquity is wrong. As a natural consequence he believes that the one ought to be followed by reward, and the other by punishment. If it be not so, are not the foundations of the world out of course? Must not wickedness prosper, and virtue perish, and earth become the theatre, not of an order that corresponds to all the best instincts of the heart, but of a disorder by which we are dismayed and ruined? When, further, we persuade ourselves that there is a righteous Governor of the world, does not the history of this, as of many another successful crime, contradict our faith, or rather mock our dream? "But as for me," cried the Psalmist, "my feet were almost gone; my steps had well-nigh slipped. For I was envious at the arrogant, when I saw the prosperity of the wicked. For there are no bands in their death; but their strength is firm. They are not in trouble as other men: neither are they plagued like other men. Therefore pride is as a chain about their neck; violence covereth them as a garment. Their eyes stand out with fatness: they have more than heart could wish. They scoff, and in wickedness utter oppression; they speak loftily, they have set their mouth in the heavens, and their tongue walketh through the earth. Therefore His people return hither, and waters of a full cup are wrung out by them. And they say, How doth God know, and is there knowledge in the Most High? Behold, these are the wicked; and, being always at ease, they increase in riches. Surely in vain have I cleansed my heart, and washed my hands in innocency; for all the day long have I been plagued, and chastened every morning" (Psa. lxxiii. 2-14). Thus the Psalmist cried, and his cry has been echoed by good men in every age, when they have seen the oppression of the poor and the prosperity of the wicked. Yet in that very psalm which has just been quoted, the cry of doubt and agony is immediately followed by the language of triumphant faith. "Surely thou settest them in slippery places: thou castest them down to destruction. How are they become a desolation in a moment! they are utterly consumed with terrors. As a dream when one awaketh; so, O Lord, when Thou awakest, Thou shalt despise their image" (Psa. lxxiii. 18-20).

No more striking illustration of this principle, or of the true results of the Almighty's government, could be afforded than that contained in the narrative before us. We are not told what length of time passed after the murder of Naboth before the incident took place. It may have been a day or two. More probably it was only a few hours. The point is of but little moment. Enough to dwell upon what is actually and distinctly recorded. Ahab was walking in the garden which he had so treacherously and cruelly acquired, and there seemed to be nothing to disturb his dream. The sun may have been shining on the slopes of Jezreel. The young plants may have been putting forth their slender stems. The air may have been balmy or filled with song; and Ahab may have been congratulating himself on the fact that he had gained his end, and that there was nothing to interfere with his enjoyment.

That was the state of things, viewed from their human side, in a world into which sin has penetrated, and which has been brought into disorder by the curse inseparably attending sin. But what a striking thing is it, when an opportunity is offered us of doing so, to turn from the human things that we see to the Divine arrangements that we do not see, and to find that God, instead of waiting only to interpose when the evil has been done, has rather been watching all along, has been marking each step in the sinner's progress, and has been fixing that moment for action which a knowledge of the end from the beginning has determined to be the best. It was so in the case of the rich man in the parable. At one instant we hear his voice, "What shall I do, because I have not where to bestow my goods? This will I do. I will pull down my barns, and build greater; and there will I bestow all my corn and my goods. And I will say to my soul, Soul, thou hast much goods laid up for many years; take thine ease, eat, drink, and be merry." We turn from the human to the Divine side; and, not *after* his fate has overtaken him, but at the moment when he speaks, and before his fall, "God said unto him, thou foolish one, this night is thy soul required of thee; and the things which thou hast prepared, whose shall they be?" (Luke xii. 17–20). In like manner is it here. We look at the human side, and Ahab is in his vineyard. We turn to the Divine side; and, undoubtedly before Ahab entered it, "the word of the Lord came to Elijah the Tishbite, saying, Arise, go down to meet Ahab, king of Israel, which dwelleth in Samaria; behold, he is in the vineyard of Naboth, whither he is gone down to take possession of it. And thou shalt speak unto him, saying, Thus saith the Lord, Hast thou killed, and also taken possession?

And thou shalt speak unto him, saying, Thus saith the Lord, In the place where dogs licked the blood of Naboth shall dogs lick thy blood, even thine."

Elijah obeyed the Divine command, and went down to the vineyard. We have already seen with what a wonderful power the conscience of man can steel itself against conviction. There is another point in the working of conscience not less wonderful —the manner in which it awakes when the sinner finds himself in the presence of others to whom his sin is known. For long he may have hardened himself, and may have reaped the fruits of his transgression without shame. At last his sin is alluded to by others, or he knows that it has reached the public ear. In an instant conscience is at work. The scorpion that seemed dead springs to life and stings. The man cannot stand the searching eye of others. The bold look departs. The delusion of innocence disappears, and the cheek burns with the blush of shame. Thus was it in the case before us. Ahab was in his garden. Suddenly the well-known figure of Elijah entered the garden and was seen approaching. The moment of awakening was come ; and Ahab started and cried, " Hast thou found me, O mine enemy ? " Elijah was not his enemy, and Ahab knew it. He was his own enemy, and Elijah had revealed to him that he was so. He remembered now all that had passed before, the bold and stern prophet, the reprover of unrighteousness, the proclaimer of the Divine judgments. He called to mind the manner in which the God of Israel had vindicated His own glory, the fire that had descended at Carmel, the slaughter at the river Kishon, and the abundant rain. Before him, with stern countenance and judgment in his eye, was the man who had been the chief actor in it all, as bold, as true, as faithful as in the day when he met face to face the four hundred and fifty prophets of Baal, and his voice penetrated to the heart of assembled Israel. That same voice shall now, he knows, penetrate his heart, and he can only exclaim, " Hast thou found me, O mine enemy ? " Verily, " the triumphing of the wicked is short, and the joy of the godless but for a moment ; " " I have seen the wicked in great power, and spreading himself like a green tree in its native soil. But I passed by, and, lo he was not : yea I sought him, but he could not be found " (Job xx. 5 ; Psa. xxxvii. 35, 36). Ahab was a different man now from what he would have seemed to us to be had we been cognizant of his thoughts a few moments earlier. His own heart and conscience anticipated what was coming, and not in vain.

Elijah answered him, "I have found thee; because thou hast sold thyself to do that which is evil in the sight of the Lord. Behold, I will bring evil upon thee, and will utterly sweep thee away, and will cut off from Ahab every man-child, and him that is shut up, and him that is left at large in Israel; and I will make thine house like the house of Jeroboam the son of Nebat, and like the house of Baasha, the son of Ahijah, for the provocation wherewith thou hast provoked me to anger, and made Israel to sin." Such was the woe denounced on Ahab himself. It was suitable to the circumstances, and to the letter it was fulfilled. Ahab had been counting not only on his own life, but on that of his family, when he seized on Naboth's garden. Not for his own pleasure only, but for the aggrandizement of his house, had he made that little plat of ground his own. It was to go down from sire to son, from generation to generation; and, as each successive representative of the royal line looked round upon his palace and gardens at Jezreel, he would naturally commend his great ancestor who, by the palaces he had built, and the gardens he had laid out, both here and elsewhere, had done so much for the happiness of his descendants. But Ahab had forgotten that, though the heart of a man deviseth his way, the Lord directeth his steps. If he had studied the history of the last half century in his own kingdom, what would he have seen? The house of Jeroboam, the son of Nebat, brought to a sudden and bloody close, when his son Nadab, along with the other members of his family, was murdered by Baasha, who introduced a new dynasty in Israel. If he had come a little further down he would have seen Elah, the son of Baasha, slain by Zimri, one of his own captains, and along with him every one of the kinsmen of Baasha, so that not a man-child was left, and a new dynasty was again introduced. Doubtless he knew these facts, but he had not studied them. He had not looked into the causes of these direful histories. Least of all had Jezebel and he, as they went over the events of these reigns (2 Kings ix. 31), laid to heart the lessons which they taught. Now, therefore, the judgment is at his own door, and he shall himself experience what he might have escaped had he taken warning from the case of others.

Nor is judgment to be confined to him. In a still more terrible

ELIJAH AND NABOTH'S VINEYARD.

manner it is to extend to Jezebel; for "of Jezebel also spake the Lord, saying, The dogs shall eat Jezebel by the wall of Jezreel. Him that dieth of Ahab in the city the dogs shall eat; and him that dieth in the field shall the fowls of the air eat."

Such was the woe denounced on Ahab and his wife; and the sacred writer appears to indicate how deeply he was impressed with the awful nature of the things which he had been compelled to utter when he interposes the remark, " But there was none like unto Ahab which did sell himself to work wickedness in the sight of the Lord, whom Jezebel his wife stirred up. And he did very abominably in following idols, according to all things as did the Amorites, whom the Lord cast out before the children of Israel." The object of these words is not to tell us that Ahab and Jezebel continued, even after they had heard the prophet's woe, to go on as they had done. On the contrary we are immediately informed of a certain measure of repentance, at least on Ahab's part. The words appear to be simply a reflection by the author on the reasons by which the judgments of the Almighty were explained.

For these judgments took effect. In referring, in our last chapter, to Jehu, we have already had occasion to speak of the main parts of their fulfilment, and it is unnecessary to repeat what was then said. Yet two additional points come here before us which it may be well to mention.

1. In exterminating as he did the house of Ahab, Jehu, however swept along by human passion, never ceased at the same time to be the instrument of the Divine judgments. He may, indeed, himself have been fierce and cruel, and there is no reason to doubt that he really was so. But it was not simply to gratify his own wild passions that he became the murderer of Ahab's son and successor to the throne, of Jezebel, and of so many direct and indirect members of the royal line. One incident in his history is in this respect peculiarly worthy of notice. On that day when Ahab took possession of the vineyard of Naboth, and when Elijah met him amidst its vines, it would appear that the king and the prophet were not alone. Two of Ahab's officers, Jehu and Bidkar, had accompanied him from Samaria, had gone with him into the garden, and had been witnesses of what had occurred between him and Elijah. Time passed away. Ahab had been succeeded by his son Joram, and Joram had been put to death by Jehu beyond the gate of Jezreel. Bidkar, Jehu's

old companion, had become captain under him, and both of them stood by the body of the murdered Joram. Then Jehu said to Bidkar, as he pointed to the corpse, "Take up, and cast him into the portion of the field of Naboth the Jezreelite, for remember how that, when I and thou rode together after Ahab his father, the Lord lay this burden upon him, Surely I have seen yesterday the blood of Naboth and the blood of his sons, saith the Lord, and I will requite them in this plat, saith the Lord. Now therefore take, and cast him into the plat of ground, according to the word of the Lord" (2 Kings ix. 25, 26). For many a day Jehu had probably thought nothing of what he had overheard. But when in the providence of God the moment came round for its fulfilment, the old scene returned upon him in all the distinctness of its outline, and he seemed to hear again, with the clearness of their first utterance undiminished by the lapse of years, the words which in the vineyard at Jezreel had penetrated his soul with horror. He felt that he had been executing the wrath of God. The same feelings animated him in the case of Jezebel. He had been the instrument of her death; but, so far as can be concluded from the narrative, only that he might rid himself of a powerful and crafty obstacle to his own aggrandizement. After Jezebel was killed at his instigation, by being thrown from an upper window into the street, Jehu yielded to a momentary emotion of pity, and gave directions for her burial. But, when his servants went to obey his commands, and found almost nothing of the body remaining, Jehu said, "This is the word of the Lord which He spake by His servant Elijah the Tishbite, saying, In the portion of Jezreel shall dogs eat the flesh of Jezebel" (2 Kings ix. 36). Nor was it otherwise when, by his instructions, the elders of Samaria had slain seventy of the sons of Ahab, and their heads, sent to Jehu at Jezreel, had been piled up in two ghastly heaps at the city gate. "Know now," he said, "that there shall fall to the earth nothing of the word of the Lord, which the Lord spake concerning the house of Ahab; for the Lord hath done that which He spake by His servant Elijah" (2 Kings x. 10). These words are not spoken by him as any apology for his deeds. In his own view he needed none. He felt no compunction. He was the child of a barbarous and cruel age, in which blood was poured out as easily as water. What the words show is this, that after his deeds were done Jehu became alive to the fact that he had been only an instrument in the hands of God in doing them; that there was a wider and a grander will than his which, without disturbing the responsibilities of human agency, directed everything to its own great ends. The lesson is a solemn one. We cannot escape out of the hands of God, or cease to be executioners of His purposes. We may rebel against Him, but we can never get beyond His power. In one way or another we must subserve the carrying out of His plans. Better surely that we do this in such a way as will advance, not His glory only, but our own everlasting happiness. We never can be our own masters. If we do not love and obey as children, we must serve as slaves.

2. The manner in which part of the woe proclaimed by Elijah was fulfilled in the case of Ahab deserves attention. The part of which we speak is contained in the words, "In the place where dogs licked the blood of Naboth shall dogs lick thy blood, even thine" (1 Kings xxi. 19). But, on the one hand, Ahab died in battle, and was buried in Samaria; and, on the other hand, the sacred writer saw this prophecy fulfilled, not in his fate, but in that of Joram, Ahab's son (2 Kings ix. 25). The explanation is not difficult, for when, as we shall immediately see, Ahab, alarmed by the words of Elijah, did to a certain degree repent, "The word of the Lord came to Elijah the Tishbite, saying, Seeth thou how Ahab humbleth himself before Me? Because he humbleth himself before Me I will not bring the evil in his days; but in his son's days will I bring the evil upon his house" (1 Kings xxi. 28, 29). God Himself, therefore, had declared, that the judgments pronounced in the first instance upon Ahab should be transferred to his son; and so it came to pass. It is less easy to solve what seems the much more trifling difficulty, that the author of these chapters appears to see the fulfilment of Elijah's prophecy in what happened in Ahab's own case rather than in that of his son, for we read at chap. xxii. 38, "And one washed the chariot (that is, the chariot in which Ahab received his mortal wound) in the pool of Samaria, and the dogs licked up his blood; and they washed his armour; according unto the word of the Lord which He spake." The woe of chap. xxi. 19, uttered of Jezreel, seems to be here transferred to Samaria. The answer to this difficulty depends in part on that correction of the translation which is given by the Old Testament Revisers—not "And they washed his armour," but

"Now the harlots washed themselves there." The latter translation shows us that the writer has the *lex talionis* in his mind. Ahab in encouraging the worship of Baal had encouraged prostitution. Behold the recompence. The harlots washed themselves in water stained with his blood. In like manner it is this *lex talionis* that the writer has in view with reference to the licking of Ahab's blood. The dogs had licked that blood of Naboth which he had been the means of shedding; in due time they shall lick his own. That, and that alone, is the point which the sacred writer has in view; and for his immediate purpose it matters not where the licking took place. It might as well be in Samaria as in Jezreel.

The threatenings of the prophet so awfully announced, so powerfully brought home to Ahab on the very spot which had been the scene of his wickedness, produced its effect. "It came to pass, when Ahab heard those words, that he rent his clothes, and put sackcloth upon his flesh, and fasted, and lay in sackcloth, and went softly." All the outward signs of humiliation and repentance are there, and there is no reason to doubt that, for the time at least, the repentance was sincere. If false or hypocritical, it will be difficult to explain the words immediately following, in which we are told that "the word of the Lord came to Elijah the Tishbite, saying, Seest thou how Ahab humbleth himself before Me? I will not bring the evil in his days, but in his son's days will I bring the evil upon his house." After this time the king of Israel was probably never so completely given up to apostasy and idolatry as he had been before.

We have followed the tragic history of Naboth to its close, and little more need be said regarding it. Yet it may be well to gather together in a few remarks the impressions which the sacred writer seems especially to have desired that story to produce.

1. He would impress us with a deep sense of the wickedness of Ahab and Jezebel. Apart even from the share which Ahab and Jezebel had had in the murder of Naboth, it may be thought that such an impression had been sufficiently produced by what we have been already told of them. Surely the apostasy of Ahab, his faithlessness to every obligation imposed upon him as Israel's covenant king, his weak submission to the revengeful and bloodthirsty Jezebel, the encouragement which he had given to the idolatrous worship of Baal, with all its attendant im-

moralities, his hardness of heart, and the miseries which, without compunction, he had been the means of inflicting upon his people, were enough of themselves to justify the charge that "there was none like unto Ahab which did sell himself to do that which was evil in the sight of the Lord, whom Jezebel his wife stirred up." What more could be needed to awaken a just sense of horror at his deeds, or to vindicate the propriety of the Divine judgments by which he himself, his wife, and his descendants were to be overtaken? But this wickedness, it will be observed, had marked Ahab and Jezebel in their public actions, and in their character as king and queen. Even with it all before our eyes we have not yet seen them as they are in themselves; and it is a fact, of which there are only too numerous illustrations, both in Church and State, that the same individual may be so different in public and in private life as hardly to be recognized in the latter, by those who have known him only in the former, sphere. Harsh and cruel in the one, he may be gentle and tender in the other. Reckless as to the means by which he accomplishes his ends in public, he may be the soul of honour and good faith in private. We can never form a true estimate of one whom we judge only as he appears in the great assemblies of his countrymen, or on the wide area of a nation's civil or religious life. To become truly acquainted with him we must follow him into the more private relations amidst which he moves, into the circle of his friends, into the family, the home, and the secret chamber. Then there may often be much to balance the derelictions of duty which stain an official career, or much to produce the melancholy conviction that the high-sounding professions by which the multitude is deceived are nothing better than the tricks of the hypocrite and the knave. So might it have been with Ahab, perhaps even with Jezebel; and it was well, therefore, that we should have the opportunity of following them to other places than the throne, and to other deeds than those of debasing the worship of Israel or persecuting the prophets of the Lord.

This the story of Naboth enables us to do; and it is impossible not to admire the skill with which all its particulars are selected, as well as the graphic power with which they are arranged, so as to make the real character of the chief actors in it appear. On the one hand our sympathy is awakened by the poverty, the simplicity, and the piety of the original owner of the vineyard, by the fondness with which he clung to the inheritance of his fathers, by his reverence for the law of God, and by his indifference to mere worldly gain or royal favour. On the other hand, our indignation is stirred by the covetousness of Ahab who, with palaces and gardens at his command, could not leave his poor subject in quiet possession of his plat of ground; while our contempt is roused by the sullen weakness with which, when he fails to accomplish his design, he goes to his house heavy and displeased, lays him down upon his bed, turns away his face, and refuses to take food. Then Jezebel comes in; and, without a scruple of conscience, or the quivering of a nerve, does her part in the dreadful tragedy. Her resolute determination, showing itself in the words "I will give it thee," the detestable inhumanity of the plan which she proposes to herself in order to secure the murder of her innocent victim, the impious daring with which she writes letters in her husband's name and seals them with his seal, the blasphemous spirit in which she employs the name of Him whose worship she had done everything to extirpate from the land, the manner in which she prostitutes judicial forms to the obtaining of a verdict of the most flagrant injustice, and, lastly, the cold-blooded indifference with which, when she heard that her plot had been successful, she said to Ahab, "Arise, take possession of the vineyard of Naboth the Jezreelite, which he refused to give thee for money, for Naboth is not alive, but dead,"—all these circumstances combine to make up a picture of wickedness that may well overpower the most callous heart, and kindle into flame the last lingering spark of justice or mercy in any human breast. And this is the effect which, we cannot doubt, the sacred historian intended to produce. In Ahab and Jezebel, he would show us, we behold not merely an idolatrous king and queen, but a wicked man and a still more wicked woman. The one weak and self-indulgent, his better thoughts, when he had them, unable to withstand temptation or the gratification of his desires; the other imperious, false, unprincipled, cruel, and remorseless—the two together present a picture of crime to which no painter can add a touch of horror, and which prepares us for the full outpouring of the vials of the Almighty's wrath.

2. The narrative exhibits the righteous retribution of God upon the sinner. The terms in which that retribution was pronounced have already been before us, and it is unnecessary

to repeat them. They are of almost unequalled severity, and with a similar severity they were actually fulfilled. A great law runs throughout the whole of Scripture, that iniquity shall not only be punished, but punished in such a way as to show the correspondence between sin and its consequences; and no more striking illustration could be afforded of the execution of this law than that which we are called upon to trace in the history of Ahab and Jezebel after the murder of Naboth. If Naboth was brought to a bloody death, so also were the king and queen by whom his murder had been instigated. If Naboth's sons shared the fate of their father (2 Kings ix. 26) so also did the doom which overtook the royal parents overtake all the members of their house. If dogs licked the blood of Naboth (1 Kings xxi. 19), not only did the dogs lick, we may be sure, the blood of Ahab's son to whom this part of the prophecy had been transferred (1 Kings xxi. 29), but they did it "in the place" where the murder had been consummated (1 Kings xxi. 19; 2 Kings ix. 25). If Ahab had encouraged harlotry in Israel, harlots washed themselves in the pool of Samaria, the waters of which his blood had stained (1 Kings xxii. 38, Revised Version). If Jezebel had been a main instrument in carrying out the wicked deed at Jezreel, her blood was eventually sprinkled upon the city-wall, and there the dogs of the city so devoured her body that men were not able to say "This is Jezebel" (1 Kings xxi. 23; 2 Kings ix. 34–37). Throughout all the history the law of retribution runs in its most marked and terrible form —that law of which David spoke,

> "Yea, he loved cursing, and it came unto him;
> And he delighted not in blessing, and it was far from him.
> He clothed himself also with cursing as with his garment,
> And it came into his inward parts like water,
> And like oil into his bones"—[1]

that law which contains the fundamental principle of all-retributive justice, both Divine and human.

Upon the unerring certainty, upon the sure accomplishment, of this law our attention is here fixed. There is nothing arbitrary in God's dealings with men. We may think of Him as of one who gives no account of any of His matters, who surrounds His throne with darkness, and who sends prosperity or adversity, health or sickness, joy or sorrow, honour or disgrace, according

[1] Psa. cix. 17, 18.

to those inscrutable counsels in the presence of which the creatures of yesterday can only wonder and adore. But it is not so. More careful observation shows us that there is a righteous order in the world, that all things "make for righteousness," and that many an individual misfortune and many a national calamity, which men in their indolence would fain represent as inscrutable events, are only features of that well-ordered government by which the Almighty has connected punishment with folly or sin.

The penalties of transgression indeed may not unfrequently be so long delayed that both the transgressor and those who witness him may begin to think that they may be altogether escaped. It cannot be. Come they will, and that often with an increased intensity proportioned to the length of time during which they have been kept back. Or, if they do not always thus come outwardly, let us remember that there are inward penalties more hard to bear than outward ones. Altogether unnoticed by the world many a man's sin meets him in that dread chamber of an awakened conscience where so many sights and sounds of terror congregate. In solitude, in secret, in dead hours of night the sinner awakes, and the long train of his transgressions passes by before him. They mock him; they reproach him; they present themselves to him in all their hideous features, with no modest reserve, no fair sentences, no smooth names to name them by, that thus their wickedness may be concealed, but bold, brazen-faced, true to what they are. In such hours the sinner trembles. How bitterly does he reproach himself, bite his lips in the anguish of his spirit, and shut his eyes only that his sins, remembered now, may peer more closely in through the closed eyelids! It is Elijah meeting Ahab in Naboth's vineyard. It is the fulfilment of the words, "What fruit had ye in those things whereof ye are now ashamed, for the end of these things is death."

The fact of this righteous judge and of this righteous judgment cannot be too deeply impressed upon us; and it is in no small degree for the sake of leaving that impression upon our minds that the story of Naboth is dwelt upon as it is. Once more—

3. The sacred writer would remind us that even He who makes Himself known to us as a God of judgment is ready to pardon. We have already more than once in the history of

Elijah had occasion to meet this great lesson, too often supposed to be the lesson of the New Testament alone, and not also of the Old. We met it in Horeb when Elijah perceived that, although the whirlwind, the earthquake, and the fire were God's, for they executed their desolating march "before" Him, it was yet in the still, small voice that He especially revealed Himself. A second time we met it on the same occasion when, in speaking of the slaughter of the rebellious sons of Israel to be effected by Hazael and Jehu and Elisha, the Almighty added, that He would leave for Himself seven thousand in Israel who had not bowed the knee to Baal and had not kissed him. Now we meet with this principle of Divine government again when, upon evidence of Ahab's repentance, our attention is called to the fact that the judgments denounced against him shall be postponed, at least in all their fulness, to the days of his son. Not that that son, though innocent himself, shall be punished for nothing but his father's sins. We must distinguish between the natural consequences of sin, and the direct pouring out of God's indignation upon the wilful and stubborn transgressor. The former may continue long after he who had been the means of introducing them has passed away, and we can see the wisdom of such an arrangement in this, that it impresses us with a deeper sense of our responsibility, and bids us beware lest we entail upon our children, or even upon our children's children, evils of which we, and not they, have been the cause. The latter does not continue unless provoked by obstinate wilfulness and stubbornness on the sinner's part. The law of Moses was express : " The fathers shall not be put to death for the children, neither shall the children be put to death for the fathers ; every man shall be put to death for his own sin" (Deut. xxiv. 16) ; and, at a later period, prophecy pointing forward to the future testified to the same truth, " In these days they shall say no more, The fathers have eaten sour grapes, and their children's teeth are set on edge. But every one shall die for his own iniquity : every man that eateth the sour grapes, his teeth shall be set on edge" (Jer. xxxi. 29, 30). Jehoram, the son of Ahab alluded to, suffered for his own sins. Though less wicked than his father "he cleaved unto the sins of Jeroboam, the son of Nebat, which made Israel to sin : he departed not therefrom" (2 Kings iii. 3), and in due time he was overtaken by the judgments threatened to the house of

Ahab. He had served himself heir to his father's wickedness, and it was a just thing, therefore, that he should meet his father's doom. But Ahab himself repented at least in part before he died, and the last impression left upon us by the sacred writer, in bringing his terrible narrative regarding him to a close, is that even He whose judgments had followed him all his days has no pleasure in the death of the wicked, but rather that he turn from his wickedness and live. His eye pitied the unhappy king as he "rent his clothes, and put sackcloth upon his flesh, and fasted, and lay in sackcloth, and went softly;" and the final motto of his melancholy story is, that, while he who dares to meet the Almighty as a foe can only perish upon the thick bosses of His buckler, he who repents and forsakes his sins shall find mercy.

CHAPTER VIII.

ELIJAH AND THE COMPANIES OF AHAZIAH (2 KINGS I. 1-16).

Elijah again retires from view—Importance of the interval to Ahab—To
Israel—Accession of Ahaziah—His character—His illness and recourse
to Baal-Zebub—Elijah appears to his messengers—His message to the
king—Ahaziah's rage—He sends first captain and his fifty; their
fate—Second captain and his fifty sent; their fate—Third captain and
his fifty—Elijah goes to Ahaziah—His message—General character of
the narrative examined—Comparison with other Scripture narratives
of a similar kind—Principles upon which such destruction of life to be
justified—Words of our Lord in Luke ix. 51-56—Methods of dealing
with nations in different ages must be different—Teaching of Matt. v.
considered—Application to state of Israel in days of Elijah—General
considerations on the subject.

WE have already seen that with the recalling of Israel to the
worship of the one only living and true God, the work for which
the prophet Elijah had been specially raised up, and with
which his name is connected in the Bible, closed. It had been
sharp, sudden, and short; but it had accomplished for the time
at least a great revolution in Israel, and had been accompanied
by revelations of the Almighty's character and ways which form
a distinct stage in the progress of His manifestations of Himself
to man. With it, accordingly, the public prophetic work of
Elijah ended, and Elisha was appointed by the Divine command to take his place. In the incident, therefore, of Naboth's
vineyard, Elijah appears the prophet of the Lord, not so much
in his public as in his private capacity; and God's dealings
are with the individual rather than the nation. In the same
character we are to meet him now when he comes into contact
with Ahaziah and his captains. Of the whole period of six

years between the calling of Elisha and the meeting of Elijah and Ahab in the vineyard of Naboth, and again of the period of four years between the latter date and the bringing down of fire from heaven upon the companies of Ahaziah, we know, so far as concerns Elijah, absolutely nothing. Where did he live? How was he employed? In what relation did he stand to Israel, in what to Elisha, in what to Ahab first and Ahaziah afterwards? No answer can be given to these questions. It has been supposed that during this time he and his successor may have been quietly though actively ministering to the cities and villages of Samaria; that the former in particular, taught by the "still, small voice" of Horeb, may have been labouring to instil into the minds of the people thoughts of God's goodness and mercy; that he may have been striving to win Israel to a purer and more spiritual service of its heavenly King; or, finally, that he may have been devoting himself to the organization and instruction of the schools of the prophets now established in the land.[1] There is no positive ground upon which such conjectures can be rested; and the sudden and unexpected appearance and disappearance of the prophet, first after meeting Ahab at Jezreel, and next after meeting Ahaziah in Samaria, would seem rather to point to the conclusion that before each of these occasions he had again withdrawn from public life, and had sought retirement, none, it may be, knowing where.

But whatever these years were to Elijah, they had been important years to Israel and to Ahab. For—

1. Ahab had at length been brought to humble himself before God. The iniquity of which he had been guilty in connection with the death of Naboth, suddenly forced home upon him at the instant when he thought himself in possession of his prize, had been more than his hardened conscience could withstand. He felt how grievously every principle of justice, truth, and honour had been violated in that deed. His own heart answered to every word of the terrible threatenings denounced against him by the prophet, and it was because of this that he rent his clothes, and put sackcloth upon his flesh, and fasted, and lay in sackcloth, and went softly. His repentance, there is no reason to doubt, was for the time at least sincere; and as such it was accepted by the Almighty when He declared

[1] Allon, in "Biblical Educator" iii. p. 189.

that, because of it, He would not bring on the calamities of which He had spoken in Ahab's days, but would reserve them for the days of his son.

2. The consequence was that a certain measure of success attended the struggles of Israel with its enemies. The insolence and impiety of Benhadad, king of Syria, were rebuked, and Ahab gained a triumphant victory over the great army which had been brought against him. Peace and prosperity might probably have followed his success had he not rebelled against what he must have known to be the will of Him who had given him the victory, and spared the life of the treacherous and cruel king who for Israel's sake had been appointed to death. As it was, peace lasted only three years, when Ahab proposed to Jehoshaphat, king of Judah, then visiting him in Samaria, that they should combine their forces for an attack on Ramoth-Gilead, the most famous fortress of which even rocky and hilly Gilead had to boast. The proposal was accepted, and, despising the warning given him by Micaiah of his approaching fate, Ahab hastened to the field. The battle of Ramoth-Gilead followed—that battle which afforded so signal a display of the vanity of all the efforts of men to defeat the counsels of the Most High. Ahab had been so far impressed by the warning of the prophet that he had disguised himself before beginning the battle, and at first his scheme appeared likely to be attended with success. The king of Syria had commanded the thirty and two captains of his chariots, saying, "Fight neither with small nor great, save only with the king of Israel." The captains beheld Jehoshaphat, king of Judah, in his royal robes, for he had not laid them aside like Ahab, and they made for him; but Jehoshaphat cried out in time for them to discover their mistake, and they turned back from pursuing him. Then a certain man drew his bow at a venture, and smote the king of Israel between the joints of his harness. That same evening he died; and they washed the chariot in which his blood had been poured out in the pool of Samaria, and the dogs licked up his blood. It was a fulfilment in part of the threatening spoken years before by Elijah in the garden of Naboth, and the minuteness with which all the particulars are detailed by the Chronicler shows the impression made upon his mind.

3. Ahaziah, the son of Ahab, now succeeded to the throne of Israel. He was a weak and guilty prince, insensible to the

wonderful dealings of God with His people during his father's days, and untouched by the discipline through which his family had been made to pass. "He did that which was evil in the sight of the Lord, and walked in the way of his father, and in the way of his mother, and in the way of Jeroboam, the son of Nebat, wherein he made Israel to sin. And he served Baal, and worshipped him, and provoked to anger the Lord, the God of Israel, according to all that his father had done" (1 Kings xxii. 52, 53). The fulfilment of the curse of God upon the house of Ahab was to begin with him; and this is the king in connection with whom Elijah once more emerges for a moment from his obscurity.

Ahaziah had been walking on the roof of his palace in Samaria, and had leant against what seems to have been a latticed fence running round the roof. The fence gave way. The king fell either into the street or into the inner court of the palace, and was so severely injured that he became alarmed for his life. After the example of his father and mother he had been a worshipper of Baal in one of the many aspects in which that divinity claimed the homage of men. In particular, Ahaziah had honoured him as Baal-Zebub, the god of flies, the god by whom in that Eastern land such plagues of flies as are well known to all travellers in the East were either sent or prevented. This deity would appear also to have been held in peculiar reverence at Ekron, the most northerly of the five great cities of the Philistines, and, therefore, nearest to Samaria. Thither, accordingly, Ahaziah sent his messengers, immediately after his fall, with the inquiry whether or not he should recover from its effects. It was a daring violation of the law of God, which had expressly declared to Israel: "The soul that turneth unto them that have familiar spirits, and unto the wizards, to go a-whoring after them, I will even set My face against that man, and will cut him off from among his people" (Lev. xx. 6). It was a countenancing of idolatry in the worst form in which it had been supported by Ahab and Jezebel. And the offence was rendered still more heinous by the recent character of that work of reformation which had been effected by Elijah.

Where the prophet was at the time we know not. But it is no sufficient objection to the view, commonly entertained, that he was at Carmel, that that range of mountains lay in a direction wholly different from that by which the messengers of Ahaziah would proceed on their way to Ekron. The distance even then would not be great before he could intercept them on their way and meet them face to face; while the expression "go up," in ver. 3 corresponds to the idea that he was to travel by the road leading to Jerusalem, still, in both God's eyes and his, the capital of the theocratic people. Whatever we may think of this, the commandment came to Elijah by "*the* angel of the Lord," not simply *an* angel, or any angel who might be employed to communicate the Divine will, and surely not the Second Person of the Trinity, supposed to have become by anticipation and for the time incarnate, but some special angel by whom the Almighty was wont to communicate His will to man in ways of which no information has been given us. "Arise," was the message, "go up to meet the messengers of the king of Samaria, and say unto them, Is it because there is no God in Israel that ye go to inquire of Baal-Zebub, the god of Ekron? Now, therefore, thus saith the Lord, Thou shalt not come down from the bed whither thou art gone up, but shalt surely die." The message at once shows the light in which the conduct of Ahaziah is to be regarded. It was a denial of the God of Israel. It was the worship of one who was no God : and the soul that so sinned was to die.

Elijah instantly obeyed "the word of the Lord," met the messengers of Ahaziah with the same startling suddenness as that with which he had before met Ahab, delivered his message, and with equal suddenness "departed." At no time was it his part to argue. He was "a voice of one crying in the wilderness." The voice was to cry at the appointed moment ; and when its cry was uttered to be silent. Let men hear or let them forbear: the work of the voice was done. The messengers of the king instantly returned.

They do not seem to have known who it was that had spoken to them, and the fact that they did not may be accepted as a proof that, during the time that had elapsed since he wrought his great reformation in Israel, Elijah had led a private, rather than a public, life. Upon the return of his messengers Ahaziah asked how it was that they had so soon come back. They answered: "There came up a man to meet us, and said unto us, Go, turn again unto the king that sent you ; " and then they delivered the message that had been given them. The king next inquired, "What manner of man was he that came up to meet you, and told you these words?" And, when they replied that he was a man with a garment of hair (Revised Version, margin), and a leathern girdle about his loins, he exclaimed, "It is Elijah the Tishbite." No doubt he suspected it before. The boldness, the daring, the sudden appearance, and equally sudden disappearance of the man who could send him such a message, were traits that could hardly belong to any but to one whom he and his father's house had so much occasion to remember. The message itself too touched his conscience; and although not the prophet himself, but his image, called up by his imagination, stood before him, he could only repeat, as it were, the exclamation of Ahab in the vineyard of Naboth, "Thou hast found me, O mine enemy."

Unlike Ahab, however, Ahaziah did not repent. He took rather the only other course which suggests itself to an awakened and alarmed conscience. He burst forth in rage against the man who had disturbed him in his false security; and, as always happens in such a case, the measure of the rage may be regarded as the measure of the degree to which the conscience has been pricked. In the present instance the rage was great, and the steps taken were of the most determined kind.

The king sent a captain of fifty with his fifty to seize the prophet at the place where he either dwelt or which he had chosen as the spot to meet them. And the captain "spake unto him, O man of God, the king hath said, Come down." The whole narrative reveals the spirit in which the words were spoken. The summons was unsympathizing, rude, and scornful, contemptuous towards God as well as recklessly indifferent to the prophet's fate. "O man of God," the captain cried, and there must have been irony in the tone, for God is immediately placed in contrast with the king, "the king hath said." It was as much as to say, "Thou professest to be a man of God, but there is one to be feared in this matter more than the God thou honourest. Thou mayest affect to dwell upon that mountain top, and there hold communion with an invisible power, but I and my fifty men will show thee that there is more in the material than the spiritual, in the seen than the unseen world." Elijah took the scorner at his word. "If I be a man of God," he said, "let fire come down from heaven and consume thee and thy fifty." The prophet had dealt with fire from heaven before. It may be that near that very spot he had seen the heavens open at his prayer and the fire came down that "consumed the burnt-offering, and the wood, and the stones, and the dust, and licked up the water that was in the trench." Thus no doubt he prayed again, and there rushed forth fire from heaven, and consumed the captain and his fifty. Not that they were merely killed; that is not the language of the sacred writer. They were "consumed," burned up by the devouring flames in the same manner as the bullock, and everything connected with it, was burned up when the Lord first answered the prophet by fire.

Undismayed by what had happened, the king now sent another captain and his fifty upon the same errand: but there is a difference in the message. It is even harsher and more imperative than before. "O man of God, thus hath the king said, Come down quickly." There was no "quickly" in the first demand. In the second there is. The message on the first occasion had perhaps not been imperative enough. A greater show of boldness may alarm the prophet. But Elijah answered as he had already done. "If I be a man of God, let fire come down from heaven, and consume thee and thy fifty." The miracle of destruction was instantly repeated: "The fire of God came down from heaven and consumed him and his fifty."

A third company was now sent, and so far apparently without any change in the king's mind. But, whether this was so or not, there was a change in the temper of the captain to whom the charge had been committed. Insolence, scorn, impiety have no place in his mind. He exhibits meekness and submission rather than arrogance and defiance. He "came and fell on his knees before Elijah, and besought him, and said unto him, O man of God, I pray thee let my life and the life of these fifty be precious in thy sight. Behold there came fire down from heaven and consumed the two former captains of fifty with their fifties: but now let my life be precious in thy sight." There is no need to think of this as mere weakness or slavish terror. That such feelings would have expressed themselves in a similar way may at once be granted, and we have no positive statement that the conduct of the third captain proceeded from any nobler motive. Yet a motive of that kind is perfectly consistent with all that is recorded, and in the circumstances it is the more natural of the two. This captain had been awed and humbled by the fate of his predecessors. He acknowledged the Divine hand in the judgments of which he had at least been made aware, and he sought to gain by entreaty what he could not compel. Nor did he seek in vain. "The angel of the Lord said unto Elijah, Go down with him, be not afraid of him And he arose, and went down with him unto the king."

But little remains to be told of this incident in Elijah's life. As on every previous occasion he at once obeyed the intimation given him of the will of God. He went down and presented himself to the king. Nothing is said of the scene but that Ahaziah was still laid upon his bed. He may have had his attendants around him. He may have been alone. Any way, it must have been a striking and solemn sight as the rugged prophet approached the couch of the royal sufferer, without hesitation in his step, or fear in his eye, or quivering in his voice, and delivered the message with which he had been entrusted, "Forasmuch as thou hast sent messengers to inquire of Baal-Zebub the god of Ekron, is it because there is no God in Israel to inquire of His word? Therefore, thou shalt not come down from the bed whither thou art gone up, but shalt surely die." The message delivered, Elijah would as usual depart in a manner not less abrupt and startling than that in which he came. But the message itself was the word of God, and not one of His words falls ineffectual to the ground. "So Ahaziah died according to the word of the Lord which Elijah had spoken," and the first part of the woe denounced upon the house of Ahab was fulfilled.

It is impossible not to feel that the events thus presented to us are of a very startling kind, and that it is not easy to reconcile them either with the conception that we form of an honoured servant of God, or with our ideas of eternal justice. Elijah rather appears to us at first sight as a proud, arrogant, and merciless wielder of the power committed to him : we wonder that an answer should have been given to his prayer : we are shocked at the destruction of so many men who listened only to the command of their captain and their king : and we cannot help contrasting Elijah's conduct as a whole with the beneficent and loving tenderness of the New Testament Dispensation.

No considerations connected with the character of the captains and their fifties are of much use in attempting the explanation. We may allow, as we have allowed, that there are traces in the narrative of a wholly different spirit and conduct between the first two companies and the third. But the men of the first two were in all probability ignorant and prejudiced, and at any rate they were simply servants doing the behests of a royal master. The men of the third again were, there is little reason to doubt, more respectful simply because they were more afraid. It was not faith in God or in any Divine mission of Elijah, but only alarm at the thoughts of the fate that might be awaiting them, which called forth their more submissive spirit. We must turn to considerations of an altogether different kind.

Before doing so it may be well, in the first place, to remember that the spirit which appears in it does not stand alone either in the history of Elijah or in the general history of the Old Testament. As to the former, we have to compare with it that destruction of the four hundred and fifty prophets of Baal at the river Kishon, the details of which have already passed under our view, though consideration of the principle upon which it was effected was reserved till now. As regards the latter, we have obvious analogies in the destruction of the Cities of the Plain (Gen. xix. 24, 25); in the slaughter of the idolaters at Sinai, when the command was given to Moses that every man should put his sword by his side, and should slay every man his brother, and when there fell of the people about three thousand men (Exod. xxxii. 28); in the earth opening her mouth to swallow up Korah, Dathan, and Abiram, and all their houses, followed by the coming forth of that fire from the Lord which consumed the two hundred and fifty men that offered incense (Numb. xvi. 31–35); in the destruction of all the inhabitants of Jericho, "both man and woman, young and old, and ox and sheep and ass," Rahab and those that were with her alone escaping (Josh. vi. 21, 25); in the nearly total extermination of the Canaanites, in obedience to the command of God, "Of the cities of these people which the Lord thy God doth give thee for an inheritance, thou shalt save alive nothing that breatheth, but thou shalt utterly destroy them," when we are told of the children of Israel that "all the spoil of these cities, and the cattle they took for a prey unto themselves, but every man they smote with the edge of the sword, until they had destroyed them, neither left they any to breathe" (Deut. xx. 16, 17; Josh. xi. 14). To these examples may be added that of the destruction of the Amalekites, when the command was given to Saul, "Now go, and smite Amalek, and utterly destroy all that they have and spare them not, but slay both man and woman, infant and suckling, ox and sheep, camel and ass" (1 Sam. xv. 3). These instances of the destruction of human life afford a parallel to that now before us; and, if they can be justified at all, they must be justified upon what are essentially the same principles. Can, then, any justification be offered of such wholesale slaughter?

One thing it appears necessary to say, that it is impossible to see how it can be justified upon the plea so often urged, that God is the Giver of life and that He may therefore justly take it away when He thinks fit. He *is* both the Giver and Maintainer of life, but He has given it upon certain conditions implied, if not expressly stated, in the gift, and in that whole system of moral government in the midst of which it is maintained. To suppose Him to act in an arbitrary manner is to deface those very attributes of His character which awaken our reverence, and draw from us that willing obedience which alone can be acceptable in His sight. The thought of mere power can never awaken those emotions in our hearts which it will be worthy either of man to offer or of the Creator and Preserver of our being to receive. We must understand His course of action; we must approve of it and honour it, before we can think of Him in any other light than that of a fetish, or a tyrant from whom we would willingly escape. It is not enough therefore to say that God, in taking the lives of the Canaanites, of the Amalekites, or of the companies of Ahaziah's captains, for it was He who took them and not Joshua or Samuel or Elijah, was only acting within His rights. It may have been so; but unless we can see that even under the Old Testament Dispensation, these rights were exercised with a due regard to His wisdom and love, we shall make the God of the Old Testament a different Being from the God of the New, and the Christian Dispensation will perish as surely as the Dispensation which preceded it.

In turning our attention, then, further to this subject, our Lord Himself must be our guide. "It came to pass," we are told on one occasion, "When the days were being fulfilled that He should be received up, He steadfastly set his face to go to Jerusalem, and sent messengers before his face: and they went and entered into a village of the Samaritans to make ready for

Him. And they did not receive Him, because His face was as though He were going to Jerusalem. And when His disciples, James and John, saw this, they said, Lord, wilt Thou that we bid fire to come down from heaven and consume them? But He turned and rebuked them" (Luke ix. 51-55). In the words of St. James and St. John there is a manifest allusion to Elijah and the companies of Ahaziah, and that even although we adopt the later reading, and find in them no express mention of the prophet. The two disciples, who, from their eager and impetuous disposition, had long before been designated by their Master, " sons of thunder" (Mark iii. 17), and whose minds were full at once of the spirit and of the facts of the Old Testament, had recalled the incident we have now before us ; and, provoked by the opposition of the Samaritans, had hastily proposed to inflict upon them a judgment similar to that with which the companies of Ahaziah had been visited. Jesus, however, it is added, turned and rebuked them. No word is spoken by our Lord in regard to the conduct of Elijah. What he finds fault with is simply the spirit of His own disciples, and the whole tone of the narrative implies that all that He would say was this, "Ye do not understand the nature of the Dispensation which I am introducing, and ye err in thinking that my mission is to be marked by the same judgments called down directly upon sinners as those which were exhibited in the Dispensation that is passing away." For anything contained in the passage, therefore, our Lord accepted the conduct of Elijah as that of a righteous servant of His Father in Heaven, and declared only that He Himself had come to fulfil all righteousness in a different way. Not, in other words, in any change in the character of God, and certainly not in the conduct of the captains and their companies, but in the outward circumstances of men, in the nature of the Old and New Testament Dispensations, as adapted to their different stages in the history of the world, is the explanation for which we are now searching to be found.

God is Himself unchangeable. The principles and aims of His government are eternally the same. The covenant promises involved in creating man in His own image and after His own likeness have been as fixed as the stars of heaven from the moment when our first parents were placed in Eden. But although God Himself does not change, His methods of administration, His ways of dealing with mankind, His modes of training the human race for the accomplishment of its destiny, may and must change with different ages; nay, we might even add, were it necessary to do so, they may be different with different peoples in the same age. It does not follow, because nations are contemporaneous, that the same truths and the same methods of instruction are equally adapted to them. Different truths and different methods of presenting them constitute an essential part of a wise discipline of the individual during his progress from childhood to manhood, and from manhood to old age. Similar treatment must mark the training of nations. Lessons fitted to be useful to one generation might be hurtful to another at an earlier or later stage of its progress. At an earlier they might overwhelm instead of strengthening a plant yet weak; at a later they might afford no nourishment to a plant now strong. We are, therefore, not entitled to expect that either the instruction, or the method of communicating instruction, that may be best adapted to one era shall be the same as that adapted to another. All that we may reasonably require is that both of these shall, in any era, tend towards the same result, or make for the same goal.

The point of which we now speak is so important that, before applying the general principle to the difficulty immediately under discussion, it may be well to illustrate it still further by the teaching of our Lord in His Sermon on the Mount. In that sermon He explains in several particulars the true nature of that relation of His to the past which he had expressed in the words, "Think not that I came to destroy the law or the prophets: I came not to destroy, but to fulfil" (Matt. v. 17). His illustrations are taken both from the Ten Commandments and from other precepts of the Mosaic Code. One of the latter is to the following effect, "Ye have heard that it was said, An eye for an eye, and a tooth for a tooth: but I say unto you, Resist not him that is evil; but whosoever smiteth thee on thy right cheek, turn to him the other also" (Matt. v. 38, 39). "An eye for an eye and a tooth for a tooth"—"Resist not him that is evil." Are not the two precepts wholly inconsistent with one another? If they come from the same fountain, do they not indicate not only that the spring is intermittent, but that its waters are at one time the very opposite of what they are at another? A little reflection will enable us to answer that question in the negative. There is neither opposition nor inconsistency. Why was the precept of the Mosaic Code what it was? And, How did it operate? It was what it was in consequence of the state of men and morals at the time. A spirit of fierce personal revenge for every injury, knowing no limits to the penalty it would inflict, and ever ready to exaggerate the offence given, filled the hearts of men. For the loss of an eye or of a tooth the injured, under a sudden and passionate impulse, might have even slain the injurer. How did the precept operate? It *restrained*, it did not *promote* the spirit of revenge. It may have enjoined a course of conduct falling far short of what is required under the Christian Dispensation, but not, when we consider the character of the age, inconsistent with it. On the contrary, it looked towards the higher standard that was to come. It taught men to check and regulate their passions, and thus it guided them onwards to a time when passion should yield wholly to the power of meekness, forgiveness, and love. The Lawgiver was the same; and He had the same end in view, both in the earlier and in the later age, but He accommodated Himself to the actual conditions of human life at the different periods with which He dealt. He raised the moral code only to the point to which it was at the time possible to raise it, in order that from that point He might make a new departure and might raise it still higher.

The principle thus laid down by our Lord may help to explain much in the Old Testament, which, although it has there the sanction of the Almighty, is yet opposed to our sense of justice and right. More particularly, that we may not leave the point immediately before us, it may help to explain that seeming recklessness in regard to the destruction of human life of which so many examples are afforded us, in the history both of Elijah and of Israel. Such deeds were far too numerous, and the motives which led to them are far too plain, to permit us to rest for a moment in the supposition that they are to be ascribed only to the unbridled passions of men, and that they had no connection with their sense of moral right and wrong. When Saul failed to obey the commandment of God, through Samuel, to exterminate the Amalekites, and afterwards met him with the words, " Blessed be thou of the Lord, I have performed the commandment of the Lord," Samuel replied, in language which from that day has shone forth as the expression of a pure Christian truth ' Hath the Lord as great delight in burnt-offerings and sacrifices as in obeying the voice of the Lord? Behold, to obey is better than sacrifice, and to hearken than the fat of rams;" and then he added the woe, "Because thou hast rejected the word of the Lord, He hath also rejected thee from being king" (1 Sam. xv. 10, &c.). Apart from all question as to the inspiration of the prophet, or his right to invoke the name of the Almighty as he did, it is clear that there is no passion in his words. He was not simply gratifying individual caprice or vengeance. He was actuated by what he felt as a high and solemn sense of religious duty, and his tone and temper thus illustrate what, in these respects, was the tone and temper of his age. There was no *spirit* of cruelty in such deeds. They were done by men who felt themselves to be the executioners of a Divine indignation against sin, which their own hearts approved.

That our moral sense would revolt against such deeds were they done now is nothing to the purpose. The very point of the explanation is that it is *our* moral sense that does so, and not that of those among whom the incidents were transacted, and that the *very same Scriptures* which demand our approval of them at the time when they occurred have taught us that they would now be inconsistent with the spirit of the Christian faith. It is not we who, in our strength, have grown beyond them. They have been superseded by a further and fuller revelation of the God of Israel; and still, in His manifestation of Himself in His Son, we behold heights of loving mercy that we have not scaled. Outward circumstances then, the condition of men, the stage at which they stood, the training needed by them at the time that, by means of it, they might be led onward to a brighter and loftier conception of what the Divine righteousness means;—these things supply the explanation of what it is otherwise so difficult to understand.

Of this condition of Israel, both long before and long after the days of Elijah, two particulars must, for our present purpose, be kept peculiarly in view.

In the first place, there was the light estimate placed on human life. We have not even to go back to the time of Elijah in order to see this principle in full operation. We may see it in the East at the present hour. Nothing is more incomprehensible to us than the state of Eastern feeling upon this point. Side by side with much that is both lofty in aim and tender in affection, with the aspirations of patriotism, the strength of friendship, and the love of wife and family, is a disregard of human life which awakens at once our astonishment and our horror. The men of the East are neither savages nor wild beasts, yet they too often look upon taking the life of a fellow creature with more indifference than we should exhibit when destroying a noxious insect. Individuals, families, communities, are slaughtered without hesitation in doing the deed, or compunction when it is done. The value of human life is estimated by a standard entirely different from that to which we are trained, and it is simply vain for us to endeavour fully to comprehend it. The consequence is that in many a case in which we should inflict a far lighter punishment justice is not satisfied unless life is taken, and that upon a scale passing far beyond the immediate offender. Now this feeling existed to at least a great extent in Israel, and it led to many acts in the Old Testament history from which we not only recoil, but which in us would indicate a general degeneracy of character that by no means accompanied them then.

In the second place, there was in Israel a view of the relation between the head and members of any organized body such as a family or a nation, largely, if not wholly, different from what prevails in Christian lands. The wife was attached to the husband, the children to the parent, the servants to the master, the soldiers to the captain, the ruled to the rulers by very different bonds from those which attach them to each other now. Canon Mozley has sought to vindicate the exterminating wars of the Old Testament almost wholly upon this ground; and, although by itself it is not enough, it must be allowed to be of great importance in the argument. " Man was regarded," he says, "as an appendage to man, to some person or some body, and therefore the idea of man being defective, the idea of justice was defective too. Hence arose, then, those monstrous forms of civil justice in the East, in which the wife and the children were included in the same punishment with the criminal himself, as being *part* of him. The idea was not always acted upon, nor did it form part, as far as one can judge, of the common routine of justice; indeed it would have caused the depopulation of countries if it had; but it was always at hand to be brought into use if wanted. The punishment of children for the sins of the fathers was, we may say, incorporated into the civil justice of the East, and was part of its traditional civil code; it was not an every-day process in the courts, but the principle of it existed in the law, and was resorted to on special occasions when a great impression had to be made. Not that the offences which were selected for the examples of this mode of retribution were chosen upon any principle, for they seem to have followed the caprice of the monarch. But they were such as, according to this irregular standard, heinous crimes, and the application of this extreme penalty seems to have carried the authority and weight of law, and to have been recognized by custom and popular opinion, and not to have been a simply arbitrary and tyrannical act of the monarch." Again, after mentioning the sentence of Nebuchadnezzar upon blasphemers of the true God, and of Darius, " a monarch who especially respected law and legal tradition, and did not make his own will his rule; a monarch who had evidently a strong sense of justice in his nature, a sympathy with the oppressed and ill-used, a respect for holy men, a pious and devout temper," the same writer adds, "These were the fruits of the idea that one man belonged to another, was part of another. The human appurtenances of the man were nobodies in themselves, they had no individual existence of their own, *their* punishment was a shadow as it affected *them*, because their own nonentity neutralized it; the *person* punished was the hateful criminal himself, who was destroyed *in* his children. The guarantee was given in this extended form of justice that no part of him escaped. Justice got the *whole* of him. The victim in himself, and in all his members, was crushed and extinguished. In the age's blindness and confusion of ideas, people did not really seem to know where the exact personality of the criminal *was*, and where it was to be got hold of; whether, in the locality of himself, was himself only, or some other person or persons also as well. They could not hit the exact mark to their own satisfaction, so they got into their grasp both the man himself and every one connected with him, to make sure. If they did this, if they collected about the criminal everything that belonged to him—wives, children, grandchildren, dependants, servants, household, the whole growth of human life about him, and destroyed it all, they were certain that they punished *him*, and the whole of him. The total of the individual was there, and justice was consummated."[1]

[1] Mozley, "Lectures on the Old Testament," lect. iv.

Even civilized India showed in our own day in the terrible institution of *Suttee* to what, as we should say, extremity of cruelty, to what depths of suffering this idea led; yet it was a religious idea, and powerful in proportion to the hold of religious ideas over the mind. We cannot judge of these things correctly without an effort: and it is difficult to persuade us that a particular act which, committed by ourselves, would drag us down to the lowest depths of degraded feeling, may often be committed by another without such a result. If it be said that the argument now led may be used to justify the horrors of the Inquisition the reply is obvious. These horrors were perpetrated in the name of a religion which demanded a spirit diametrically opposed to that which they displayed. They were perpetrated by men moving amidst scenes and influences expressly designed to foster the highest principles of compassion, and tenderness, and love. The more we explain what are to us the dreadful deeds of Old Testament prophets by the nature of the Dispensation under which they lived and of their times, the more do we condemn those who would have rolled back the course of ages, and who stabbed to the heart the system they were bound to foster and promote. Nor is there, in saying this, any mere shifting of the difficulty, from the men who acted by a standard which we would be wrong in adopting, to the Dispensation which supplied that standard. Our argument is that that Dispensation was adapted to its age. Without the severities of which we have spoken men would not have received a sufficiently deep impression of the heinousness of the sins which led to them, or of the frightful immoralities and disorders which these sins must have produced, if left unchecked by the only checks they could understand. Here it is that the immoralities of the time, that the relaxed condition of all law, both Divine and human, necessary to the welfare of society, ought to be taken into account. The sins of the original inhabitants of Canaan, or of the idolatrous worshippers of Baal in Ahab's days, are often appealed to as if, *in themselves*, they justified the terrible punishments inflicted. It may be doubted if we can really feel that they did so. But that is not the point. What we have to deal with is, that such was the general condition of things that those who were beginning to awake both to the nature and the tendency of the iniquity surrounding them could not but acknowledge the justice of the punishment, and could not but allow that nothing else could have presented a barrier to its ruinous course. With the stirring of incipient moral feeling, men were thus helped to rise to higher stages. Beginning to recognize the importance of law they beheld, in the severity with which transgression of law was punished, what was fitted to deepen in the general mind a sense of the magnitude of the sin of transgressing law. Beginning to recognize the necessity of protecting the weak against tyrannical power, they beheld in the idea that the wife, the child, the slave was part of the husband, the father, the master, a certain guarantee for their protection: he who attacked the property attacked its master, and the master was the stronger of the two.

Dreadful as the system was according to the standard given us in Christ, it yet helped to educate men; and the want of some such educating influence is often felt now in our dealings with those who are as yet far beneath the elevation to which the nations of Christendom have been raised. By not sufficiently recognizing the fact that the power of conscience is as yet only imperfectly developed among many whom we would instruct, it may be feared that we not unfrequently destroy our influence over subject tribes and deprive ourselves of anything in them to which to appeal. Their ideas of justice are different from ours, and they do not understand us. Of the rights which we allow to every fellow creature they have little or no conception. Our motives are misinterpreted. Our aims find no answer in their breasts. Kindness they think to be treachery; mercy they attribute to fear; and we soon learn, to our disappointment and dismay, that the very purity of the spirit in which we act, because not regulated by a prudent consideration of circumstances, becomes one main cause of the overthrow of our hopes. Let us not blame that spirit in itself, or yield to the discouraging impression that all labour must be vain. The fault is not in our spirit, but in its too hasty and unreserved application, at a time when those whom we would elevate are unable to receive it. The history of England in dealing with the less advanced portions of the empire, might afford many illustrations of this truth.

The principles now spoken of must be borne in mind when we would judge aright of the destruction brought through Elijah upon the companies of Ahaziah as well as upon the four hundred and fifty prophets of Baal at an earlier period. In neither case is there the least appearance of merely human passion, or of a spirit of revenge that knew not where to pause. In both the prophet acts as one who feels that he is the messenger of God, clothed with His commission, under an obligation to execute His will—and that will was regulated by thought of the condition of those who were then training for better things.

One remark more may be made before passing from this scene in Elijah's life. What, it leads us to ask, is the direct end of punishment? It is often answered, to reform the criminal, or, to deter others from being guilty of his sin. Neither answer is completely satisfactory. No doubt both these ends may properly be kept in view by the authority which punishes, and both may be in part attained. But they are the ultimate issue rather than the immediate aim of properly regulated retribution. We can easily imagine cases in which both effects might be secured, and yet neither the conscience of the criminal, nor the public conscience be satisfied. The crime may have been so great that the latter demands satisfaction to violated law. It honours the majesty of law, and is well aware that upon the vindication of the law the welfare of the community depends. It proceeds upon the feeling that there is an eternal distinction between right and wrong, alike in themselves and in the results to which they lead. This distinction must be maintained for its own sake, and no reformation of the criminal, no deterring others from following his example, touches that. The crime demands punishment, and the criminal must suffer.

Only thus, too, is the reformation of the criminal or the deterring of others from a similar crime really reached. No criminal is reformed by the mere dread of punishment; for, if that be all that influences him, he will again be guilty of the same transgression whenever he hopes that he may commit it with such secrecy that punishment may be escaped. That is not reformation. There is no change in the heart out of which are the issues of life. The outside of the cup or the platter may have been cleansed, but within it may be as full as ever of extortion or excess. Not the fear of punishment is the reforming element, but the stirring up to the thought of righteousness, the rousing within the breast of the conviction that there is a moral order in the world, and that only in conforming to it shall we reach truth, and beauty, and happiness. Punishment of sin as sin may awaken this; and when it does so the foundation of reformation is laid. But punishment can go no further; and unless we can bring other influences to bear upon the criminal classes of any country we shall find that all that law can do for us will end in disappointment and defeat.

CHAPTER IX.

THE ASCENSION OF ELIJAH (2 KINGS II. 1-12).

Elijah drawing near the close of his life—Gilgal—Departure of Elijah from Gilgal—Elisha persists in accompanying him—Bethel and the sons of the prophets there—Jericho and the sons of the prophets there—Jordan—Passage opened through the river—Converse of Elijah and Elisha—The request of Elisha and its meaning—The translation of Elijah—Difficulty of the passage—No merely "natural" explanation can suffice—But not on that account are we to be indifferent to the amount of miracle involved—Modes of thought of the writer and of his age to be kept in view—Application of these principles to the narrative—The true meaning of its different parts—Elisha's cry—His return to the Jordan—River again opened—Vain search for Elijah—Concluding observations on the translation of Elijah.

THE appointment of Elisha as his successor had brought to a close Elijah's short public career as the prophet of God in Israel. Like John the Baptist, however, in similar circumstances, he had again been brought out from his retirement to testify before a king to the cause of righteousness. After the Baptist had withdrawn in the presence of Jesus he comes once more upon the scene to rebuke Herod for his sin. After Elijah had withdrawn to make way for Elisha, he, too, once more meets us to pronounce judgment upon Ahaziah. Both prophets are the same as they have all along been. At the close, as at the beginning of their course, they laid the axe to the root of the tree, and then they passed away, faithful to the last.

It would seem from the narrative in the Second Book of Kings that Elijah had a presentiment of what was before him. He may not have known all the particulars, but this much at least he knew, that the hour of his departure was at hand. He had been residing at Gilgal. The place thus mentioned is generally allowed to have been different from that of the same name associated with not a few of the memorable events in the history of the children of Israel. That Gilgal was in the immediate neighbourhood of Jericho. It received its name from the fact mentioned in the book of Joshua, that the Israelites were there circumcised immediately after they had entered into the promised land : "And the Lord said unto Joshua, This day have I rolled away the reproach of Egypt from off you. Wherefore the name of that place was called Gilgal (or rolling) unto this day" (Josh. v. 9). Many other important incidents were connected with it, upon which we have no call to dwell. The Gilgal mentioned in connection with the closing days of Elijah lay to the north-west of the other and at a level higher than Bethel, which was again twelve hundred feet higher than the level of Jericho. Hence the expression of the narrative before us, in which it is said that Elijah and Elisha "went down to Bethel," while in the books of Joshua and 1 Samuel, the nature of the road from the other Gilgal to Bethel is described as an ascent.

Of this Gilgal nothing is positively known ; nor is any mention made of a connection between it and Elijah. It may indeed be inferred, with no small degree of probability, from what is stated in the verses before us compared with what is afterwards said in chap. iv. 38, that Elisha had his residence here, and this would harmonize well with the idea that, on the present occasion, Elijah had come forth from his own retirement, wherever it was, to seek out his pupil and successor in the prophetic office. With a vague notion at least of what was to happen he knew also that Elisha was not less deeply interested in it than himself. One other remark may be made on the second Gilgal, because it may throw light upon some of the circumstances related in the following narrative. We may justly infer from what is stated in 2 Kings iv. 38, that a school of the sons of the prophets had been planted there—a school, that is, where an education corresponding to the necessities of the time, but probably extending to little more than music and the ceremonial observances of the law, was given.

To this Gilgal, then, Elijah now came, and there he found Elisha. They left together, but had probably not gone far when "Elijah said unto Elisha, Tarry here, I pray thee, for the

THE ASCENSION OF ELIJAH.

Lord hath sent me as far as Bethel," which lay further on his way towards the Jordan and the city of Jericho. Elisha would not listen to his voice. "As the Lord liveth," he said, "and as thy soul liveth, I will not leave thee. So they went down to Bethel."

At Bethel was another school of the sons of the prophets, and there we can hardly doubt Elijah and Elisha rested. The same mysterious anticipations which had taken possession of Elijah, and had certainly also passed from him to Elisha, now found their way to the pupils of the prophetic school which they had reached; and, eager to gain further information as well as to express their feelings, these pupils came forth to Elisha, and said unto him, "Knowest thou that the Lord will take away thy master from thy head to-day?" And Elisha answered, "Yea, I know it: hold ye your peace." The subject was far too serious and weighty to be made a topic of curious conversation or inquiry. The hand of God was to be visibly present in the events about to happen whatever they might be; and in such circumstances the devout mind can only pause and wait. "Be still, and know that I am God," is the language in which the Almighty addresses us on the eve of any special manifestation of His glory; and "silence in heaven" is the attitude of the Church before the breaking of that seventh seal which is to set before her the judgments about to be executed for her sake upon a guilty world (Rev. viii. 1). Elijah now renews his request to his companion prophet. He said to Elisha, "Tarry here, I pray thee, for the Lord hath sent me to Jericho;" but the same earnest answer as before is given—"As the Lord liveth, and as thy soul liveth, I will not leave thee. . . . So they came to Jericho."

At Jericho was another of the prophetic schools which we have already found in existence at Gilgal and at Bethel; and there again Elijah and Elisha paused. Once more premonitions of something wonderful about to happen occupied the minds of the pupils; and once more, like those at Bethel, they came to Elisha and said unto him, "Knowest thou that the Lord will take away thy master from thy head to-day?" Elisha simply repeated his old reply, "Yea, I know it: hold ye your peace."

Even at Jericho, however, Elijah was not to rest. He turned to Elisha and said, "Tarry here, I pray thee, for the Lord hath sent me to Jordan." But, as to the sons of the prophets, so to his master, the same reply as before was given—"As the Lord liveth, and as thy soul liveth, I will not leave thee. . . . And they two went on." There was silence in all probability between them. They were solemnized by the consciousness of a Divine presence, by the feeling that they were every moment approaching nearer to an as yet unknown manifestation of the Divine counsels, by the persuasion that one of them at least was standing on the threshold of the unseen world. Under impressions such as these Elisha had already declined conversation with the sons of the prophets at Bethel and at Jericho. Under the same impressions he was silent now. Nor would Elijah be inclined to speak. His departure itself, and not the words with which he might accompany it, was to be the lesson to his companion and friend. When we stand by the death-bed of the child of God our impulse is not so much to speak as to learn the lessons that are taught us by the scene. Thus Elijah and Elisha—" they two went on."

Others, however, were also witnesses of the hour. "Fifty men," we are told, "of the sons of the prophets went, and stood over against them afar off." The interest was natural, and it exhibits itself in every age wherever the emotions of the heart are allowed free play, especially, therefore, among the young and the poor. These sons of the prophets were well aware that they were taking the last look of their master, and that something extraordinary was about to happen. No wonder that they watched.

At length Elijah and Elisha stood by Jordan. Once before in the history of Israel that river had flowed between Israel and the promised land, and had seemed to bar the passage of the people to their inheritance. But Joshua had commanded the priests to bear the ark of God into the river, and had given Israel the assurance that, when this was done, the host should pass over upon dry land. The promise was fulfilled, and "all the Israelites passed over upon dry ground, until all the people were passed over Jordan" (Josh. iii. 14-17). In a similarly miraculous manner did the Almighty now interpose on behalf of His servants. The river was before them, an apparently insuperable obstacle; but Elijah took his mantle and wrapped it together, and smote the waters, and they were divided hither and thither, so that " they two went over on dry ground." As the rod of Moses had been the symbol of his prophetic power, and by his lifting it up the waters of the Red Sea had been divided, so the mantle was the symbol of the prophetic power of Elijah, and smitten by it the Jordan was to yield a dry passage across its bed. The use of the "mantle" had undoubtedly a meaning. It had been the most characteristic token of the prophet's work. As a garment of rough hair, it reminded both him and all who witnessed the use to which it was put, of his privations in the wilderness, of his loneliness, of his toils, of his self-denials, and of his sufferings, in the execution of his mission. It was associated with the thought of a good fight fought, of a course finished, of faith kept. Why should it not be a source of strength to him in a departing hour? It had covered him alike in his struggles and in his triumphs, in his sorrows and his joys. He rolled it together as his rod, struck the waters of the river with it, and he and Elisha passed over dry-shod.

The Jordan was crossed, and Elijah was on the borders of Gilead, that Gilead which he had left many years before at the commandment of God to be His prophet in Israel. Even in an outward sense, therefore, it may be said that he was returning home. But such words may also be used with a far deeper meaning, for the hour had arrived when the doors of his eternal home were about to open to him. On the eastern side of the Jordan the ground rises into the hills and rocky heights of Gilead ; and to one, without a doubt to one of the nearest, of these points Elijah and Elisha began to move. But the master, well aware of what was immediately to be accomplished in him, would not leave his disciple without a blessing. "And it came to pass, when they were gone over, that Elijah said unto Elisha, Ask what I shall do for thee before I be taken from thee." The answer of the disciple illustrated the devotion of his heart, and justified the selection made of him long before as the prophet of Israel in Elijah's room. "And Elisha said, Let a double portion of thy spirit be upon me."

These words of Elisha have been very variously interpreted ; and we must endeavour, both for his sake and Elijah's, to understand them. It is almost needless to say that the promise related only to spiritual blessings. The tone of the whole narrative distinctly shows that, as in the case of Solomon, when the Lord appeared to him in a dream, saying, "Ask what I shall give thee?", Elijah could neither have thought of offering, nor

Elisha of receiving, any temporal **boon**. Spiritual blessings alone were in the minds of both.

Again, it is impossible to adopt the idea that Elisha, in requesting a double portion of his master's spirit, has reference to an evangelical spirit which, when compared with the spirit of the Law, may be regarded as the doubly powerful spirit of the two. Elisha knew little more of the spirit of the Gospel than Elijah did. He belonged, not less than his master, to the Dispensation of the Law; and, even though it were possible to prove that he was many steps nearer to the later Dispensation than he really was, he could not have received as a gift from Elijah what the latter did not possess.

The most curious supposition upon the point is that of Menken who, in his homilies upon the history of Elijah, understands that prophet to mean that in the eternal world he will remember Elisha, and to ask what he can do for him when he has been removed to heaven. "Beloved," he supposes Elijah to say to Elisha, "we are about to be parted from one another: I go to the Lord for whom I have lived and laboured, and thou remainest still here below in His service, for the hallowing of His name, and the spreading of His kingdom upon earth. Hast thou in thy heart any request that thou wouldest make of me, make it now before I am taken away from thee. If to thee I can be anything with the Lord in that land to which I go, believe me that I will be it. Hast thou anything pressing upon thy mind discover it to me now, and ask for thyself what I may do for thee when I return to our Lord." On the supposition that this interpretation is correct, the meaning of the prophet is that Elisha shall give him a commission for the world beyond the grave, to the Lord whom he will there see face to face, and who will doubtless deny him no spiritual blessing that he can ask for a servant so holy and so true.[1] Such is Menken's view; and it possesses interest as that of a man both able and devout in dealing with a difficult passage of the Bible. Nor is it open to the objection that it encourages the Romish doctrine of prayers to the saints, for Menken distinctly repudiates any such supposition. Elijah "speaks," he adds, "as though after his departure there could be no further intercourse between Elisha and him. Hence the words, 'Ask what I shall do for thee, before I be taken away from thee.'"

[1] Menken, "Werke," ii. p. 236.

Yet it is impossible to accept the interpretation. The probability is that Elijah, no more than Elisha, knew what was before him, or what would be his precise relation to the God of Israel in that new scene on which he was about to enter. Besides which his whole language bears upon its face that what he would now confer upon his disciple was the last gift it would be in his power to bestow.

We turn from all these suppositions and look again at Elisha's words, " Let a double portion of thy spirit be upon me." There is nothing in them of selfishness or ambition on the part of the younger prophet. The words have reference to that law of the Mosaic Dispensation by which the eldest son in a family was entitled, as compared with the other children, to a double portion in the inheritance of his father. They are thus simply equivalent to the request that, as the eldest son, as the most expressly called, in the family of the sons of the prophets, Elisha may receive such a measure of Elijah's spirit as to fit him for the task to be performed by him when his spiritual father is gone (comp. Deut. xxi. 17). Even that was much ; and Elijah felt that it was not his to grant. It could come only from the God who had bestowed upon him his own gift ; and to Him, therefore, the petition was to be referred. And he said, "Thou hast asked a hard thing, nevertheless, if thou see me when I am taken from thee, it shall be so unto thee ; but if not it shall not be so." Thus did he cast the whole matter upon Him who is the sole fountain of strength, either to His prophets or His people, and who gives or withholds according to the counsel of His own unerring judgment.

Of the further conversation of the two prophets with one another, as they went upon their way, no information is afforded us. We are simply told that, "as they went on, they talked." The sacred writer hastens on to the incident by which the career of the prophet, whose history he is tracing, was closed : " And it came to pass, as they still went on and talked, that, behold, there appeared a chariot of fire and horses of fire, and parted them both asunder, and Elijah went up by a whirlwind into heaven."

It can occasion no surprise that the incident thus related should have been at once the scorn of unbelief and a stumbling-block to faith. Some brief considerations connected with it are therefore imperatively required,

1. No explanation supplied by the naturalist school of interpreters can banish the miraculous element from the scene. No calling in of lightning and tempest is sufficient to meet the difficulties of the case, or to reduce the statement of what happened to the level of an ordinary occurrence. Even allowing for an instant that we have before us only the description of an Eastern storm, and of a flash of lightning which ended the career of the prophet of Israel, we have gained nothing in the direction for which such an explanation is supplied. We shall still have to account for the obviously præternatural expectation of Elisha, that his removal from this world by some extraordinary method was at hand; for the degree to which that expectation was shared, not only by Elisha, to whom his master might have communicated it, but by the sons of the prophets whose language shows that to them at least no such intimation had been given; for such an expression as that which tells us that Elijah "went up into (or towards) heaven;" and for the fact that the sons of the prophets having, despite the warning of Elisha, sought the body of Elijah for three days returned without finding it. Such an explanation, too, not merely defeats the clear intention of the narrator, but substitutes for it one directly opposed to what all readers must acknowledge he had in view. To represent Elijah as struck down by lightning or overwhelmed by a tempest, would have been to make him share the fate of those of whom it is said, "Upon the wicked God shall reign snares; fire and brimstone and burning wind shall be the portion of their cup" (Psa. xi. 6), or of those idolatrous worshippers of Baal, the judgment prepared for whom had been represented in this very narrative as the whirlwind, the earthquake, and the fire (1 Kings xix. 11, 12). Where then would have been the honour bestowed upon the prophet, or the crown of glory with which, at the end of his earthly course, it is the unquestionable desire of the historian that we should behold him crowned? Or if, instead of the naturalistic, the mythical interpretation be resorted to, the untenable supposition is implied in it that, on the one hand, the whole history is mythical, and that, on the other hand, a mode of departure is here related which finds no parallel in Scripture accounts given us of extraordinary departures of God's saints, either in earlier or in later times.

2. It does not follow from this that we may be indifferent to

the *amount* of miracle involved in any Scripture narrative, or that the utmost extreme of miraculous interposition that can be put into a passage is to be as readily welcomed as the smallest introduction of the same element that is consistent with fairness to the words with which we deal. If we may err in diminishing, we may equally err in magnifying the degree in which such interposition takes place. As God ordinarily works by common means, we are not unnecessarily to push the miraculous element into quarters into which He Himself has not distinctly introduced it.

3. The circumstances of a writer, his modes of thought and the modes of thought of his day must be invariably kept in view by the interpeter. Details, at first sight apparently miraculous, may be little else than a mould of thought different from ours, that mould being determined by the age or mental development of those among whom the portents are said to have occurred. The principle now laid down is, of course, attended with great difficulty in its application—with not less difficulty, indeed, than what is known as the doctrine of "accommodation," of which it is a part. Few, however, will deny that the doctrine of "accommodation," looked at in its most general light, is both true and indispensable to the interpreter of any ancient work. The difficulty of using it, therefore, can neither affect the validity of the doctrine nor destroy our responsibility for its legitimate use.

4. A fourth observation may still be made, but that of so obvious a kind that almost nothing need be said on its behalf. Our first duty, in considering such a passage as that which we have here before us, is carefully to determine what it actually says, without allowing ourselves to be carried away by traditional interpretation, however long continued or widely prevalent.

Let us apply these principles to the translation of Elijah. In doing so, the first thing that will strike the reader even of the Authorized Version (and the Revised Version does not differ from it, except in one small word having no effect upon the sense) is, that Elijah is not said to have gone up into heaven *in* a chariot of fire with horses of fire. On the contrary, it is distinctly stated that "Elijah went up by a whirlwind into heaven." No doubt the chariots and horses of fire appeared, but they are so spoken of as to show that they were rather the *accompaniment* than the *means* of the translation. Again, in our effort to understand the "chariot of fire, and horses of fire," the analogy of Scripture must be taken into account, and fortunately we have in this respect more than usual to help us here. In this very book we are told that when the king of Syria, then warring against Israel, was informed that all his plans were discovered by Elisha, he determined to seize the prophet. For this purpose he sent to Dothan where Elisha was "horses and chariots and a great host; and they came by night, and compassed the city about." In the morning, Elisha's servant was alarmed when he saw "an host with horses and chariots round about the city," and he hastened to report the fact to his master. Elisha answered, and his answer is to be particularly noted, "Fear not; for they that be with us are more than they that be with them;" and then, praying that the young man's eyes might be opened, they were opened, and he saw: "And behold the mountain was full of horses and chariots of fire round about Elisha" (2 Kings vi. 8–17). It is hardly possible to doubt as to the meaning, in the circumstances, of these horses and chariots of fire. They are in direct contrast to the horses and chariots of the Syrians twice spoken of before. We are not compelled to think that the mountain was full of actual horses and actual chariots of fire, but only that under appearances of such a nature was represented that strength, higher than that of the Syrian host, which had been commissioned by the Almighty to be on the prophet's side. Let us take another passage. When in the scene before us Elisha beheld his master ascend towards heaven he cried out, "My father, my father, the chariots of Israel and the horsemen thereof" (ver. 12). The last words have occasioned no small perplexity to commentators. We doubt if it is possible to explain them except on the supposition that they are suggested by the horses and chariot that Elisha had immediately before seen. He would express the might that had always accompanied Elijah, the commanding part that he had been enabled to play in Israel, the irresistible power with which God had swept all his enemies before him; and for the figure by which he would express this he seizes upon the appearance in which the Divine presence had so recently been made known to him. Once more, let us recall such passages as these, 'He rode upon a cherub," " He walketh upon the wings of the wind," "The chariots of God are twenty thousand, even thousands of angels," "The Lord encampeth round about them that fear Him, and delivereth them" (Psa. xviii. 10; civ. 3, lxviii. 17; xxxiv. 7), and we shall see that statements are often made with regard to God's opposition to His adversaries and protection to His friends to which no one would dream of giving a literal interpretation.

In the light of all that has been said, we thus seem to be perfectly justified in saying that the mention here made of a chariot of fire and horses of fire does not require us to believe that either the one or the other literally exists in the world beyond the grave. What Elisha saw was a symbol of the strength of Him of whom it is said, "The Lord is a man of war" (Exod. xv. 3), presenting itself in that appearance of a chariot and horses of fire which most strikingly represented at once His own destroying judgments and the burning zeal of the prophet whom he had been chosen to succeed. It was a fulfilment of the promise, "He shall give His angels charge concerning thee," those angels or ministers which, if at times they appear in gentleness, are at other times "a flame of fire" (Exod. iii. 2; Psa. civ. 4). Such appearances Elisha actually beheld waiting, as it were, upon Elijah in the last moments of his life upon earth; and then, with that glory as his attendant satellite, he saw him swept away by a whirlwind towards heaven. Thus with all reverence for the Sacred Word may we be permitted to speak of the translation of Elijah. All we can say is that, not in calm peacefulness like Enoch, but in a whirlwind, and with attendant angels or messengers of heaven corresponding to the whole of his prophetic life, Elijah closed his earthly career, and entered on his eternal reward.

The translation of Elijah was witnessed by Elisha. It was not in vain that the servant had clung, as he had done, to his master in these the closing hours of his life; and now God bestowed upon him his reward. He witnessed the sight withheld from the fifty sons of the prophets who stood afar off for the very purpose of beholding what might happen—his master translated bodily from earth to heaven.

"And," when he saw it, "he cried, My father, my father, the chariots of Israel, and the horsemen thereof." Both clauses are descriptive of the now departed prophet, though in different aspects of his character. He had been a father to Elisha, and the latter felt it now as probably never before. He could recall many a token of the loving care and tender bearing of one whom the world had known only in his sterner moods: and all these came back upon his memory at the moment when he was separated from him. As Elijah, accordingly, went up into heaven he cried after him, "My father, my father."

Nor was this all. Elijah had been more than a father. He had been "the chariot of Israel, and the horseman thereof." The words, as has been already said, were in all probability suggested by the spectacle just witnessed of the chariot and horses from heaven, combined with what Elisha could not fail to regard as an appropriate accompaniment of the scene, that this strength of God's true Israel should disappear, as he had lived, in fire. Chariots and horsemen were then the bulwark of a nation in its times of war. They were that arm of its military force on which it placed most reliance, and of which its enemies were most afraid. "Some," says the Psalmist, "trust in chariots and some in horses" (Psa. xx. 7). Such a bulwark of the truth, such a defence to the faithful among whom he lived, such a terror to the faithless, had Elijah been. His whole life is summed up by his disciple in that parting cry with which he followed him on his path to heaven—"My father, my father, the chariots of Israel, and the horsemen thereof:" and, as he saw him no more, he gave utterance to his sorrow after the manner of the time, by taking hold of his own clothes and rending them in two pieces, *i.e.*, "from top to bottom, as a sign of the greatest grief and of the deepest sorrow."[1]

One earthly token, however, of the great prophet of Israel remained, a symbol of the precious inheritance that he left, and of the fact that, although he himself was gone, his work was to be continued by his successor, and that Elijah was still to speak through him. His "mantle," that rough, hairy covering in which he had appeared before Ahab and assembled Israel, and which had been the sign of his prophetic work, fell from him as he ascended into heaven, and "Elisha took up the mantle of Elijah that fell from him, and went back, and stood by Jordan." He knew now that his request made but a little before to his master had been granted, that he was called to take his place as the first-born in the family of the sons of the prophet, and that he was summoned to carry on the work which

[1] Lange, "Commentary on the Old Testament," *in loc.*

THE ASCENSION OF ELIJAH.

his spiritual father had begun. With this inspiration upon him he stood by the banks of the Jordan, the waters of which again filled its bed, "and he took the mantle of Elijah that fell from him, and smote the waters, and said, Where is the Lord, the God of Elijah?" He was heard and answered, for "when he had smitten the waters they were divided hither and thither; and Elisha went over." He might not linger on the spot where he had been separated from Elijah. His life was still before him, his work had to be done, and it was necessary that he should return to them both.

A few closing particulars are now mentioned by the sacred writer with the view not so much of establishing the truthfulness of his narrative, as of showing that the arrangements of the Almighty were accepted by men, and that the new order of things was recognized. The sons of the prophets, who had gone out to witness as far as possible the solemn events connected with the departure of Elijah, beheld Elisha on his return; and, when the waters were again divided exactly as they had been a little before, they exclaimed, " The spirit of Elijah doth rest on Elisha. And they came to meet him, and bowed themselves to the ground before him." To pay him reverence, however, was not all their aim. They had not actually seen the translation of Elijah; and, under the impression that he might still be found on earth, they desired to search for him. " Behold, now," they said, "there be with thy servants fifty strong men: let them go we pray thee, and seek thy master; lest peradventure the spirit of the Lord hath taken him up, and cast him upon some mountain, or into some valley." They believed that he was gone; and that he had not, in the manner of his past life, simply returned to solitude after having shown himself for a moment to men. Perhaps they thought that, as he had disappeared not far from Mount Pisgah, his fate might have been similar to that of Moses, and that it was due to him therefore to make immediate inquiry after his body. Elisha, whether he told them fully what had happened or not, declined to comply with their request. He said, " Ye shall not send;" and only after they had urged him to such an extent that he was ashamed to persist in his refusal did he say, " Send." The fifty men were sent, and three days were spent in the search, but without their finding that of which they were in quest. They therefore returned to Jericho where Elisha had in the meanwhile tarried·

and, when they reported to him the failure of their mission, "he said unto them, Did I not say unto you, Go not?" Thus they were reproved, and the shame that a moment before was spoken of as Elisha's passed to them.

In looking back upon the remarkable narrative before us several considerations suggest themselves which it may be well to notice with the utmost brevity.

1. The difficulties of the narrative are unquestionable, and may be frankly acknowledged. But we have seen, on the one hand, that the popular impression as to the manner of Elijah's translation is not warranted by the text; and that, on the other, it is not necessary to interpret each expression of the narrative with the utmost literalness. We can easily form to ourselves a clear idea of what the statement was intended to convey and would convey to those for whom it was originally written. It would undoubtedly tell them that Elijah was translated from this world to the next without having tasted death, and that his translation took place in a manner corresponding to the course of his previous life. He had been the prophet of fire: in fire he was removed from the scene of his labours; and this fact is clothed in a garb adapted to the Eastern mind, when it is said that the angelic host which came to accompany him to his rest appeared as "a chariot of fire and horses of fire." "Both fact and figure," says a writer whose soundness in the faith and reverence of spirit are unquestionable, "Both fact and figure are here. The essential fact is that Elijah was translated without dying. Not only does the credibility of the history demand this; but the entire Biblical conception demands it also. If the Gospels do not accept myths as veritable history, if the transfiguration of our Lord be a fact, and not a mere vision or legend, if there be any significance in the representation of Moses and Elias appearing with Him in glory, we must literally accept the representation that Elijah was translated without tasting death. No doubt the manner of his translation is figuratively represented; all that the description necessarily means is, that he was caught away as in a fiery storm-cloud,[1] poetically God's 'chariot and horses of fire;' 'as a fire,' Elijah 'broke forth;' in a fiery storm-cloud he was taken

---

[1] It will be remembered that our conception of what passed has slightly differed from this.

away; the prophet of fire to the end."[1] The miracle it is impossible to remove, and those who reject miracles must reject the narrative as a whole. But it is unnecessary to multiply obstacles to faith, and if an undoubted characteristic of Jewish modes of thought helps to make easier our acceptance of details we are entitled to resort to it.

No other difficulty meets us in connection with the passage. It is true that at the instant of his translation Elijah was a man not only in full possession of his mental powers, but clothed with his bodily frame; and the Apostle Paul, writing to the Corinthians, has said that "flesh and blood cannot inherit the kingdom of God; neither doth corruption inherit incorruption." But the same apostle immediately added, "Behold, I tell you a mystery; We shall not all sleep, but we shall all be changed, in a moment, in the twinkling of an eye, at the last trump; for the trumpet shall sound, and the dead shall be raised incorruptible, and we shall be changed" (1 Cor. xv. 50–52). The translation of our Lord Himself from His earthly to His heavenly body must also have been instantaneous, or nearly so. There was no time for a gradual process either during the period that He lay in the tomb or during the forty days that intervened between His resurrection and His ascension. When He rose from the dead it must have been with His natural body, for the grave was empty. When he issued from the grave it must have been with His glorified body, for immediately afterwards He said to Mary, "Touch ME not."

Thus also was it with Elijah. The same Divine power which translated him from earth to heaven would make him instantly ready for the change. The corruptible would put on incorruption, the mortal immortality. Possessed at one moment of a "natural body" he would the next moment acquire the "spiritual body," with which alone he could enter the house not made with hands, eternal in the heavens.

2. The scene reminds us of the Ascension of our Lord. He, too, returned to His Father in the presence of none but His disciples. His miracles He had wrought before the multitude, but His disciples alone He led out to Bethany on that day when He returned to "His Father and their Father, to His God and their God." It is remarkable that in each great division of Holy Scripture we should thus have the record of an ascension, and only one. We are told, indeed, of Enoch that

[1] Dr. Allon, "Bible Educator," iii. p. 159.

"he walked with God; and that he was not, for God took him," but the words are too indefinite to permit us to think of what is meant by an ascension, and at any rate no details are given. The one ascension of the New Testament is the ascension of our Lord; the one of the Old Testament is the translation of Elijah. In the one, the Christian scheme of salvation culminates: in the other, especially when we call to mind that closeness of connection between Elijah and the Baptist of which we have yet to speak, we reach the highest point of the preparatory dispensation. Both dispensations rise from earth to heaven. The goal to which they lead us is the same.

Not only so. Each of the two, the translation and the ascension, corresponded to the nature of the dispensation, to which it belonged. In the whirlwind which swept Elijah into the eternal world we see the fitting end of a work which had been throughout a work of storm and judgment. In the narrative of the evangelist we see the fitting end of a work which had been throughout one of mercy and grace and blessing—"And Jesus led the disciples out until they were over against Bethany: and He lifted up His hands and blessed them: and it came to pass, while He blessed them, He parted from them, and was carried up into heaven, and a cloud received Him out of their sight" (Luke xxiv. 50, 51; Acts i. 9).

In the one case, there is everything to awe if not even to overwhelm with terror; in the other, there is everything to soothe and to console. In the one case, Elisha returned alone to resume a work in many respects like his Master's; in the other, the disciples returned together that they might be messengers of glad tidings to the utmost ends of the earth. In both cases, however, the animating power comes not from the seen, but from the unseen world. It was the spirit of the translated Elijah that rested upon Elisha. It is the spirit of the ascended Lord that is in every age the strength of His apostles and ministers. The spiritual alone gives the victory over the material, the unseen over the seen, the eternal over the temporal. A ministry the strength of which is drawn from earth and not from heaven is self-condemned, and will, as it must, be powerless.

One other remark is so closely connected with the subject we have been considering that it is impossible to omit it.

3. The translation of Elijah conveyed to the Old Testament Church an intimation of immortality. It was at least a step in the process of the education of the people of God for their future destiny. No doubt life and immortality are brought clearly to light only in the Gospel of Christ. Of Him alone who rose on the third morning from the grave can we say that He hath abolished death, and hath given us the assurance that an hour is coming when mortality shall be swallowed up of life. But, as for all the other truths of the Christian dispensation, so for this great truth there was a preparation made before Jesus came. The Old Testament Church was not left so completely without hope of a future inheritance as it is often represented to have been. Enoch was translated that he should not see death; and, whatever ideas they who read the brief narrative of his removal might entertain as to the particulars connected with it, they could hardly fail to gather the general impression that he continued to live in some region beyond the present scene. We are distinctly taught by the writer of the Epistle to the Hebrews that those saints of old who received the promises, and were led, in doing so, to confess that they were strangers and pilgrims on the earth, thus plainly declared that they sought a better country, even an heavenly (Heb. xi. 16): and throughout the prophets there are not a few passages which show that the expectation of life in a world to come was rising upon the mind of Israel with increasing clearness as time ran on. Such views the translation of Elijah must have deepened and confirmed. It must have helped to lift Israel above those things of sense in which it was so prone to be immersed, until at last He came by whom the great truth is taught that to the believer, even during his life here below, death is past; and that, in this the vestibule of that life there has already been bestowed upon him a complete and everlasting temple, which he has only to make more and more worthy of the unclouded glory and the uninterrupted happiness of its inner shrine.

CHAPTER X.

LETTER OF ELIJAH TO JEHORAM, KING OF JUDAH—CHARACTER AND WORK OF THE PROPHET (2 CHRON. XXI. 12-15).

Elijah's letter to Jehoram king of Judah—Difficulties connected with it—Most probable solution—Contents of the letter—Character of Jehoram—Fulfilment of Elijah's warnings—General considerations on Elijah's character and work—The circumstances amidst which he appeared—The school out of which he came—Prophecy in Judah and in Israel—The particular work given Elijah to do—The leading features of his character—His simplicity of faith and singleness of aim—His fearlessness of action—His sternness of spirit—Comparison with Elisha—Estimate of the prophet in after times—Book of Ecclesiasticus—New Testament references—His grandeur and uniqueness.

WE have followed the prophet Elijah to the close of his career on earth, and to the moment when he entered upon the eternal world. One other incident, indeed, connected with the prophet meets us, belonging, in the opinion of not a few inquirers, to the period after his translation, and thus attended with difficulties of its own. To this we may now direct our thoughts; after which, before proceeding further, it will be well to take a general survey of the prophet's character and work.

The incident of which we speak is related in the Second Book of Chronicles, where, in the account given us of Jehoram, king of Judah, we read that "there came a writing to him from Elijah the prophet, saying, Thus saith the Lord, the God of David thy father, Because thou hast not walked in the ways of Jehoshaphat thy father, nor in the ways of Asa king of Judah; but hast walked in the way of the kings of Israel, and hast made Judah and the inhabitants of Jerusalem to go a-whoring, like as the house of Ahab did, and also hast slain thy brethren of thy father's house, which were better than thyself: behold, the Lord will smite with a great plague thy people, and thy children, and thy wives, and all thy substance; and thou shalt have great sickness by disease of thy bowels, until thy bowels fall out, by reason of the sickness, day by day " (2 Chron. xxi. 12–15).

No difficulty connected with this writing need arise from the fact that it is not noticed in the Books of Kings, and that the account of it is given only in the Books of Chronicles. Elijah was the prophet of Israel in the limited sense of the northern kingdom, and the Books of Chronicles are devoted to the fortunes of Judah, the southern kingdom. So far, therefore, because addressed to a king of Judah, the writing is entirely in its place. Again, there is nothing to surprise us in the fact that a prophet of Israel should address himself to a king of Judah. Instead of recognizing the division of the twelve tribes into their two portions as legitimate, Elijah saw in it one of the strongest proofs of the apostasy of his people from the God of their fathers. He believed in the national unity as an arrangement ordained of God, and destined to continue; and, when on Carmel he erected the altar on which to call down fire from heaven, he built it of twelve, not ten, stones as a symbol that in the Divine ideal all the sons of Jacob, however outwardly separated, were one. It was no more than natural, then, that his interest in the fortunes of Judah should be only second, if even second, to his interest in those of Israel. Both kingdoms were God's. At Jerusalem was their common temple. And both were so related to each other by birth, by proximity of country, by the traditions of the past, the duties of the present, and the hopes of the future, that they could hardly fail powerfully to influence one another whether for good or evil.

The difficulty connected with the writing to Jehoram is entirely different from those now spoken of. In the opinion of many commentators Elijah was now dead, or rather translated to heaven; and the narrative has thus afforded great scope for the ridicule of those whose delight is to do everything possible to bring Scripture into contempt. We are not called upon in this work to enter into the elaborate and obscure chronological inquiries by which alone a distinct conclusion as to the date of Elijah's departure can be reached. Even were it allowed that it had taken place before any date of which the writing to Jehoram can be assigned, the difficulty connected with that writing may be easily surmounted. Nothing is more natural than to think that Elijah, as a prophet, anticipated the character of Jehoram and the nature of his reign ; that, as the future rose before him in prophetic vision, he beheld the wickedness of that king, and the evil that he would do ; and that thus he was led to address to him a warning which, preserved in the meantime amongst his prophetic writings, or amongst the other writings in the schools of the prophets, might be handed to him for whom it was intended when the fitting moment came.

Although, however, such a supposition is by no means unnatural, and although it is sufficient to meet the difficulty with which we have to deal, it is not necessary to resort to it. The probability is great, that at this period of Jehoram's reign, Elijah was still alive. The following words of the "Speaker's Commentary," on 2 Kings ii. 1, apparently by Rawlinson, are worthy of quotation : "There are reasons for believing that the events of this chapter are related out of their chronological order. Elijah's translation did not take place till after the accession of Jehoram in Judah (2 Chron xxi. 12), which was not till the fifth year of Jehoram of Israel (2 Kings viii. 16). It would seem that the writer of Kings, having concluded his notice of the ministry of Elijah in chap. i., and being about to pass in chap. ii. to the ministry of Elisha, thought it best to insert at this point the final scene of Elijah's life, though it did not occur till several years later." The explanation is simple, and in harmony with well-known principles of structure by which Jewish historians were guided. Even in the New Testament parts of St. Matthew's Gospel are, it is generally admitted, arranged upon this principle. Much more may we expect to meet it in the Old Testament, at a time when the historical sense was much more imperfectly developed than in the days of Christ. Nor is any serious difficulty created by the circumstance that, if this explanation be correct, we must suppose that Elisha entered upon his public work several years before the translation of his master. There is no reason why he should not have done so. But in fact Elijah's proper work terminated with the vision at Horeb, and the appointment of Elisha in his room which immediately followed it. Any act performed by him after that was more of a private than a public nature ; and we may be sure that, from the day when he cast his mantle upon Elisha at Abel-meholah, Elijah would never fail to recognize in him a prophet of Israel raised above himself.

From the outward circumstances attending this writing of Elijah's we may now turn to the contents. They are a warning in the whole spirit of Elijah's life to a rebellious and apostate king. Jehoram had succeeded Jehoshaphat upon the throne of Judah, but was displaying a spirit very different from that of either his father or his grandfather (2 Chron. xvii. 3-6; xiv. 2-4). Notwithstanding the examples set before him, and the traditions of his house, Jehoram, when he succeeded to the throne, pursued a policy of the most reckless wickedness, and the most daring impiety. His first act was to slay his six brethren lest any of them should afterwards make pretensions to the crown, together with others of the princes of Israel. Then he yielded, like Ahab in Samaria, to the corrupting influence of an idolatrous wife (2 Chron. xxi. 6, 11). The threatenings of Elijah's writing thus neglected were soon terribly fulfilled. Jehoram had received them in the beginning of his reign. He refused to listen to them, and the remainder of his life was spent in misfortune, defeat at the hands of his enemies, loss of all that he valued, and the sufferings of a painful and incurable disease (2 Chron. xxi. 10, 16, 17, 19). He even died unhonoured and unlamented. "His people made no burning for him like the burning of his fathers. He departed without being desired; and they buried him in the city of David, but not in the sepulchres of the kings" (2 Chron. xxi. 20).

The last act of Elijah is not the least striking of his life, and it ought especially to interest and instruct us because the prophet appears in it working beyond the boundaries of Israel. Neither in His mercies nor in His judgments is the Almighty limited by national boundaries. He has made of one blood all the families of men that dwell upon the face of the earth. They are placed under one government, have one responsibility, are capable of being brought to own, if not always at the same moment, the same truths, and are preparing here for the same destiny hereafter. The revelation of God therefore knows no limits to its possible sway: the messenger of the cross no boundaries which he may not pass: the Church of Christ no nation which, on the plea that she is national, she is not to bring under her beneficent sway. "The field is the world," and truth is as universal as it is eternal.

In the previous chapters of this book we have considered in detail the particular incidents recorded in the Old Testament of the great prophet of Israel whose life we have been engaged in tracing. If few in number, they are more than usually important. Nor are they only important. They are encompassed with greater difficulties than commonly meet us even in those narratives of Scripture which present the greatest obstacles to faith. It can be no matter of surprise, and certainly it ought to infer no reproach, if many a humble and devout reader of the Bible pauses before such records as those of the feeding of Elijah by the ravens, or his translation from this earth by a whirlwind with the accompaniment of a chariot of fire and with horses of fire, and asks himself whether he has understood these passages aright. Upon the other hand, he may equally wonder whether it is possible by any honest or unsophisticated reasoning to justify the slaughter of the four hundred and fifty priests of Baal at the river Kishon, or the destruction by fire from heaven of the two captains of Ahaziah, each with his fifty men. Doubts as to the literal meaning of the passages recording the two miracles may well be excused when we consider that the Bible itself has taught us that the performance of miraculous acts in which we are to recognize the working of God is dependent upon their occasion, their design, and their moral character; while hesitation as tot he possibility of vindicating the two terrible instances of destruction of human life may naturally enough be entertained when we remember that the New Testament has been our guide to a gentler spirit of dealing with our erring brethren. It may not be without use, therefore, before we leave the prophet and his work on earth, to endeavour to form some estimate of his character and labours as a whole. Still further light than that already spoken of may thus be reflected upon the individual parts of both. We begin with the prophet's work.

1. The circumstances amidst which he appeared first demand our attention. It was a crisis in the history of Israel. The time was altogether different from any that had preceded it since the days of Jeroboam, when the ten tribes first constituted themselves into a kingdom distinct from Judah. There had been degeneracy, idolatry, forgetfulness of God, before. Now there was complete apostasy. There was an attempt, only it would seem too successful, to introduce among the chosen

people the Baal worship of the ancient Canaanites, with all the abominations that belonged to it—that very worship which was so full of the foulest and most wicked rites that, in order to effect an entire separation between it and the chosen people, the children of Israel had been instructed to exterminate the old inhabitants of the land. The steps, too, taken to introduce it had been conceived not so much in a religious, though falsely religious, as in a worldly and secular spirit. Jezebel, it is true, was a fanatic in her own faith. There is no reason to think the same of Ahab. That king could hardly have blotted out from his mind the past history of his people. His readiness to yield to the application of the test suggested by Elijah at Carmel; his cowering before the prophet in the garden of Naboth; his subsequent repentance; and his conduct at Ramoth-Gilead, when he endeavoured to escape death in a manner so different from that of the defiant Jezebel when her hour came,—all these things show that Ahab had never completely shaken off the conviction that there was a God in Israel, for whom it might not be possible to substitute with impunity the objects of Tyrian worship. But Ahab was of an irreligious spirit; intent on schemes of worldly aggrandizement; more interested in the outward than the inward glory of his kingdom. The laying out of his gardens, the building of cities, the erection of his ivory palace—these two last achievements commemorated in the Book of the Chronicles of the Kings of Israel (1 Kings xxii. 39), occupied his thoughts. In this spirit he had in all probability formed his alliance with the house of Ethbaal king of the Sidonians. Disregarding the danger to religion, it was enough for him to hope that he might thus share in the commercial prosperity of Phœnicia, and might thereby enrich, whatever else might be the consequence, both himself and Israel.

To act in such a way, however, was to ignore, and, as far as man could do it, to defeat the end which the Almighty had in view when He dealt with Israel as He dealt with no other nation. Religion was the foundation of the Hebrew commonwealth, the purpose of its existence, the end of its calling, and the secret of its strength. "To Jehovah Israel owed, not only the blessings of life, but national existence and all the principles of social order; and through His priests, His prophets, but above all His anointed king, He was the source of all authority, and the fountain of all law and judgment in the land."[1] Substitute for religion either that exclusive pursuit of material ends which is fatal to the religious spirit in every form, or that idolatry which is incompatible with true religion; much more substitute for it both of these together, and Israel as a people would not only have degenerated; the end of its national existence would have been destroyed, and the purpose of God's providential dealings with it would have suffered disastrous and permanent eclipse. The moment, therefore, when Elijah was raised up was that of a great crisis in his nation's history, and the man who should meet that crisis needed to possess more than common force of character, singleness of aim, and readiness to hazard everything in the cause committed to him.

2. The school out of which Elijah sprang. In one sense it is impossible in his case to speak of any school. There is not the slightest reason to believe that he belonged even to those schools of the prophets which Samuel had long before instituted, and which, to say nothing of other parts of the land, were still in existence in Elijah's day at Gilgal, at Bethel, and at Jericho. That he took an interest in these institutions may fairly enough be inferred from the fact that, upon his way to the spot whence he was translated, he paused for a little at the three places named, and that Elisha who accompanied him held intercourse with the scholars in each place. But everything recorded of Elijah leads to the belief that, like his great follower the Baptist, he was the child of the desert, and that, though he may have been educated to some extent at least as youths then were, he was really trained by God Himself in the wilderness for the task to which he was to be called.

We use the word "school" in a wider sense. Elijah belonged to Israel, not to Judah; and it was in Israel, not in Judah, that at this period of the nation's history the most marked development of the prophetic spirit occurred. There is much to account for this. Judah possessed Jerusalem, the holy city; the temple of Solomon; the ordinances which the Almighty had appointed for His people; and the priesthood without that corruption of its regular line which had been introduced by Jeroboam, and had probably continued to the days of Ahab. With these things the desires of the pious Israelite were satisfied. He did not stand in need of the extra-

[1] W. Robertson Smith, "The Prophets of Israel," p. 48.

ordinary provision for his religious necessities with which he was supplied by the prophet rather than the priest; while, at the same time, there may have already existed some degree of that selfish interest in the preservation of the ancient order of things which, in the days of our Lord, goes so far to account for the difference between the stolid insensibility of Judæa to the Redeemer's teaching and the more open mind of Galilee, ever ready for religious as well as political revolution. In addition to this the actual condition of the ten tribes in the days of Elijah had a greater tendency to call forth the prophetic voice than that of the two tribes which had continued faithful to the house of David. The prophet, it must be remembered, was not a mere predicter of the future. Prediction, considered in itself, was not even his main function. When he did predict it was, if we may not say always, at least for the most part, because he would unfold some principle of the Divine government, or would point to something which, when accomplished, might show that God had a plan that He was steadily carrying out, notwithstanding all the obstacles that might oppose it. To correct moral and religious abuses, to proclaim the great moral and religious truths which are connected with the character of God, and which lie at the foundation of His government, was the prophet's task. He had to face the moral and religious corruptions of his age whether among the mass of the people, in the sanctuaries of the priesthood, or in the palaces of kings.

If so, we are prepared to find that, in Elijah's days there should have been a deeper and more widespread manifestation of the prophetic work in Israel than in Judah. It is not for naught that the great Captain of salvation sends His armies into the field. When He summons them there is a work to do. When there is a work to do He summons them. But we have already seen what the spiritual condition of Israel, as compared with that of Judah, in the days of Elijah was; and we have seen this, alike in the wretched character of its kings, in its impurely appointed priesthood, in its apostate prophets, and in the corrupt state of its community as a whole. The very extent of the corruption, then, helps to explain the thoroughness and severity of the remedy provided.

Whether, however, these considerations account fully for the fact or not, there seems no cause to doubt that about the days of Elijah prophecy had received a development in the northern, which it had not yet received in the southern, kingdom. The great prophets of the latter belong to a later date. About the time of Elijah we find them for the most part in the former. In Samaria, indeed, with the exception of a few, they had been either slaughtered by the cruelty of Jezebel, or had apostatized to the service of Baal. Those that escaped persecution, or remained true to the God of Israel, had been silenced. Obadiah had hidden a hundred of them in caves, but they were thus removed from public life, and Elijah believed that he, and he alone, was left to vindicate the honour of God.

By circumstances such as these he could not fail to be influenced. The prophetic atmosphere of his land would penetrate even to his desert solitude. He would be stirred by the darkness and corruption around him to a feeling of the greatness of a prophet's work, and to the need for a larger than ordinary degree of boldness, determination, unhesitating self-sacrifice, and unflinching zeal, in the effort to discharge it.

3. The particular work given him to do. That work was restoration; the bringing back of a state of things from which Israel had fallen away; not an inculcation of new views or a call to new duties, but the re-awakening of the conscience of the nation, the rousing it to an old rigidness of rule and strictness of discipline which had been weakened by the temptations of worldly prosperity. Restoration, we have said, was Elijah's work, and we have our Lord's distinct authority for saying so. When asked by His disciples to explain how it was that the scribes considered the coming of Elijah to be a necessary preliminary to His own coming, He replied, "Elijah cometh first, and shall restore all things" (Matt. xvii. 11). He refers no doubt in this reply to John the Baptist, the second Elijah; but, in doing so, He clearly implies that the work of the first Elijah was that of restoration.

What, therefore, we understand by the work of an ordinary prophet was not that required at Elijah's hand. No Messianic prophecies were to be put into his mouth. No new revelation of the God of Israel was to be committed to his care, and we have already seen that that part of the vision at Horeb, which contained fresh principles of God's method of procedure, he did not fully comprehend. He was not even commissioned to enunciate new moral and religious truths. What was needed in his day was to go back to the old foundations, to make a stand upon the ancient paths, to proclaim anew the one self-existent and absolute Jehovah who had originally constituted the Jewish people as a nation, but who had now been placed on a level with, or even inferior to, that of the gods of the heathen.

It was this that in the time of Ahab Israel particularly required—that an old truth should be restored to its proper place, that an old impression should be revivified, that the principle, sinfully forgotten, upon which God was dealing with His people at that stage of their history should be again held up to view, so that the pious might once more rejoice at the proclamation of the holiness of God, and the wicked be once more brought to tremble at His judgments. Elijah's work was thus in one sense singularly simple and direct. One idea runs throughout it all. At his first appearance before Ahab at Carmel, at Horeb, in the vineyard of Naboth, in his dealings with the captains of Ahaziah, and at his translation into heaven, he has one truth to enunciate and one lesson to enforce. He is the embodiment of law. He stands in a position wholly different from that of the evangelical prophets of the Old Testament. He is a second Moses. He is the prophet of judgment and of fire. All this demanded a man of action more than a man of words. It demanded more than ability either to reason or instruct. No one could fulfil such a function who was not stern, bold, and unflinching even unto death.

ii. In these circumstances Elijah was raised up to be the prophet of God in Israel. Let us glance at one or two of the leading features of his character. We cannot fail to be struck with—

1. His simplicity of faith and singleness of aim. He forms no plans of his own. He places himself wholly in the hands of God. He waits upon the Lord, that he may be of good courage, and that his heart may be strengthened. Almost every great act of his life seems to be preceded by a special call addressed to him to do it. No mention indeed is made of this in the case of his first appearance before Ahab, though it is probably involved in the words then addressed by him to the king, "The Lord God of Israel, *before whom I stand.*" But after that, when he took refuge by the Cherith, it was because "the word of the Lord came unto him." When he left the Cherith for

Zarephath; when he a second time showed himself to Ahab; when he returned from Horeb by the wilderness to Damascus; when he went down to meet Ahab in the vineyard of Naboth; when he intercepted the messengers sent by King Ahaziah to Ekron; when he came forth from his solitude to visit that king upon his sick bed; when, preparing for his translation, he went from Gilgal to Bethel; when from Bethel to Jericho; and when from Jericho to Jordan—on every one of these occasions the same or a similar formula is used (1 Kings xvii. 2, 8, xviii. 1, xx. 13, xxi. 17; 2 Kings i. 3, 15, ii. 2, 4, 6). Once only does it fail. It is not found in connection with the prophet's flight from Jezebel. Then we simply read, "And when he saw that he arose and went for his life, and came to Beersheba, which belongeth to Judah, and left his servant there" (1 Kings xix. 3). This, however, was the moment of Elijah's weakness; a moment similar to that in the life of the Baptist when, as he "heard in the prison the works of the Christ, he sent by his disciples, and said unto Him, Art Thou He that cometh, or look we for another?" (Matt. xi. 2, 3). But just as then Jesus not only resolved the doubts of His forerunner, instead of reproving him for want of faith, but did so by a revelation of mercy—" The blind receive their sight, and the lame walk, the lepers are cleansed, and the deaf hear, and the dead are raised up, and the poor have good tidings preached to them"—so now God had compassion on the weakness of His servant, sent His angel to him, and granted him that manifestation of Himself at Horeb in which He appeared, not in the tempest, the earthquake, or the fire, but in the still small voice.

To return, however, to the point more immediately before us, the simplicity of Elijah's faith. His dependence was wholly upon God. In every event of his life he looked to Him, and to Him alone, for guidance. He had neither wishes nor purposes of his own. Like the Saviour Himself, he would have said to any one calling him to action at an instant when he had not yet heard the voice of God speaking to his soul, "What have I to do with thee? Mine hour is not yet come." And, anxious as he must have been that his work should be continued by Elisha, he could yet only reply to his disciple as he asked that a double portion of his spirit might be granted him, "Thou hast asked a hard thing: nevertheless, if thou see me when I am taken from thee, it shall be so unto thee; but if not, it shall not be so" (2 Kings ii. 10). He cast the whole matter upon God. Thus he was always ready for any service to which he was summoned; and, the moment he had accomplished it, we hear no more of him till the next summons comes. In this simplicity of faith lay the foundation of that strength so eminently displayed by him.

With this simplicity of faith, again, was closely connected his singleness of aim. We can hardly imagine that he was insensible to the political condition of Israel in his time, or that he had no concern for the temporal welfare of his people. He must rather have been more concerned for such things than other men, because more than other men he had entered into the spirit of that dispensation the purity of which he was endeavouring to restore, and because temporal prosperity was so essentially associated with a faithful adherence to the covenant. Yet his one aim was the religious revival of the nation. Even though the immediate result of his work might have been to check that temporal prosperity which the schemes of Ahab promised, he could not have helped himself. He had one thing to do, to re-awaken the religious life of Israel, and to that he directed all his efforts, assured that the final issue must be for the common welfare, and that, if we seek first God's kingdom and righteousness, all things will be added unto us. In this respect, he embodied the essence of the true prophetic spirit; and his character thus possessed all the force which belongs in every age to men who become so possessed by one great cause that for its sake they are ready both to live and die.

2. His fearlessness of action. This characteristic of his nature was closely connected with that last spoken of. Nothing gives strength and fearlessness in action like simplicity of faith. We have then the might of God upon our side. "Thou hast given a banner to them that fear Thee;" "In God have I put my trust, I will not be afraid: what can man do unto me?" Psa. lx. 4; lvi. 11.) Three times Elijah appeared before Ahab, despising danger, scorning the fear of death; and on each occasion there is a marvellous directness in his words, in refreshing contrast to the honeyed phrases and the dexterous circumlocutions of too many a modern prophet, who manages to combine apparent faithfulness with soothing instead of alarming the consciences of those to whom he speaks. On the first occasion he says to Ahab, "As the Lord God of Israel liveth, before

whom I stand, there shall not be dew nor rain these years, but according to my word." As if he would say, " Thou art king, and all the authority of the kingdom appears to be at thy command. But there is a living God in Israel, and my word, as His servant, shall show itself to be greater than thine." On the second occasion Ahab addresses him with the angry question, "Is it thou, thou troubler of Israel?" and is immediately met with the reply, "I have not troubled Israel, but thou and thy father's house;" and when, upon the third, the conscience-stricken king exclaims, " Hast thou found me, O mine enemy?" he at once, without hesitation, answered, " I have found thee; because thou hast sold thyself to do that which is evil in the sight of the Lord." It is the bracing gale of the mountain, quickening the pulse and imparting strength and vigour to every limb. Of Elijah it may be truly said that he "never feared the face of man."

3. His sternness of spirit. In this respect Elijah leaves upon us the impression of a man of still sterner mould than either of the other prophets of the Old Testament or John the Baptist. The latter, indeed, we meet even less among the softer scenes of life than his great predecessor in the prophetic line. But that dying swan-like song of his, when he felt that he was passing away in the presence of One mightier than himself, reveals a depth of tenderness in his heart to which we find no parallel in any language ascribed to Elijah : " Ye yourselves bear me witness that I said, I am not the Christ, but that I am sent before Him. He that hath the bride is the bridegroom ; but the friend of the bridegroom, which standeth and heareth him, rejoiceth greatly because of the bridegroom's voice: this my joy therefore is fulfilled. He must increase but I must decrease" (John iii. 28–30). Not indeed that Elijah can have been without tenderness. His conduct towards the widow of Zarephath when her child died ; his language to Elisha when the latter begged that, before finally departing upon that mission to which his life was thenceforward to be devoted, he might be allowed to kiss his father and mother ; his consideration for the same prophet, and the gentle solemnity with which he speaks when Elisha insists on accompanying him to that close of his life which was shrouded in such mysterious darkness ; above all, perhaps the attachment of Elisha to him, and the devotion which will not permit him to quit his side even for

an instant before the end—all these things show that there must have been veins full of the life-blood of pity and sympathy in Elijah's nature.

Yet such is not the impression that he makes upon us. We see in him rather little else than sternness, ruggedness, severity unsoftened by any melting mood. From this point of view he has been often contrasted with Elisha, his successor; and we are invited to mark in the one a type of the Baptist, in the other of the tender and loving Saviour. The miracles of the two prophets have been set over against each other, as if those of Elijah were illustrations of a Dispensation of judgment, those of Elisha of a Dispensation of mercy. Instead of the slaughter of the priests of Baal, or the destruction of the captains and their fifties, we are asked to think of the deliverance of the kings of Israel and Judah and Edom from the sweeping scourge of the Moabites; of the increasing of the widow's oil; of the procuring the gift of a son for the Shunammite woman; and at a later period, when the child had died, of its restoration to life; of the healing of the poisoned food at Gilgal; of the multiplying of the loaves of barley so that the large company ate and left thereof; of the cure of the leprosy of Namaan; of the recovery of the axe-head from the river Jordan; and, finally, of life restored by the touch of his body to the corpse which had been buried hastily beside him; and then we are further asked whether these miracles do not bear upon them the marks of visitations of mercy, whether they are not "the very opposite of those judicial inflictions with which, through Elijah, the power of God broke forth to punish evil and to overawe the guilty."[1] The contrast, however, has been overdrawn. That there was a wide difference between the two prophets may be at once allowed. The difference appears even in their names; and the great importance attached in Scripture to names as expressive of the realities of things must be borne in mind in order that the full force of the difference may be felt. "Elijah" means "Jehovah is my God," "Elisha" means "My God is salvation"—the one name leading us to the thought of the power and the majesty, the other to the compassion and grace, of the Most High. Yet with the mantle of Elijah, Elisha inherited his master's spirit. Apart even from the thought of the destruction of the children by bears out of the wood near

[1] Wilberforce, "Heroes of Hebrew History," p. 349.

Bethel, which is obviously represented as an effect of the curse then pronounced by him (2 Kings ii. 24), we have the words spoken to Elijah at Horeb, "Him that escapeth from the sword of Hazael shall Jehu slay, and him that escapeth from the sword of Jehu shall Elisha slay" (1 Kings xix. 17); and these words, whatever we understand by the "sword" of Elisha, can only mean that the pupil was to walk in the same steps and to exhibit the same spirit as his teacher. The fact that he was to do so makes it also clear that the time for a revelation of the Divine mercy was not yet come, and that in the severity of Elijah we meet no more than was needed by, and adapted to, the requirements of his day.

Why, indeed, should we judge otherwise? We can look back to the sternness, even the violence, of leading actors in the German and Scottish Reformations with the feeling that the spirit displayed by them on many an occasion was justified by the circumstances of the case. Because we could not defend it if exhibited now, it does not follow that we cannot defend it as it was exhibited then. We owe to it in no small degree all that is most precious in the inheritance of religious and civil liberty transmitted to us by our fathers. We justly recognize in it, not the coarse outbreaks of human passion alone, but a stern, uncompromising severity demanded by a condition of things of which we have no experience.

Thus, then, it was with Elijah. The state of things around him was such that gentleness of dealing with the sins and errors of the people would either have produced no impression, or have been completely misunderstood. With nothing short of the most unbounding sternness and severity could he effect the object of his mission. And this must have been allowed by all. There is not the slightest trace in any part of the sacred narrative that he was thought to have been too severe. He lived in the memories of men as a noble example of that zeal for the glory of God which secures the Divine approval; and it was the very narratives at which so many now stumble that transmitted this estimate of his character to future ages. What that estimate was we learn from the striking description of the prophet in the apocryphal Book of Ecclesiasticus: "Then stood up Elias the prophet as fire, and his word burned like a lamp. He brought a sore famine upon them, and by his zeal diminished their number. By the Word of the Lord he shut up the heaven and also three times brought down fire. O Elias! how wast thou honoured in thy wondrous deeds! And who may glory like unto thee! who didst raise up a dead man from death, and his soul from the place of the dead, by the Word of the Most High; who broughtest kings to destruction, and honourable men from their bed; who heardest the rebuke of the Lord in Sinai, and in Horeb the judgment of vengeance; who anointedst kings to take revenge, and prophets to succeed after him; who wast taken up in a whirlwind of fire and in a chariot of fiery horses; who wast ordained for reproofs in their times to pacify the wrath of the Lord's judgment, before it brake forth into fury, and to turn the heart of the father unto the son, and to restore the tribes of Jacob. Blessed are they that saw thee" (chap. xlviii. 1–11).

Later even than the apocryphal books, however, a similar estimate of him continued to exist in Israel. It has been remarked that no one of the old prophets is so frequently mentioned in the New Testament; and his name never occurs except in a connection which testifies to the deep impression that he had made. His memory was cherished with admiration and reverence. The priests and Levites could not comprehend the Baptist's right to baptize unless he was either the Christ, or the great prophet that was to come, or Elijah (John i. 25). St. Paul refers to an incident in his history to give force to his argument that Israel was not wholly cast away (Rom. xi. 2). St. James sees in him the most striking illustration of the power of prayer (James v. 17); and our Lord's disciples quote him as one whose deeds afforded a justification of what they were anxious to do to the inhabitants of the village that would not receive their Master (Luke ix. 54). It was the rugged sternness and severity of his character which most of all left this impression upon men's minds. They had an instinctive feeling that it had been needed, and that there was no one by whom it had been so strikingly and consistently displayed.

Possessed of elements of character like these, Elijah stands out on the page of Old Testament history the grandest and most unique of all its figures except the great law-giver Moses. He was the prophet of fire, and it was most of all, by being so, that he prepared the way for Him who was the Hope at once of Israel and of the world.

CHAPTER XI.

THE SECOND ELIJAH.

Passages in the New Testament in which we read of a second Elijah—An integral part of Messianic hope—John i. 19-21; Luke ix. 7, 8; Matt. xvi. 14, xvii. 10, xi. 13, 14; Mark xv. 34, 35—Rabbinical testimonies to same belief—Founded on Malachi iv. 5, 6—Inquiry whether such passages are fulfilled in the coming of the Baptist—Alford, Moberly—Examination of Luke i. 17; Matt. xvii. 11, 12—Character of the Baptist's work—Conclusion that in the Baptist we have the second Elijah—Reference of the words in Malachi, "The great and dreadful day of the Lord"—Applicable to the beginning as well as the close of the Christian era—Jewish mode of looking at the Messianic age—Christian mode of doing so—Character of the age, not historical development, at first thought of—Judgment not less than mercy connected with it—Objection from 2 Thess. ii. 1-3—Objection answered—General conclusion that no second appearance of Elijah to be looked for.

A REMARKABLE class of passages occurs in the New Testament in which we read of a second Elijah; and our view of the great prophet who bore that name in the Old Testament would be incomplete were we to leave these passages without notice. A consideration of them ought also to open up questions both of variety and interest in connection with the mission and the purposes of our Lord Himself.

It seems to have been an integral part of that Messianic hope by which, immediately before the coming of Jesus, the Jews were animated, that the approach of the coming Deliverer would be heralded by the re-appearance of Elijah. When John the Baptist appeared, and so shook Jerusalem by his preaching as to lead men to suppose that the great religious crisis so long waited for was at hand, a vague idea took possession of the minds of many that, if not the Messiah, he might be that prophet of the Old Testament for whom they had been waiting. "They asked him, What then? art thou Elijah?" (John i. 21). When Herod the Tetrarch heard of the wonderful works of Jesus and His disciples, we are told that "he was much perplexed, because that it was said by some that John was risen from the dead, and by some that Elijah had appeared" (Luke ix. 7, 8). When, a few days before the transfiguration, Jesus asked His disciples, "Who do men say that the Son of Man is?" they answered, "Some say John the Baptist, and some Elijah" (Matt. xvi. 14). And when, after that event, the men who had witnessed upon the mount the glory of their Lord, were unable to account for the fact that He should thus manifest the brightness of His kingdom, without having been preceded by the return of the ancient prophet whom they expected, they came to Jesus with the question, "Why then say the scribes that Elijah must first come?" (Matt. xvii. 10). The strength of the popular impression was recognized indeed by Jesus Himself, when, addressing the multitudes who had gone out to hear the Baptist in the wilderness, He said to them, "For all the prophets and the law prophesied until John. And if ye are willing to receive it, this is Elijah which is to come" (Matt. xi. 13, 14); while, finally, a striking illustration is afforded of the hold which the idea had of the minds of the people by their interpretation of the Saviour's words upon the cross, "*Eli, Eli, lama sabachthani*," "This man calleth Elijah" (Mark xv. 34, 35).

These passages leave no doubt as to the widely-spread and deeply-rooted expectation in the days of Christ that, before the coming of the Messiah, Elijah was to return to the world in order to proclaim His approach, and to bring Him forth from the obscurity in which He was to remain until thus pointed out and consecrated to His work; and the inference is confirmed by quotations carefully collected from the surviving literature of the time by those who have written on the Messianic age (comp. Drummond, "The Jewish Messiah," pp. 222-224). Nor can there be any doubt that, in cherishing such expectations, the Jews thought of Elijah himself, not of one who should possess the spirit and power of the prophet, but of the prophet in flesh and blood; of the same prophet who, in the days of their fathers, had played so important a part in the history of Israel. At the hands of the scribes, too, the idea had even further degenerated, and had been surrounded with many of those trifling puerilities with which the formalists of the time corrupted all that was fairest and best in God's revelation of Himself to His ancient people.

Such then was the state of feeling in Israel with regard to the return in person of Elijah, and it rested on the words of the prophet Malachi, the very last words spoken before the voice of ancient prophecy was silent, "Behold, I will send you Elijah the prophet before the great and terrible day of the Lord come. And he shall turn the heart of the fathers to the children, and the heart of the children to their fathers; lest I come and smite the earth with a curse" (chap. iv. 5, 6).

Two questions of importance meet us in connection with these words, and with that expectation of the return of Elijah to which they gave rise.

I. Was the expectation as to the return of Elijah in person just, or was it fulfilled in the coming of John the Baptist, and are we no more to look for him?

II. If this question in its latter form be answered in the affirmative, how are we to explain the prophecy of Malachi?

I. It is at once admitted by all that in a certain sense at least, John the Baptist is to be regarded as the second Elijah. The words of our Lord upon different occasions are too precise to admit of any other conclusion. When He spoke to the multitudes of the greatness of the Baptist He said, "Verily, I say unto you, Among them that are born of women there hath not arisen a greater than John the Baptist. And if ye are willing to receive it, this is Elijah which is to come" (Matt. xi. 11, 14). And again, when His disciples asked Him, "Why then say the scribes that Elijah must first come?" He answered, "Elijah indeed cometh, and shall restore all things: but I say unto you that Elijah is come already" (Matt. xvii. 10-12). Of these passages it is said that "they cannot be understood to mean that the prophecy in Malachi iv. 5 received its *full completion* in John"; but that, "as in other prophecies, so in this, we have a partial fulfilment both of the coming of the Lord and of His forerunner, while the great and complete fulfilment is yet future —at the great day of the Lord " (Mal. iv. 1); that the expression in the original " Elijah which is to come " is not used from the Old Testament point of view, but, as proved more especially

by the words, " shall restore all things " in chap. xvii. 11, is
"*strictly future*"; and that the " double allusion (to Elijah and
the Baptist) is only the assertion that the Elias (in spirit and
power) who foreran our Lord's first coming was a partial fulfilment of the great prophecy which announces the *real Elias* [the
words of Malachi will bear no other than a personal meaning],
who is to forerun His greater and second coming." [1] The same
view is expressed by the late Bishop Moberly, in a posthumous
sermon recently published, in which that able and excellent
prelate speaks as follows : " Are we then to look forward to the
actual and literal fulfilment (of the prophecy of Malachi) ? Are
we to expect that Elijah himself . . . is to come back with his
glorified body upon the earth, and turn the hearts of the fathers
to the children, and the children to the fathers, before the
coming of the great and dreadful day of the Lord? Brethren,
I would not speak with any positiveness on a matter of this
kind ; but I will own that I so read the prophecy. I believe
that it will have a literal fulfilment. . . . In some sort he may
be said, and may be understood, to have come already; for *John*
is come in his spirit and power, and has proclaimed repentance
before the First Advent. He had been a likeness, a shadow, of
the real messenger, the real herald ; just as the first humble and
peaceful Advent is a likeness, a shadow, an assurance of the
great and dreadful Advent which is yet to come." [2]

The passages now quoted clearly indicate the nature of the
question with which we have to deal. Was the prophecy of
Malachi fulfilled in the person of the Baptist, or was the Baptist
no more than a partial fulfilment, a shadow and a likeness of
the real and personal Elijah who is to reappear before the
second Advent of the Lord?

1. We turn to the words addressed by the angel to Zacharias,
when announcing to him the birth of a son, " And he shall go
before his face in the spirit and power of Elijah, and turn the
hearts of the fathers to the children, and the disobedient *to*

---

[1] Alford on Matt. xi. 14, xvii. 12 ; comp. Schaff in Commentary, published by Clark; Olshausen *in loc.* See the names of many ancient
expositors who took this view in Wordsworth's Commentary on Mal. iv. 5
Wordsworth not unnaturally supposes that the Greek fathers may have been
led to a similar conclusion because the LXX. read, not " Elijah the
prophet," but " Elijah the Tishbite," thus individualizing the prophet still
more. [2] " Parochial Sermons," p. 16.

walk in the wisdom of the just; to make ready for the Lord a people prepared *for him*" (Luke i. 17). No meaning can be assigned to these words but one—that John should be the forerunner announced in the prophecy of Malachi, and that in him the mission of the forerunner, with the exact meaning of which we have at this moment no immediate concern, should be fulfilled. The words of the Old Testament prophecy are quoted with almost literal exactness, and it is declared that the prophetic function which they express shall be accomplished in John. Omitting for the present the difficulty arising out of the mention by Malachi of "the great and dreadful day of the Lord," it is clear that the mission of Elijah is transferred in its fulness to the Baptist, that, with his birth, the Elijah spoken of in the Old Testament will have come, and that no other is to be looked for at a later day.

2. More distinct, however, than the language of the angel to Zacharias is that of our Lord Himself to His disciples, when they asked Him why it was said by the scribes that Elijah must first come—" Elijah indeed cometh, and shall restore all things; but I say unto you that Elijah is come already, and they knew him not, but did unto him whatsoever they listed" (Matt. xvii. 11, 12)—while His language to the multitudes is to the same effect, "And if ye are willing to receive it, this [viz., the Baptist] is Elijah which is to come" (ὁ μέλλων ἔρχεσθαι, Matt. xi. 14).

Looking first at the latter of these two passages it seems almost unnecessary to say that the word "if" with which it begins does not make the meaning of the assertion with which it closes dependent upon its reception or rejection by the hearers, as if our Lord would assert that, only in the event of their acknowledging the truth of His remark, was the Baptist to be regarded in the light in which He was presenting him. His assertion could be affected neither by their faith nor by their unbelief. The Baptist was, and must have been, what he was, independent of any views of theirs. Our Lord can only mean, "I have a statement to make which is of importance for you to hear and understand. Ye may not be willing to receive it. Under the influence of your prepossessions, ye may harden your hearts against it; nevertheless, it is true, and is fraught with momentous consequences, that the John whom you have hastened to the wilderness to see is far more even than you have supposed. He is the very 'Elijah, which is to come.'"

Nor can it be urged that the expression "which is to come" leads us to the thought of an Elijah who was to appear at some future time. In such a case our Lord could only have spoken of a shadow or type of Elijah. He could not have said, "This *is* Elijah," or led His hearers to understand that Elijah was already come. The words "which is to come" are obviously spoken from the point of view of the Old Testament, and from the fact that the language in which Elijah had been long anticipated had become a technical designation for the man. The same thing is to be observed in that mention of the "age" or the "world to come," which often meets us in the New Testament (Matt. xii. 32; Luke xviii. 30; Heb. ii. 5, vi. 5, x. 1), and which marks out, not the future world, as distinguished from the present, but a period already come, the Christian age as distinguished from the age of preparation that went before.

If now we turn to the first of the two passages quoted above (Matt. xvii. 11), it will be seen that some of these remarks apply equally to it. Our Lord there speaks of Elijah as of one who "cometh," not who "shall come," and that expression, like the words of chap. xi. 14, "Elijah which is to come," is the designation by which His hearers were wont to describe the prophet. It is true that our Lord immediately adds, "and shall restore all things," words which, taken up by themselves, would unquestionably lead us to the thought of the future. Yet in the light of the words immediately following, such an interpretation is impossible: "But I say unto you that Elijah is come already, and they knew him not, but did unto him whatsoever they liked." Here all the verbs used point to a distinct and definite past, and nothing can be plainer than the statement, that the expectation entertained by the scribes, that Elijah was still to come, was false. He "was come already." The disciples immediately recognized the meaning of what was said (ver. 13). The words of ver. 11, therefore, can have only one meaning. Our Lord puts Himself into the position of Old Testament expectation. He says as it were, "I allow the truth of the expectation of Elijah from the point of view occupied by those who do not, and will not, see that already in My person the new order of things has been introduced. It is a part of Old Testament revelation that Elijah cometh and shall restore all things. But that promise has been fulfilled, and men ought to admit that, in its fulfilment, lies not only the coming of the forerunner, but of Me of whom he spoke."

While the teaching of Scripture upon the point before us is thus clear, it is confirmed by—

3. The character of the Baptist's work. The later prophet corresponded so closely to the earlier that he might well be looked upon as his double, and be styled a second of that name. Even outwardly it was so—the same connection with a wild and wilderness country; the same long retirement in the desert; the same sudden startling entrance upon his work (1 Kings xvii. 1; Luke iii. 2); even the same dress, a hairy garment, and a leathern girdle about the loins (2 Kings i. 8; Matt. iii. 4).

If the two thus corresponded in the outward, they equally corresponded in the inward aspects of their mission. We have already seen that the work of Elijah was not a new revelation of God; it was a restoration of the old, of the old theocracy, of the old worship instituted, and of the old law given through Moses.

Such also was the work of the Baptist. The angel indeed who announced his birth to Zacharias applied to him the very language in which the prophet Malachi had described the Elijah that was to come. He was "to turn the hearts of the fathers to the children, and the disobedient to walk in the wisdom of the just"; while Malachi had said of the Elijah of whom he speaks, that he would come "to turn the heart of the fathers to the children, and the heart of the children to their fathers." The exact meaning of these latter words is indeed difficult to determine; but there can be little doubt that in a general sense they express a work of reformation and restoration. The "children," in short, should be to such an extent the worthy descendants of a worthy ancestry; the "fathers" should have such satisfaction in their children, that the later age of the nation would exhibit the accomplishment of what the earlier had aimed at, and that both fathers and children would thus be knit together in similar bonds of submission to the will of God.

We have, however, more to guide us than this general description of what John's work was to be in comparison with Elijah's; we have the work itself. It is essentially an Elijah-work. Like his great predecessor, the Baptist was a prophet of

THE SECOND ELIJAH. 199

the law. The chief note of all his preaching was "Repent, for the kingdom of heaven is at hand." Making no distinction of persons, with a boldness that knew no fear, with a plainness of speech that went directly home to the heart, he addressed himself to every class of the community from the lowest to the highest urging upon them the great lessons of righteousness which had been the constant theme of those Old Testament prophets whose line culminated in him (Luke iii. 10–14). With holy indignation against sin even in the most exalted circles of the land he met Herod face to face as Elijah had met Ahab, and Herodias as the same prophet of the Old Testament had met Jezebel. Nothing daunted him in the execution of his task until he paid the penalty of his faithfulness with his life. His whole career was that of one separated from the world, pierced to the heart by the irreligion that prevailed around him, burning with zeal for the honour of God and for the memories of the theocratic kingdom. It is true that John witnessed to the coming and presence of the Redeemer in a way that Elijah did not, and in his circumstances could not do. But this arose from the necessities of his position, as that of one who terminated the series of the prophets of Israel, and who announced that a moment had arrived when He of whom all the prophets spake had actually come and was even standing among the people, though they knew Him not. John's main work, however, was to preach repentance, and to baptize with a baptism of repentance, "unto," to prepare for, to lead to, "a remission," a putting away, "of sins," so that all flesh might see that "salvation of God," which consists not only in pardon and acceptance with Him whose wrath we have provoked, but in a righteous and holy life led in Him to His glory and the fulfilling of His designs for the perfection and happiness of His creatures.

The clear and definite conclusion to which the whole of this discussion leads is that in the Baptist we have the second Elijah, and that we are not to look for a future appearance of that prophet.

But if so, the second question spoken of in connection with this subject demands our attention.

II. How are we, on the supposition now advocated, to explain the prophecy of Malachi? The Elijah of whom the Old Testament prophet speaks is to come before "the great and dreadful day of the Lord." Is not this the day of judgment, the close of the present dispensation? In that case, another appearance either of Elijah or of John is still to be expected, and all that has been just said has been beside the mark. The point is one of no small moment for the interpretation of numerous passages both of the prophets and of the New Testament, and an effort must be made to understand it.

(1) It is to be observed that the passage before us is not the only one in the prophecy of Malachi in which we read of a "day" which shall be peculiarly marked by judgment, which "burneth as a furnace," in which "all the proud and all that work wickedness shall be as stubble," which shall "burn them up," and they shall be "ashes under the soles of the feet" of God's people, and they shall "be trodden down" (Mal. iv. 1–3). In an earlier part of the prophecy we read of a "day" that comes with such a penetrating and searching power that the prophet says of it, "But who may abide the day of His coming? And who shall stand when He appeareth? for He is like a refiner's fire, and like fullers' soap: and He shall sit as a refiner and purifier of silver, and He shall purify the sons of Levi, and purge them as gold and silver.... And I will come near to you in judgment" (chap. iii. 2, 3, 5). But this latter "day" is introduced by the words, "Behold I send My messenger, and he shall prepare the way before Me; and the Lord whom ye seek, shall suddenly come to His temple, even the angel of the covenant, whom ye delight in, behold, he cometh, saith the Lord of Hosts" (ver 1). These words, again, are distinctly applied by our Lord to the Baptist who preceded His own coming in the flesh (Matt. xi. 10; comp. Mark i. 2; Luke i. 76). The "day" therefore spoken of in Malachi iv. 5 as "the great and dreadful day of the Lord" refers as much to the first as to the second advent, and we are not entitled to confine it to the latter. Even Bishop Wordsworth, commenting on Malachi iii. 1, says, "The day of the Lord *began*, in a certain sense, with our Lord's first appearance upon earth; and it will have its climax and consummation in His second advent." There is no ground, however, for speaking of "a certain sense." The teaching of the passage is precise that, not with the day of final judgment, but with the first manifestation of the Father in the Son, the "day" of the Lord began. To a similar effect is the language of Heb. i. 1, 2. Finally, we may refer upon this point to the language of the prophet Joel, with the comment upon it by the

apostle Peter in his first sermon at Jerusalem. After a glowing description of the Messianic age Joel thus speaks, "And it shall come to pass afterward that I will pour out my spirit upon all flesh; and your sons and your daughters shall prophesy, your old men shall dream dreams, your young men shall see visions; and also upon the servants and upon the handmaids in those days will I pour out my spirit. And I will show wonders in the heavens and in the earth, blood and fire and pillars of smoke. The sun shall be turned into darkness, and the moon into blood, before the great und terrible day of the Lord come. And it shall come to pass that whosoever shall call upon the name of the Lord shall be delivered: for in mount Zion and in Jerusalem there shall be those that escape, as the Lord hath said, and in the remnant whom the Lord shall call" (chap. ii. 28–32). These words are declared by St. Peter to have been fulfilled in the outpouring of the Spirit upon the day of Pentecost; for, explaining what had just taken place upon that day the apostle, "standing forth with the eleven, lifted up his voice, and spake forth unto the multitude, saying, This is that which hath been spoken by the prophet Joel" (Acts ii. 14, 16), and then he quotes the prophecy which we have given. With the day of Pentecost, therefore, "the great and terrible day of the Lord," the same expression as that used in the prophecy of Malachi (chap. iv. 5), had dawned, and these words cannot be restricted to a day only to dawn at the close of the present dispensation.

The truth is that we lose the force of all such passages as these by not placing ourselves with sufficient clearness in the position of the Jews at the beginning of the Christian era. With eighteen centuries of Christian history behind us it is difficult for us to regard the Christian age in any other light than as a long course of historical events; and, so regarding it, we imagine that the Jews also must have regarded it, and the voice of prophecy described it, in a similar light. But this was exactly what the Jews and prophecy *did not do*. By them the period to follow the first appearance of the Messiah was not looked at in the light of what we would style a course of historical development. They dwelt upon the *character*, not the *extension*, of the crisis, or æon, or age, which should then be introduced. They gathered together all its particulars into one. It was a season separated by a broad line of demarcation from the season going immediately before, the termination of which had now been reached. To have spoken therefore to a Jew of a first and second advent of the Lord would have been to use language which to him would have been unintelligible. His hope was fixed upon *one* coming of the Great Deliverer, and the kingdom and the glory which he expected were associated with it alone.

The question may be asked, Was it not otherwise in the early Christian Church? And, when that Church learned by hard experience that, instead of being admitted to the outward rest and splendour of the Messianic kingdom, she was summoned to persecution and trial and death, was she not led to think of two distinct "comings" of the Lord, the one past, in humiliation, the other still to come, with a brightness that should realize every hope she had learned to entertain? To this question in its strictest sense an answer must be given in the negative. The ideas of the early Christian Church were at least in this respect essentially the same as those of the Church of the older covenant. To the former as well as to the latter the Christian age did not present itself as a long historical development such as the age preceding it had been. To the Christian as well as to the Jew it presented itself as a crisis, or æon, or age, the *nature* rather than the *extension* of which was to be the subject of his thoughts. No doubt the idea of historical development gradually forced itself upon the minds of men as time ran on and the fulness of their first expectations was not realized; while the struggling together of the expectation and the experience led to that slight wavering in the meaning of such words as "day of the Lord" that we find in the New Testament. Yet in the main the whole Christian era was to the first disciples one. It began with the first advent of Christ, and that advent introduced it in its reality and essence. Christ was not "to come." He was come already. Acccording to His promise, "Lo, I am with you alway, even unto the consummation of the age," He was present in His Church. The word *Parousia*, so often used in this connection, cannot mean "future coming." It can mean only "presence," although that particular presence may have associated with it the thought of a degree of glory only to be *manifested* at a future day; and it is to be regretted that the New Testament Revisers were not bold enough to transfer this rendering from their margin to their text. That, accordingly for which the first Christians looked was not so much Christ's coming as the "manifestation" of His coming. Amidst their many and sore troubles they felt that though Christ was come, the idea of His coming was not exhausted. As yet He was hidden with the Father. But a day would break when His glory would be *manifested*, and when He who for a time had made Himself known only in the lowly condition of the "flesh," and was now concealed from view, would be *revealed* in all the brightness that belonged to Him. This, however, was not strictly speaking a Second Advent. It was simply the completion of the First Advent. It was not a "day of the Lord" wholly new. It was only a filling out of the idea of that day in all its completeness.

One difficulty must still be noticed. It may be asked how it comes to pass that, if the prophets of the Old Testament thus looked upon the whole gospel age as the day of the Lord, they should associate with it ideas of terribleness and of judgment, instead of ideas of mercy and grace alone. Is it possible that Christian times should be regarded in any other light than as times of the revelation of the love of God? And, when we find so many images of terror connected with the "day" of the Lord, is it not a proof that we are wrong in thus embracing the "day of salvation" not less than the day of the final judgment under the idea of one coming of the Lord?

To this it may be answered in part, that there is often in prophetic language what may at first sight appear to be not only a singular, but even an inexplicable, mingling of the gentle and severe, of the encouraging and the terrible, in reference to the same event. The clauses of such a passage as that of Isaiah lxiii. 4, "The day of vengeance is in mine heart, and the year of My redeemed is come," may be a sufficient illustration of this; although the same principle lies at the bottom of those words of the Epistle to the Hebrews, in which the sacred writer, after having given what is perhaps the most glowing description of the privileges of believers contained in the New Testament, exclaims, "Wherefore, receiving a kingdom that cannot be shaken, let us have grace whereby we may offer service well pleasing to God with godly fear and awe; for our God is a consuming fire." It is plain from passages such as these that according to the conception of Scripture two views of God and of our relation to Him, generally deemed inconsistent, may well accompany each other.

But there is more to be said, for a little reflection may show us that the annunciation of *judgment* must be one of the deepest and most essential elements of the prophetic spirit. The prophets are false who "speak smooth things, who prophesy deceits" (Isa. xxx. 10). It is the hatred of all sin; it is the profound sense of its evil as committed against God, and as the source of all misery to man, combined with the conviction that it ought to be and can be forsaken; it is a heart bursting with sorrow as it contemplates the burden of human woe, and swelling with indignation at its cause, that draws the true prophet forth. He sees the captive in his chains; he hears the groaning of the prisoner and the cry of the oppressed; his spirit is overwhelmed as he meditates on the sufferings of God's saints who have no earthly comforter. Then he knows that, in spite of all this, there is a just Governor of the universe, that there is a reward for the righteous, that verily there is a God who judgeth in the earth—and when these considerations and others of a similar kind rush in upon him like a flood, what can he do but cry for judgment? Judgment in such a case is not vindictiveness or vengeance. It is the necessary preliminary to the restoration of order. It is the vindication of truth. It is the punishment and the banishment of sin. It is a step that must be taken before the foundations of that kingdom can be laid which is "righteousness and peace and joy in the Holy Ghost."

The true prophet therefore must look, and long, and cry for judgment. So far from being inconsistent with the love of God judgment is rather to him one of the forms in which the love of God is manifested. The same Redeemer who on one occasion said, "I came not to judge the world, but to save the world" (John xii. 47), said upon another, "For a judgment came I into this world" (John ix. 39); and in a striking passage in the Revelation of St. John the proclamation of judgment is even represented as a gospel—"And I saw another angel flying in mid heaven, having an eternal gospel to proclaim unto them that dwell on the earth, and unto every nation and tribe and tongue and people; and he saith with a great voice, Fear God, and give Him glory; for the hour of His judgment is come; and worship Him that made the heaven and the earth and sea and fountains of waters" (chap. xiv. 6, 7).

To what has now been said it may, indeed, be still objected

that, in 2 Thess. ii. 1–3, St. Paul appears to teach that the "day of the Lord" is not yet come, and that it will not come until an important series of events, dwelt upon in the following verses of the chapter, shall have taken place. It is not difficult, however, to understand that the terms applied to the whole age which was to be the final age of the present dispensation should have been transferred to its closing period, when it was seen that the events inseparably connected with the thought of it could be expected only in the future. Such expressions as "the day of the Lord," or the "coming" or "presence" of the Lord, though originally applicable to the Christian era, at its beginning as well as at its end, were pushed onward to the latter point because then only would all the hopes associated with them be fulfilled.

In the light, therefore, of all that has been said, we can have no hesitation in referring such words as those of Malachi when he speaks of "the great and dreadful day of the Lord," to the whole Christian Dispensation, and not merely to the particular "day" at which the Lord comes to final judgment.

But, if so, the chief difficulty connected with Malachi iv. 5, 6, disappears, and we at once see that there is nothing in the words there used to make it necessary to think of an Elijah yet to come. The Baptist was the only second Elijah promised to the Church, and we do not look for another. Why, indeed, should another come? He would have no work to do. When the day of final judgment arrives men will be divided into the two great classes in which they have chosen their respective places—the believing, waiting Church upon the one hand, the unbelieving world that has steeled itself against Christ, upon the other. The former need no Elijah-work. The latter would not profit from it. No time of new probation then begins, but only the full and perfect manifestation of a probation ended. Even now the course of time is running on lines which do not change, which only reach their terminal issues in the world's great assize—"He that is unrighteous, let him do unrighteousness still, and he that is filthy let him be filthy still; and he that is righteous let him do righteousness still, and he that is holy let him be made holy still" (Rev. xxii. 11).

www.ingramcontent.com/pod-product-compliance
Lightning Source LLC
Chambersburg PA
CBHW051052160426
43193CB00010B/1158